The Mirror of Our Anguish

The Mirror
of Our Anguish

A Study
of Luigi Pirandello's
Narrative Writings

Douglas Radcliff-Umstead

Rutherford • Madison • Teaneck
Fairleigh Dickinson University Press

London: Associated University Presses

© 1978 by Associated University Presses, Inc.

Associated University Presses, Inc.
Cranbury, New Jersey 08512

Associated University Presses
Magdalen House
136–148 Tooley Street
London SE1 2TT, England

174825

Library of Congress Cataloging in Publication Data

Radcliff-Umstead, Douglas.
The mirror of our anguish.

Bibliography: p.
Includes index.
1. Pirandello, Luigi, 1867–1936—Prose.
I. Title.
PQ4835.17Z754   853'.9'12   76–742
ISBN 0–8386–1930–4

The author wishes to thank the editor of *Italica*, Olga Ragusa, for permission to reprint material from his "Pirandello and the Puppet World," *Italica Magazine* 54, no. 1 (1967): 13–16.

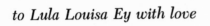

to Lula Louisa Ey with love

Contents

Preface

It is only recently that critics in Italy have tried to revaluate Luigi Pirandello's narrative writings. This text represents an effort to introduce to the English-reading public the seven novels and the most typical tales of that Sicilian writer, whose literary fame still rests upon his achievements as a dramatist. Few writers of this century, Shaw and Gide included, have engendered such passionate debate as has Pirandello. Anyone who has endeavored to compile a comprehensive bibliography of Pirandello studies soon recognizes the staggering dimensions of the task. Despite the almost innumerable studies, Pirandello in his usual humoristic fashion seems as always to elude critical definition. The anguished masks in Pirandello's works, narrative or dramatic, will perhaps remain forever enigmatic in spite of every critical effort to strip them away to a naked truth. The inquiry and the effort are necessary, however, for to understand Pirandello is to comprehend ourselves.

Throughout this text I have cited page references to

Pirandello's novels from the Omnibus publication by Mondadori in 1945. For the dates of the author's novelle I have followed the chronology established by Manlio Lo Vecchio-Musti in *Bibliografia di Pirandello* (Milan, 1937). In cases of problematic dating for the composition of certain tales, I have consulted the listing by Frederick May for his translation of *Pirandello's Short Stories*.

As always with my scholarly projects, it is to Lula Louisa Ey that I have turned for the sustaining faith that has carried me through many trying moments.

I wish to express appreciation to the National Endowment for the Humanities for an award to begin work on this project and to the John Simon Guggenheim Memorial Foundation for a fellowship to complete it as part of a study of alienation in modern literature. Thanks should also be extended to Professors Donald McGrady, of the University of Virginia; Aldo Scaglione, of the University of North Carolina; Javier Herrero, of the University of Pittsburgh; Franco Fido, of Brown University; René Girard and the late Henry T. Rowell, of Johns Hopkins University, for their encouragement.

Douglas Radcliff-Umstead
Kent State University

Chronology of Luigi Pirandello's Life

1867   Luigi Pirandello born on June 28 in Girgenti (Agrigento), Sicily.
1880   Moves to Palermo to continue secondary school studies in classical languages and literatures.
1887   In the attempt to break off an engagement to his cousin Lina Pirandello, transfers from the University of Palermo to the University of Rome.
1888–1892   Continues studies in romance philology at the University of Bonn, where he receives a doctorate in 1891 with the dissertation *Sounds and Phonetic Development of the Dialect of Girgenti*.
1889   Publishes in Palermo his first collection of verses, *Mal giocondo (Joyful Ill)*.
1891   Publishes in Milan a second verse collection, *Pasqua di Gea. (The Easter of Gea Tellus)*.
1893   Establishes self in Rome as a member of Luigi Capuana's literary circle. Writes first novel, *L'Esclusa (The Outcast)*.

1894   Publishes at Milan first volume of novelle, *Amori senza amore* (*Loves without love*). Marries Antonietta Portulano, the daughter of his father's business partner.

1895   Publishes *Elegie renane* (*Rhenish elegies*). First son, Stefano, born.

1897   Begins teaching career at Instituto Superiore di Magistero (Women's college) in Rome. Daughter Lietta born.

1899   Son Fausto born.

1901   Publishes *L'Esclusa,* in serial form.

1902   Publishes second novel *Il Turno* (written in 1895).

1903   Early period of relative serenity and financial security ends with landslide and flood that destroy his father's sulfur mine. Mental and physical breakdown of his wife, who never recovers from paranoia. Teaching position becomes major source of income.

1904   Publishes novel *Il Fu Mattia Pascal* (*The Late Mattia Pascal*).

1908   Publishes two treatises, *L'Umorismo* (*Humor*) and *Arte e Scienza* (*Art and Science*).

1909   Serial publication of novel *I Vecchi e i Giovani* (*The Old and the Young*).

1911   Publishes novel *Suo Marito* (*Her Husband*).

1913   Performance of his play *Il Dovere del Medico* (*The Physician's Duty*) in Rome.

1915   Publishes in serial form novel *Si Gira* (*Shoot!*). Performance of first full-length play, *La Ragione degli Altri* (*The Rightness of Others*). With Italy's intervention in the First World War, both of his sons enter military service.

1916   Theatrical success of Sicilian dialect plays *Pensaci, Giacomino!* (*Think it over, Giacomino!*) and *Liolà*.

1917	Performances of plays *Cosi è se vi pare* (*It is so if you think so*) and *Il Berretto a Sonagli* (*Cap and Bells*).
1919	Commits wife to a mental institution. Stage productions of dramas *L'Uomo, la Bestia e la virtù* (*Man, Beast and Virtue*) and *La Patente* (*The License*).
1921	Performance of *Sei Personaggi in Cerca d'Autore* (*Six Characters in Search of an Author*) in Rome on May 10th creates a riot.
1922	Triumphal performances of *Enrico IV* (*Henry IV*) and *Vestire Gli ignudi* (*Dress the Naked*).
1923	International success of *Sei Personaggi* with Parisian production by Georges Pitoëff. Visits New York for cyclic performances of his plays.
1924	Premiere of drama *Ciascuno a suo modo* (*Each in His Own Way*).
1925	Publishes last complete novel, *Uno, Nessuno e Centomila* (*One, None and a Hundred Thousand*). Having joined the Fascist Party, receives government sponsorship to form the Art Theatre of Rome. Begins production tours with drama company throughout Europe and the Americas.
1926	Premiere in German translation of drama *Diana e la Tuda* (*Diana and the Tuda*) at Zurich.
1928	Roman premiere of play *La Nuova Colonia* (*The New Colony*). Dissolution of his Art Theatre.
1929	Chosen by the Fascists to become a member of the new Accademia d'Italia. Performance of play *Lazzaro* (*Lazarus*).
1930	Performances of *Questa sera si recita a soggetto* (*Tonight we improvise*) and *Come tu mi vuoi* (*As you desire me*).
1932	Performance of *Trovarsi* (*To Find Oneself*).
1933	Premiere of *Quando si è qualcuno* (*When you are someone*) in Buenos Aires.

1934   Fascist claque hisses *La Favola del Figlio Cambiato* (*The Fable of the Changeling*) off the stage in Rome. Receives Nobel Prize for Literature.

1936   Dies in Rome on December 10.

1937   Florentine performance of incomplete final play, *I Giganti della Montagna*.

Introduction: The Marionette in the Mirror

The World of the Grotesque

Since ancient times the puppet theater has served as a small-scale mirror of man's precarious adventure in this world. Marionettes, which were used in religious ceremonies, have been discovered in Egyptian tombs. Socrates and Plato compared human passions to the wires that controlled puppets. The Roman marionette theater, which borrowed heavily from the Greeks and introduced Italic variations, included a large repertoire of plots and puppet-figures to please every social class. With the triumph of Christianity the puppets moved to the church, when priests ordered the erection of wooden stages where marionettes in costly costumes acted out the lives of the Virgin and saints. By the time the Council of Trent finally attempted to proscribe puppet plays in church, the marionettes had returned to the secular theater. The Commedia dell'Arte and the Italian puppet theater developed on parallel lines. Italian puppetry artists traveled all over Europe, finding especially favorable audiences in France. The eighteenth century became a golden age of puppetry.[1]

In the twentieth century there has occurred a grotesque inversion of roles: instead of puppets' serving to represent human actions, men of flesh and blood have seemingly turned to wood and taken on the characteristics of puppets. This is the period when an artist like Giorgio De Chirico has depicted man as a faceless puppet, a powerless clothing-store dummy sometimes serene but often tormented and threatening; man is either a marionette awaiting some puppeteer to come and manipulate his strings or an automaton controlled by a hidden mechanism.[2] This exchange of roles between man and marionette can be noted as early as Heinrich Kleist's essay *Über das Marionettentheater*, written at the start of the nineteenth century.[3] Kleist asserts that puppets are more graceful than humans, whereas modern stage dancers are extremely affected and artificial in their movements. After man ate of the Tree of Knowledge, he lost his original innocent grace to acquire a civilized consciousness. Only where reflection grows weaker does grace become more vigorous and resplendent. Man would have to become a god in order to regain that original spontaneous charm. Humans would have to enter through the Infinite to recapture the grace that an unthinking puppet or a god with infinite consciousness possesses. The last chapter of world history is to be man's returning to eat again of the Tree of Knowledge. Kleist's essay is a perfect introduction to German romanticism, with its goal of infinity through becoming. The crisis of modern man arises because he has not been able to reach the divine, infinite consciousness that Kleist spoke of, but instead has had to enclose himself in the complete void of a puppet's unconsciousness.

Kleist's scorn for the human actor later found emphatic reiteration in the theoretical writings of the British stage reformer Edward Gordon Craig, who in his essay *The Actor and the Übermarionette* of 1908 declared, "The actor must go and in his place comes the inanimate figure—the Übermarionette." [4] Craig wished to return to the original use of puppets in religious rituals. His "divine puppet" is not the doll-like imitation of human actors that could be viewed in any crude Punch and Judy show but a modern re-creation of the stone images in ancient temples. The Übermarionette would perform the symbolic and rhythmical gestures that could be observed in temple ceremonies. The human actor for Craig seemed a clumsy creature who lacked the puppet's "noble artificiality," especially since the individual actor permitted his own emotions to interfere with the sentiments that he was trying to represent on stage. Craig rejected acting as an art of impersonation that made the actor an exhibitionist in competition with real life. The Übermarionette symbolizes a Platonic perfection, the Ideal realized in a theater that would not be a place of entertainment, but a holy precinct where man's most profound feelings would be reenacted in a solemn drama.

Although Craig later stated in the preface to his book *On the Art of the Theatre* (1911) that he never intended to replace living actors with things of wood and that the Übermarionette was only the actor whose performance was fired by the spark of divine inspiration, the fierce aversion to the human actor and the distrust of the human body as a vehicle of sincere theatrical expression that his essay proclaimed were echoed in the subsequent manifestoes of the Italian and French Futurists, who wanted to see man made over into a robot, a dynamic continuum to glorify mechanical processes. In 1909, the year when the Futurist movement was launched, Tommaso Marinetti published his play *Poupées Electriques (Electric Puppets)*.[5] Its central character is the American inventor John Wilson who has created two life-size electric puppets, which he keeps in the parlor of his French Riviera villa. John and his wife, Mary, make love behind the backs of the puppets, M. Prudent and Mme.

Prunelle, just as if they were cheating on two elderly chaperones. The puppets can speak, snore, cough, hold up newspapers, and knit. In their intimate relations John has begun to treat his wife as if she were a mechanical puppet. When she weeps, he says he has pushed the button for tears. John finally forces his wife to destroy herself after she fails to escape his control by finding the love of another man. Marinetti portrayed how humans can be transformed into automata with push buttons to elicit desired emotional responses.

Other Futurists, such as Enrico Prampolini, followed Craig by affirming that the human actor was no longer necessary in the theater. Prampolini's manifesto, *Scenografia Futurista* (1915), advocated a mechanistic actor with funnel-shaped ears and a mouth like a megaphone. The human actor, now regarded as an utterly worthless interpretative element, was to disappear before an automaton moving according to a stage dynamism determined by a "plasticity" of light and space. Prampolini was later to become one of the stage designers for Luigi Pirandello's plays. In 1918 Fortunato Depero produced his marionette ballets, *Balli Plastici*, at the Roman Palazzo Odescalchi (afterwards to become the home theater for Pirandello's professional company); marionettes represented clowns, chickens, and bears. For the Futurists the human actor with his confessional manner of portraying emotions was not half so effective as a "spot of color" on the stage.[6]

One of the key notions of twentieth-century art and its reduction of man to a marionette is implied by the name usually given to a group of Italian playwrights who emerged during the First World War: the Theater of the Grotesque ("Teatro del Grottesco"). The term came from Luigi Chiarelli's play *La Maschera e il Volto* (*The Mask and the Face*) of 1916, which the author called a "grotesque in three acts." By *grotesque* Chiarelli meant a deliberate burlesque of the social games that persons have to play because of ridiculous bourgeois conventions. The grotesque is not an artistic form or category, but a manner of expression that works through conscious deformation of characters and customs. The Italian grotesque play that best illustrates the "marionet-tesque" transformation is Rosso di San Secondo's *Marionette, che passione!* (*Marionettes, What Suffering!*) of 1918. Even though Rosso di San Secondo was very sensitive to influence from North European Expressionism, the human puppets in his play have an everyday quality about them. He expressly stated in a prefatory note to actors that the characters remained human, but humans reduced to marionette roles and therefore deeply deserving of pity. Rosso's marionettes are social misfits who have lost individual features and are identified only by a detail of dress, like the lady with a blue fox, the man in mourning, and the man in gray. By acting as puppets guided by traditional motives and attitudes, the characters in the Rosso play become little more than impersonal representations of various degrees of sensual love.[7]

Outside of Italy and France, the aesthetic estrangement of the grotesque manner and the preference for the puppet-actor characterized the works of the Spanish decadentist Ramón del Valle-Inclán and the Flemish playwright Michel de Ghelderode. In his dramatic pieces (*esperpentos*) like *Los Cuernos de Don Friolera* (*The Horns of Don Friolera*), Valle--Inclán looked down at his fictional characters from the vantage of a puppet-master and deliberately deformed the human figure, making it a gargoyle, a mechanized doll, or a mask from the Commedia dell'Arte. The Spanish author wished to hold a concave mirror before reality, since he believed that farcical distortion could be the only genuine manner of representing life's absurd situations. Ramón del Valle-Inclán worked from a basically anti-sentimental aesthetic, creating an artistic distance between his grotesque characters and the puzzled spectators, who would not know whether to laugh or recoil in horror before the ludicrous dramas. Whereas the puppet figure in the Spanish writer's works symbolized man's stunted spirit, the marionette seemed to Michel de Ghelderode a magical figure, whose wax and wood body showed greater flexibility than the easily fatigued limbs of flesh- and blood-performers. In the third of his Ostend interviews the Flemish dramatist expressed the hope that through marionettes he might find the freedom to break from the restrictions of conventional theater in order to restore drama to its original savage state. He called his play *D'Un Diable qui prêcha merveilles* (*About a Devil who Preached Wonders*), a "mystery for marionettes," and included an introductory note to the puppet-master stage director on the drama's inverted morality. Valle-Inclán and Ghelderode demonstrate respectively the two principal representations of the puppet figure in twentieth century literature: as the mirror image of modern man's freakish nature and as a totemistic being inherently superior to humans.[8]

Pirandello's Humoristic Vision

It is to the writings of Luigi Pirandello that one must turn to find characters who, although they appear to be made of wood, are truly contracted in a desperate tension. Afraid of their emotions and crushed by overwhelming circumstances, Pirandellian characters voluntarily surrender their humanity in order to escape the pain of living by taking refuge in the wooden passivity of marionettes. Pirandello began his literary career at a particularly disillusioning moment in Italian history when the patriotic fervor of the movement for national unification (the *Risorgimento*) had died away under a corrupt government. To the young Pirandello, who came from a family of ardent Sicilian fighters for unity, life in the new Italy seemed a sham play. Even as a nineteen-year-old student at the University of

Palermo he had confessed to his sister Lina his moral bewilderment:

> We are like the poor spiders, who in order to live need to
> weave their slender webs in some corner; we are like the poor
> snails, who in order to live have to carry their fragile shells
> on their backs; or we are like the molluscs with their shells
> at the bottom of the sea. We are spiders, snails and molluscs
> of a more noble species; to be sure, we would not want a
> spider's web or the shelter of a shell—that goes without
> saying—but a little world, both to live in it and to live on it.
> An ideal, a feeling, a habit, an activity—there's the little
> world, there's the shell of that over-sized snail or man as he's
> called. Without it life is impossible. When you end up with-
> out an ideal, because when you look at life, it seems like an
> enormous puppet show, without ever any connections or
> explanations; when you no longer have a feeling left because
> you have ended up no longer respecting or caring for persons
> and things, and therefore you cannot develop habits and you
> despise specific activities—when you, in a word, live without
> life, think without a thought, feel without your heart—then
> you won't know what to do: you will be a wayfarer without
> a home, a bird without a nest. (Letter of October 31, 1886) [9]

Unable to clothe his life with the exterior form of intellectual pursuit, sentiment, or intense occupation, Pirandello saw himself as a morally naked individual. As an artist
he was later to investigate how others covered their nakedness with the masks of society's formal thoughts and activities; his total theater bears the title *Naked Masks*. Life for
the young writer appeared a mechanical process repeating
itself without any authentic feeling. At the close of his
adolescence the Sicilian writer viewed human relations as a
ridiculous puppet play; for the idea of life's "puppet show"
he used the word *pupazzata*, from *pupo*, the puppet operated
by the fingers. [10] In a post-heroic age when all ideals were
dead, man ceased to exercise control over his destiny and
became a manipulated creature.

Society, in the opinion of the young Pirandello, bore the blame for imposing the puppet role on men by compelling them to lead essentially false existences. In the essay *La Menzogna del Sentimento nell'Arte* (*The Falsification of Sentiment in Art*), written in 1890 while the author was working for a doctorate in romance philology from the University of Bonn, he pointed out that even though life in present times could be intensely dramatic, an overdeveloped sense of duty forced persons to stifle their natural feelings. As a result of his obedience to contemporary morality, modern man lacked the inner harmony that had permitted the ancient Greeks to contemplate their errors serenely and to portray them in tragedies. The Greeks, unlike their Roman imitators, had possessed the clear vision and spiritual honesty to represent in drama the conflict between rigid duty and natural passion that must result in disaster. But according to Pirandello, when a society came to be founded on mendacity—as Italy was at the end of the nineteenth century—art could only reflect the falsification of genuine sentiments under an inflexible code of conduct. That lying moral conscience, which represses natural impulses and misrepresents them in compliance with taboos, deprives man of tragic stature and reduces art to being the maidservant of social, religious, and legal obligations. As a writer, Pirandello aspired to demolish the façade of bourgeois respectability in order to reveal the pathetic truths of the inner man.[11]

An attempt to explore the confusion and despair of the author's generation is evident in the essay *Arte e Coscienza d'Oggi* (*Today's Art and Conscience*), published in 1893 after Pirandello's return to Italy. He states that God at the end of the nineteenth century could merely be a dark void; hence men's longing to reestablish contact with the divine, as advocated by representatives of the older generation like Count Tolstoy, was symptomatic of the sense of loss caused by the discoveries of science, which had shattered the an-

thropomorphic vision of the world. The old might very well
ignore science and materialistic philosophy and take refuge
in the simplicistic faith of an earlier age, but the young—
like the twenty-six-year-old author himself—were torn between their natural curiosity to understand the world and a
crippling realization of their emptiness. Pirandello constantly stresses the pathology of his generation, who suffered
from the absence of any purpose in life. To point out the
perplexity of youth, the author employs the figure of an
inner mirror, which reflects the chaotic emotions of those
who shift from one direction to another in the hope of
finding the right way out of their confusion. In the writings
of Pirandello's maturity the mirror image returns again and
again to indicate his characters' efforts to strike a pose that
will protect them before the world. The author also introduces the major idea of the masks that men assume to
hide the fear that is gnawing away within them: "We
almost all in the meantime show scorn for every traditional
opinion, as if to mask the muffled discouragement that is in
the depths of us all along with the presentiment of obscure
fears. We simulate with a proper air of haughtiness indifference for everything we do not know, and which in truth
we wish to know, and we feel ourselves as if gone astray,
indeed lost in a blind immense labyrinth, surrounded all
about by an impentrable mystery. There are so many ways;
which is the true one? . . ." [12] To discover the proper direction
in life appeared to be the paramount problem of Pirandello's
generation.

Confusion naturally arose before the distressing number
of *isms* that offered moral solutions or aesthetic programs.
Walter Bagehot's theory of Social Darwinism tried to prove
that vigorous, civilized nations could break the inhibiting
"cake of custom" to achieve social progress in a competitive
world. The positivistic philosophy of Auguste Comte showed
that Europe had passed through the stages of theological
and metaphysical knowledge and was ready for a unified

government based on incontrovertible facts. In literature realism and naturalism were on the wane while symbolism and mysticism held sway, but Pirandello understood only too well that new merchants of thought would soon arrive to sell their wares in what he derided as the "international fair of madness." The general reaction of the times seemed to the Sicilian author a state of pessimism, skepticism, nausea, exaggerated emotionalism, unconscious falsehood, or a cowardly surrender to a crude phenomenalism. At this early moment in his life Pirandello could not accept the pantheistic withdrawal into the loveliness of nature that was typical of some of his contemporaries and that was to provide the existential solution for several characters in his future fictional writings. He believed that the cosmic displacement brought about by astronomy and the law of evolution had rendered contemporary man little more than a raving lunatic; as an artist Pirandello was to study the insanity hidden behind the mask of indifference or excessive self-confidence.

Between those who looked back to the past for a way out and those who ran feverishly to take up the latest *ism*, the author placed a third group of individuals, who in the total shipwreck of the times made themselves strangers to life by retreating from its vulgar struggles. Perhaps Pirandello considered himself in this group that reacted with disgust or ennui before the feelings and beliefs of others. But, to apply the author's own terms, was that disgust genuine or was it a mask for a sense of alienation from the overwhelming majority of committed persons? At this point Pirandello affirms still another of his cardinal ideas: the relativity of all things in a world where the absolute can never be verified. The strangers to life could find no firm point of reference since all the old norms had collapsed. Here the author begins to elaborate his theory of human constructions: history has recorded how some few noble individuals have succeeded in realizing their ideals, but

always in the mistaken belief that they had created something permanent; life, however, does not stand still and in
time all of man's ideal constructions will crumble. If permanence is impossible, what reason is there to enter the
struggle? In Pirandello's final analysis man appears a passive
creature, bound in chains and left to life's discretion while
the world seems a ravenous machine that consumes its victims.

Pirandello wrote his essay during a period in European
history that was characterized by an optimistic faith in
materialistic progress and parliamentary democracy. The
general belief of the era was that perfection was near at
hand in a world that would be free of wars and disease. The
contemporary cult of science indicated a desire to master
the truth and control reality. According to the German
biologist and philosopher Ernst Haeckel, even the human
mind was to be considered a physical entity; the only riddle
left unsolved at the end of the nineteenth century was, in
Haeckel's words, the existence of God, and it did not merit
further investigation. In part Pirandello's pessimism derived
from a political awareness that his parents' generation had
been betrayed in their patriotic aspirations by a mediocre
and vitiated government. The year when the essay on contemporary art and conscience appeared in print was an
especially scandalous moment in the history of the new
kingdom of Italy, as Pirandello was later to descibe in his
novel *I Vecchi e i Giovani* (*The Old and the Young*) of 1909.
His despondency also rested on the firm conviction that
science had taken more away from man than it had given.
Neither positivism nor Spencerian synthetic philosophy
could restore to man the self-assurance of pre-Copernican
and pre-Newtonian times. The author excluded as visible art
forms those that exalted democracy or the triumphs of
science. Throughout the pages of his essay there predominates a sense of anguish, which resembles the nausea or
the ennui of twentieth-century existentialists, even to the

terminology of *nausea* and *noia*. But instead of the metaphysical freedom that Sartre was to contend was possible
after the nauseous experiencing of life's absurdity, or the
revolt and subsequent attempt to live authentically that
Camus was to affirm, the young Pirandello saw only man's
enslavement—the puppet in chains. At best he hoped for the
coming of a liberator, and his essay concludes with the pre-
diction that his generation stood on the eve of a great event.

The essay on art and conscience demonstrates that Pirandello must be classed with the small group of sensitive mal-
contents, like the decadentists that he attacked, who in the
midst of their age's complacent satisfaction with material
progress recognized the fragility and hollowness of late-
nineteenth-century-values. Their doubts were to be con-
firmed by the catastrophic events of the First World War
and the ensuing emergenge of dictators. The anti-rationalis-
tic Pirandello was to clamor for Italian intervention in that
war, and he afterward welcomed Mussolini as his nation's
Messianic liberator. Like William Butler Yeats, Pirandello
belonged to the early group of apocalyptic modernists who
felt that their age was drawing to a close and would be reborn with the advent of a leader.[13] During the worst period
of his government's corruption in the final decade of the
last century, however, the young Sicilian writer favored the
socialist radicals; and when a new administration brought
reform and prosperity to Italy by the early years of this
century, Pirandello joined the moderates.

In truth the only *ism* with which Pirandello became
associated during the formative period of his literary career
was Verism, the school of regional realism in writing, which
emphasized fidelity to truth. Giovanni Verga, the greatest
of Italian Verists, had asserted in a letter preceding his
Sicilian tale "L'Amante di Gramigna" ("Gramigna's Mistress") of 1880 that a work of art should never show the
author's hand; instead it must give the impression of having
created itself like a fact of nature. The Veristic impersonality

of style depended on the author's eclipsing himself in the creative process. After Pirandello took up residence in Rome, he entered the circle of authors gathered around Luigi Capuana, the acknowledged theorist of Verism. Influenced by Balzac and Zola, Capuana thought modern literature should resemble a carefully structured and painfully collected case history full of intricate details on the personal background of the fictional characters. To their artistic credit, the Italian Verists rarely displayed the pseudo-scientific recourse to the "laws" of heredity and environment that mar the novels and dramas of the French Naturalist school. With their common Sicilian origin, Verga, Capuana, and the young Pirandello wished to depict the customs and problems of life in their native island : the declining aristocracy, the peasants' distrust of the central government in Rome, the clergy's double-dealing, and the ruthlessness of entrepreneurs in the sulfur industry. In the creation of character they stressed the explosively violent passions of the deprived peasants.[14]

Because of his adherence to the principles of Verism and its goal of producing human documents, Pirandello doubted whether he could fashion morally positive characters. The tale "La Scelta" ("The Choice"), published in 1898 but written at least three years before, examines the artist's dilemma. In it the author recalls how as a child he went to the annual Sicilian toy fair, which is held on All Souls' Day. No matter how much the aggressive toy vendors fought with each other to persuade the little boy to purchase a tin trumpet or a train set, he invariably returned to the puppet stall with its figures taken from the epic songs of Charlemagne, Roland, and the paladins of France. Every year the child's irascible tutor Pinzone tried to dispel the puppets' magical attractiveness for the boy by pointing out the poor workmanship in the carving and painting of the faces; Pinzone also complained that the paladins were not worthy of admiration since they were either insane or treacherous knights. Now, as an adult, the author still goes to the fair, not the toy fair of childhood but the larger fair of life where, instead of selecting wooden marionettes, he chooses the heroes and heroines for his tales and novels. But his tutor's critical voice continues to speak to him and find fault with his selections, compelling the writer to recognize the falseness and misery of his models. In a deceitful and un-heroic world, an author desiring to write in a manner true to life will fail to represent exemplary characters. Pirandello wonders what the faithful writer can do with the "wretched, inane worrisome puppets that the daily fair only offers. . . ." For puppets, the author here uses the word *fantoccio,* the mechanism articulated by a wire; it is the term that he will employ most frequently to designate man's reduction to an impotent puppet. If life's drama is without sense, then its actors can function only as miserable creatures incapable of positive decisions. This early tale of the writer's choice illustrates Pirandello's highly critical attitude toward his own literary characters: their wretched nature so often dis-pleased him that he refused sometimes to realize them in a coherent work of art. The germinal situation of his most famous play, *Sei Personaggi in cerca d'autore* (*Six Characters in Search of an Author*), can be detected in this story written in his youth.[15]

In the essay on contemporary conscience and art, Piran-dello commented that man's pathetic place in post-Coper-nican cosmology ought to serve as the subject for a poem by a humoristic writer. But at that early moment in his development as an artist, the Sicilian author did not explain what he meant by humor. The fullest theoretical statements of Pirandello's attitudes toward art and life are to be found in the treatise *Umorismo* (*Humor*) of 1908. Unfortunately, this work has rarely received the critical attention that it deserves. Yet its poor reception and the absence of transla-tions in several foreign languages are not at all surprising if one considers the circumstances of the treatise's composition. Pirandello's theories on humor grew out of a series of courses he taught at the Women's Normal School in Rome, and he published the treatise in 1908 in order to secure a permanent post at that institution. One must read nearly one hundred pages of dense prose, heavy with Teutonic-style erudition, before the text comes to life; and then almost another twenty-five pages are required before the author arrives at an explanation of the true nature of humor.[16] The text should be studied in its entirety, however, since it represents far more than a general tract on humor in literature. Pirandello's *Umorismo* is an intense self-investigation, a document that illustrates the author's aesthetic doctrine and reveals his compassionate vision of human existence. This treatise sheds much light on humor in Pirandello's narrative writings, and a detailed analysis of it at this point will enhance subsequent evaluations of his stories and novels.

Part One of the treatise starts with a semantic discussion of the Italian word *umore*, which the Sicilian writer traces to its original physical meaning in Latin to refer to the four fluids of the human body and their effect on temperament. He at once distinguishes *umore* from the British *humour*, inasmuch as the Italian term does not include the meaning of "good humor" unless it is specifically modified so. Then he reviews the common confusion of humor with the comic, burlesque, satiric, grotesque, and trivial, or literary forms like caricature, farce, and epigram. Pirandello admits that most persons consider humor the form of writing that arouses laughter, and states that often humoristic authors have called themselves *ironists* to avoid being labeled buffoons, since the word *humor* had fallen in low repute. According to Pirandello irony can assume one of two natures, neither of which is truly humoristic. First he distinguishes irony as a rhetorical figure, a fictional wordplay between what is said and what is really intended. A highly sarcastic writer like Dante would fit Pirandello's definition of the rhetorical ironist but could never be considered a humorist. Aside from the merely verbal contradictions of rhetorical irony, there also exists philosophical irony, whose definition the Sicilian writer attributes to German Romantic literary theorists like Tieck and Friedrich Schlegel as a perpetual parody or a transcendental farce. Philosophical irony is the pin prick that deflates the world's vain appearance, and it serves as the instrument only of those authors who have so fully mastered the game of creation that they are not taken in by it but always recognize the irreality of their works.[17] Pirandello sees inherent in irony a pitiless, caustic quality that is absolutely inconsistent with his own interpretation of humor.

Before he can attempt a definition of literary humor, the Sicilian writer pauses to consider certain preliminary questions. Is humor exclusively a modern phenomenon? Is it foreign to Italian literature and therefore native to Anglo-Saxon literatures? Pirandello's method of answering these questions would never serve as an example of clear, logical demonstration and organization.[18] Despite the heavy erudition with references to Taine, Leopardi, and Jean Paul Richter, the author's quest into the nature of humor is not a matter of intellectual research but a deeply personal examination of the views that different writers have held about humor. At times Pirandello seems to seize upon certain basic distinctions, only to abandon them after close scrutiny of his sources. A case in point is his reference to a novella by the contemporary Italian humorist Alberto Cantoni, who imagined a confrontation between classical humor and modern humor. Cantoni visualized Classical Humor as a plump, jolly old fellow while Modern Humor appeared as a thin, highly reserved character with a mocking expression on his face. The two meet before the monument to Donizetti in Bergamo, and they challenge each other to attend the country fair at Clusone and afterward to return to the monument in order to relate their impressions, each according to his own humoristic temperament. Classical Humor's wit recalls the pleasantries of Boccaccio, Firenzuola, and Bandello, whereas his modern counterpart displays the dry humor and preference for the incongruous of writers like Sterne and Heine. The highly sensual and somewhat vulgar old man rebukes Modern Humor for the way he conceals tears of grief behind a smiling mask. Pirandello's use of the Cantoni story at first appears to differentiate between two applications of humor: the joyous, serene comic spirit of classical literature as opposed to the reflective, rather melancholy wit of more recent eras. But then the Sicilian author observes that Cantoni's modern humor is only a rather refined and subtle derivation of the classical form of the comic; Pirandello expressly refuses to accept the everyday confusion between humor and comedy. The Cantoni novella has served to lead the investigation into a blind corner.[19]

Humor for Pirandello is not an attribute of a literary genre but a quality of expression that requires the greatest possible linguistic freedom. The major weakness of Italian literary tradition has been the tyranny of rhetoric, which reduces writing to a series of rules for perfect composition. That rhetorical stress on exterior composition destroys the spontaneity that is absolutely necessary for the creation of humor. According to Pirandello humor has flourished in Italy only in vigorous dialectal poetry, in the Macaronic contamination of Latin with Italian, and in the writings of those few authors who broke away from artificial standards. Style for this Sicilian is inner creation of form, and in the section of his treatise entitled "Comic Irony in Chivalric Poetry" he examines the three most important Italian Renaissance chivalric poems that each exhibit a distinctly individual style: Luigi Pulci's *Morgante* (1478–1483), Matteo Maria Boiardo's *Orlando Innamorato* (*Roland in Love*) of 1494, and Lodovico Ariosto's *Orlando Furioso* (*Mad Roland*) of 1516. Pirandello notes that even before the chivalric epic entered Italy, its French originators had ceased to believe in the ideals of knightly life and the glory of Charlemagne's court and had already started the parody of the *chanson de geste* that was later carried to its most extreme development in Italy. Pulci's *Morgante* would fall under the definition of philosophical irony, since it deliberately travestied epic subject matter in a burlesque, plebeian style that reflected the taste of Laurentian Florence for exaggerated imitation of rustic poetry. Pirandello does not detect a trace of genuine humoristic spirit in Pulci's poem, although he acknowledges the artistic mastery over grotesque material that the *Morgante* displays.

Boiardo's *Orlando Innamorato* is condemned as a failure because the Ferrarese poet did not possess the imagination to participate seriously in the world of chivalric virtues like loyalty, valor, and courtesy, which he claimed to admire. If neither Pulci's riotous comedy nor Boiardo's gentle amusement conforms to Pirandello's idea of humor, Ariosto's smiling comprehension of human folly might appear to possess a genuinely humorous nature. The Sicilian writer admits to the magical quality of Ariosto's style that infused the enchanted world of the poem with the vividness of real life. In the bewitched gardens and castles of the *Orlando Furioso,* Ariosto placed characters who were motivated by true human passions as they frenetically sought to realize their fondest illusions. Ariosto succeeded in carrying his drama to the moment where reality causes illusion to vanish, as when the palace of the magician Atlante disappears like a puff of smoke and the liberated ladies and knights express their sorrow at the loss of the dreams that held them prisoners in the palace. But because Ariosto did not wish to explore the feelings of his characters after their illusions crumbled, Pirandello does not consider him a true humorist. When Ariosto's central character, Orlando, learns that his dream of love and beauty as incarnated by Princess Angelica is irrevocably lost to him, a destructive insanity sweeps over him. He never arrives at a superior perception of his illusions wherein he could recognize his essentially comic pursuit of Angelica. Orlando's madness is for Pirandello a tragic condition, and he judges Ariosto's unwillingness to fuse the tragic with the comic as totally alien to true humor.

Scholarly investigation finally assumes a deeply lyrical animation in the text of *Umorismo* when the Sicilian writer studies the first author he feels to be a humorist: Cervantes, with his *Don Quixote*. Cervantes' anti-hero meets defeat after he tries to impose his mad vision onto reality; the pathetic knight errant bears within himself a legendary view of life that clashes with the real world. Pirandello wonders why a heroic individual like Cervantes ever happened to write such a devastatingly critical parody of the chivalric romance, and he does not accept the Spanish author's avowed intention merely to destroy the powerful vogue of books of chivalry in his times. Surely Cervantes, veteran of Spanish wars against the Turks, would more easily have been expected to compose an epic glorifying the exploits of Charles V and the struggle of Christianity against Islam. But when Pirandello reflects on the moment in Cervantes' life when he conceived the figure of Don Quixote, the Sicilian writer begins to understand the Spaniard's motives. For the courageous Don Miguel Cervantes de Saavedra, who lost the use of a hand at the battle of Lepanto and later suffered five years of captivity among the Turks in Algiers, was languishing in a Spanish jail in La Mancha when he first envisioned the knight of the mournful countenance. Excommunication, betrayal, and imprisonment were Cervantes' reward for his lifetime of noble devotion to country and religion. In the jail of La Mancha the Spanish patriot at last saw himself clearly, realizing that he had led a Quixotic existence ever since his birth in 1547 at Alcalá de Henares. That flash of insight into his own life, forcing Cervantes to behold the contrast between his self-sacrificial aspirations and the wretchedness of his personal situation, made him into a humorist. When he came to recount Quixote's misadventures, Cervantes did not look in scorn at the knight's inability to tell the difference between giants and windmills, an army or a flock of sheep. Reflection on his long lifetime of mistakes inspired Cervantes with what Pirandello calls the "sentiment of the contrary" (*"sentimento del contrario"*), the realization of the sadness behind Quixote's apparently ridiculous errors. Instead of with scorn, the humorist regards his characters with sympathetic indulgence. Pirandello in *Umorismo* recognizes the author of *Don Quixote* as a kindred soul, one of the few writers who ever understood the autonomy of his fictional characters as creatures independent of their maker. Just as the Sicilian writer was to compose imaginary interviews between himself and his characters, so he concludes the Cervantes section with the Spanish author's holding an audience in his jail cell between Don Quixote and El Cid. Whereas El Cid enjoyed the good fortune of living in an age when courageous deeds and legend could fuse into one and the same heroic tale, poor Quixote's ardent faith brought him only painful blows.[20]

In the final section of the treatise's first part, Pirandello does answer his preliminary questions. Humor, he affirms, is a rare faculty in literature, but it is not exclusively a modern phenomenon, for even the ancient philosopher Socrates possessed it. Nor can humor be thought the private property of dry-witted Anglo-Saxons, since Italian writers like the novelist Alessandro Manzoni and the poet Giuseppe Giusti have displayed that "sentiment of the contrary" which Pirandello holds to be intrinsic to humor. In Part Two of his treatise the author proposes to expound on the essence, characteristics, and subject matter of humor. He points out that humor is a twofold process. He gives the example of an old woman who dyes her hair in a hideous manner, smears make-up over her wrinkled face, and wears clothes that are too youthful in fashion for her. One's first reaction is to laugh at the woman for her unbecoming appearance. Pirandello terms that initial, laughable impression the comic level or the "awareness of the contrary" (*"avvertimento del contrario"*), the recognition of the contrast between the ridiculous appearance of the old woman and what should be her respectable manner of dress and make-up. Humor arises when the laughing beholder starts to reflect on the reason for the old woman's appearance. She takes no delight in looking like a parrot, but she hopes to cheat the years and hold onto her young husband. From the "awareness of the contrary," the beholder has passed to the "sentiment of the contrary" through the thought process of reflection; from comic laughter he changes to compassion for the sad old woman who does not want to lose the man she loves. Pirandello in fact presents just such a wretched wife in his novella "Le Dodici Lettere" ("The Twelve Letters") of 1897, where Signora Baldinotti deceives herself that she can prevent the infidelities of her philandering husband by wearing smart clothes and arranging her hair in what she thinks is a seductive coiffure. Pity, rather than derision, for human error comes from the sentiment of the contrary. Humor for him includes compassion, seeing beyond the ridiculous superficial appearances into man's inner misery.

Humoristic reflection need not proceed from an awareness of comic incongruities. Pirandello analyzes Giuseppe Giusti's poem "Sant'Ambrogio" ("Saint Ambrose") to demonstrate the different ways reflection can work to awaken a sympathetic response. Giusti relates in his poem how one day he chanced to enter the Milanese church of St. Ambrose, which he found crowded with Austrian soldiers who stood there rigid in their military posture. As an Italian patriot, Giusti looked with hatred at the soldiery of the nation that held his country in bondage. After the military band began to play the chorus "Oh, Lord, out of our native home" from Verdi's *I Lombardi*, the music so enthralled the poet that his hostility started to melt away. Even when

Giusti tried to resume his initial attitude of resentment, he was forced, after they sang a melancholy German hymn, to see in those soldiers not his country's enemies but unfortunate human beings. The sad harmony of that hymn made the poet recall nostalgia for home, a desire for peace, the dread of exile. Giusti then realized that those poor soldiers had been separated from their homes and families in Bohemia and Croatia solely to satisfy the imperialistic ambitions of the Austrian government. Behind the soldiers' wooden stiffness he beheld the lonely men who were conscripted into a life of harsh discipline in a country whose natives despised them. The rapture that the hymn had inspired caused Giusti to forget his patriotic grievances, and his sympathy grew so strong that he had to flee from the church or otherwise he would have embraced one of the soldiers. Reflection, by arousing the sentiment of the contrary, changed Giusti's reaction, from one of enmity toward the soldiers as oppressors to a feeling of sorrow for those oppressed men.

A humorist must penetrate beneath appearances in the hope of discovering the vital truth that persons feel compelled to mask. In creating fictional characters a humorist must always show the self-contradicting situations into which life thrusts its victims, so that the author's attitude toward his characters' weaknesses will not be one of contempt but of sympathetic understanding. Alessandro Manzoni's portrait of the cowardly priest Don Abbondio in the novel *I Promessi Sposi* (*The Betrothed*), Pirandello asserts, would illustrate perfectly the humorist's method in conceiving a fictional character. Don Abbondio is a timid creature who makes a very grave error, that of refusing to marry a young couple out of fear of a local tyrant who has designs on the bride-to-be. This failure to carry out his clerical responsibility might at first make the priest appear a contemptible figure, but Manzoni takes great care to let his readers know that the danger to Don Abbondio's life is very great. In the novel's opening scene the priest encounters two cutthroats barring the way to his home. Don Abbondio's inability to escape the encounter, his physical discomfort in the assassins' presence, and his trembling before their orders are all described with a great comic verve, especially when the novelist concludes that the priest was not born with the heart of a lion. From that comic understatement Manzoni goes on to reflect that since Don Abbondio was neither rich nor noble by birth, his position was almost defenseless. The author's attitude toward his character avoids anger at the priest's neglect of duty, momentarily laughs at the cleric's terror, and then through reflection ends by pitying his helplessness in a society that does not enforce its laws. Pirandello observes that Manzoni's sympathy for the priest's all-too-human failings is particularly impressive because the novelist also succeeded in presenting morally positive characters like Cardinal Borromeo and the monk Fra Cristoforo as incarnations of the ideals of clerical responsibility and courage before danger. In his own fictional writings Pirandello was unable to include ideal characters, since his times—as he had commented in the early tale "La Scelta"—offered only examples of inane puppets. The Sicilian writer's situation was therefore more disconsolate than Manzoni's, because the entire human race required his compassion.

Pirandello returns to his favorite theme of the mirror when he compares humor to other artistic forms of expression. Reflection usually functions in the conception of a work of art as a mirror where sentiment can regard itself. But in the conception of a humoristic work, reflection serves as a special kind of mirror: the mirror surface of icy water where the flame of sentiment is not only reflected but is also quenched. Pirandello's use of imagery, like the simile between reflection and icy water, astounded and irritated some of his first readers, who did not expect poetic style in a scholarly treatise.[21] This style is essential to humor, for every humorist must be both poet and a critic of fantasy (*"critico fantastico"*) in order to create an art form that depends on a series of anitheses. No sooner does one idea arise in the humorist's mind than its opposite immediately suggests itself to him. Pirandello explains this process as a "phenomenon of doubling in the act of conception." The humorist conceives through polar oppositions, and a close scrutiny of Pirandello's fiction will reveal that a great many apparent contradictions must be attributed to the bipolarism of his vision. While other art forms work through synthesis, humor works through analysis to decompose every thought or sentiment that an author examines.

The humorist is a psychological analyst who breaks down the fictions of man's soul. His reflection resembles a little demon who dismantles a machine to see how it functions. He must expose the powerful sway of self-deception in human existence. Many of Pirandello's ideas on man's hypocrisy as a necessary psychic response to social pressure came from a popular text at the turn of the century: Giovanni Marchesini's *Le Finzioni dell 'anima* (*The Fictions of the Soul*). Society is founded on the falsehoods of honesty, friendship, trust, freedom, and love; people lie to themselves and to each other by pretending to accept those falsehoods as undeniable truths. In his youth, when he wrote his essays on falsification in art and the crisis of contemporary conscience, Pirandello reacted with nausea and scorn to his lying age. By the time he published *Umorismo*, his reading of authors like Marchesini and the troubled events of his own life (the loss of the family fortune and his wife's subsequent insanity) caused Pirandello to view mankind's deceptions and illusions with profound pity. The humorist recognizes lies as a form of social adaptation, and he tears them apart to arrive at an understanding of man's various roles in society.

From his examination of social lies the humorist begins to entertain doubts about the human personality. He comes to believe that no man can be absolutely sincere with himself. Man is forced to set certain limits on his conscious personality. There are times, however, when those barriers are broken down, and a wholly unsuspected self is manifested. Pirandello derived this theory of multiple personality from Marchesini's study and from Alfred Binet's *Les Altérations de la personalité*. The humorist rejects the notion of human personality as a unity and instead views man as fragmented in the struggle among his instinctive, moral, emotional, and social souls. The personality that one shows to the world and to himself is an ideal construction, and here the Sicilian author employs the term *costruirsi:* to construct for oneself a lasting form that will resist life's onslaughts. In *Umorismo* Pirandello does not yet resort to the facile dialectic of Life versus Form that will characterize his essays and stage writings after 1922 and that can be attributed to the influence of the literary critic Adriano Tilgher.[22] He views life as a continual flux that men try to halt by fixing it in permanent forms. The public mask, the *persona*, is no more than just another of those forms which are constructed with great care over the years but which only a brief moment of vital passion can destroy. Man's instrument for building the fictitious personality is logic, which the supremely anti-rationalist Pirandello assails as an "infernal little machine," a pump and filter running from the brain to the heart so that feelings can be cooled down to abstract ideas. Logic works insidiously to make life's mobility appear stable, to give absolute value to what is only relative. Through logic man builds the seemingly solid ego state, which Pirandello as humorist rejects.

Yet no man, no matter how stable his personality may appear, lives in full assurance of his being. For everyone there come moments of inner silence when the soul strips itself of its everyday falsehoods and vision acquires a power of penetration to see life in its arid nakedness. In a lightning flash one gazes on a reality utterly different from the normal reality. At this moment the soul begins to lose itself in the surrounding and menacing void, and in an attempt to save himself man rushes to a mirror, where he hopes to readjust his mask. But Pirandello's final mirror stage causes the on-looker to step outside of himself, to see himself living (*vedersi vivere*) in a painful experience of depersonalization. Most of the Sicilian writer's characters become haunted by doubts about their personality, as if their being were floating away from them; and their tormented gesturing before the mirror of self-examination represents an effort to gain the permanent and nonliving image of a statue. Although the Sicilian writer was to work apart from the current of Freudian thought, he arrived independently at a theory of the mirror stage that the neo-Freudian Jacques Lacan would later define as the most significant moment in an individual's life, when he based his personal identity on the images projected by other persons. Pirandello's humor works to reveal the falseness of an individual's ego, for it is founded on an Imaginary order between the self and others.[23]

The humorist exposes the artificiality of man's fabrications; he rips apart logical mechanisms to prove that life is not coherent. To uncover the pettiness of human existence the humorist reverses a telescope and looks at man through the large lens; all of man's grandeur then becomes infinitesimal. Since man is the animal that clothes itself, the humorist will divest man of his artificial garments to show the natural nakedness. While other writers construct their characters, the humorist takes his apart to exhibit their inconsistent personality. Pirandello as humorist is not interested in outwardly deforming his fictional characters through his art; rather, he seems to say that life is the force that deforms men physically and spiritually, twisting them in body and soul. His is not the art of a grotesque writer like Valle-Inclán in the *esperpentos*. Pirandello's humoristic art has to be a faithful mirror of man's outer and inner deformation.

Even in his youth Pirandello viewed life with the humorist's sentiment of the contrary. His first volume of verse, written between 1882 and 1888, bore the antithetical title *Mal Giocondo* (*Joyful Ill*) on its publication in 1889. At the University of Bonn Pirandello became acquainted with the German Romantic theory of humor as a sympathetic reconciliation of laughter and suffering.[24] The writings of pre-Freudian psychologists like Marchesini and Binet provided him with case-history evidence of the disintegration of personality and the deceitful patterns of character roles in society. From his day-to-day torture of living with an insanely jealous wife, Pirandello grew aware of the absolutely logical and wholly constructed reality of madness. By the time *Umorismo* appeared in print, the author had published five books of verse, three novels, and six volumes of novelle —all suffused with the compassionate spirit of his humor.

On his first arrival in Rome the twenty-year-old Pirandello had already decided on a career as a dramatist. It took almost another thirty years before he could realize his adolescent dream and write for the Italian stage those works which brought him international fame and revolutionized modern drama. The limited resources of the Italian theater before World War I made it impossible for the provincial writer from Sicily to have his first dramatic works staged. With Capuana's encouragement Pirandello turned to narrative writing. A critical study of the totality and originality of his literary accomplishments must include the narrative works, for Pirandello was neither a novelist *manqué* who found in the theater the ideal means of communication for his humoristic style, nor was he a narrative author who went astray by writing experimental plays. Even after his emergence as a major playwright he continued to write novelle and produced what might very well be considered his most important novel. At the time of his death the writer was contemplating a novel to be entitled *Adamo e Eva* (*Adam and Eve*) that was to be his final statement on the human search for inner peace. Pirandello did not evolve into a

dramatist. Instead he eventually found in the theater—
thanks to the innovative spirit of the Italian stage during
the world war—an opportunity for a living representation
of the themes and situations that he had first treated in his
narrative works. Examination of his novelle and novels must
precede consideration of his plays. In conducting this investigation I shall employ many of the literary theories and
analytical tools of critics like René Girard, Georges Poulet,
and Gaston Bachelard. The world of Pirandello's narrative
writings reflects the creative consciousness of an author in
search of a significance that remains painfully absent. As a
critic I intend to study the recurring patterns and obsessive
themes of this quest in narrative form and language.

The Mirror of Our Anguish

I

The Jests of Love and Death

Pirandello's Novellistic Art

Before his death Luigi Pirandello hoped to write a novella
for each day of the year and to gather them in the series
Novelle per un anno of twenty-four volumes, each consisting
of fifteen tales. By 1937, the year after his death, fifteen
volumes had appeared in print. In all, Pirandello succeeded
in completing two hundred and thirty-three novelle. The
earliest tale dates from his seventeenth year, and the final
surrealistic dream stories belong to the last five years of his
life. Between 1894 and 1920, before Pirandello conceived
the plan for *Novelle per un anno,* he published his tales in
a series of volumes with humoristically antithetical titles
like *Amori senza Amore* (*Loves without love,* 1894), *Beffe
della Morte e della Vita* (*Jests of Death and Life*), first series,
1902; second series, 1903, *Quand'ero matto* (*When I was*

mad, 1902), *Bianche e Nere* (*White and Black*, 1904), *Erma Bifronte* (*The Two-faced Herma*, 1906), *La Vita Nuda* (*Naked Life*, 1910), *Terzetti* (*Tercets*, 1912), *Le Due Maschere* (*The Two Masks*, 1914), *La Trappola* (*The Trap*, 1915), *Erba del Nostro Orto* (*Grass from Our Garden*, 1915), *E Domani, Lunedì* (*And Tomorrow, Monday*, 1917), *Un Cavallo nella Luna* (*A Horse in the Moon*, 1918), *Berecche e la Guerra* (*Berecche and the War*, 1919), *Il Carnevale dei Morti* (*The Carnival of the Dead*, 1919). Besides inclusion in those volumes, many novelle appeared on the story page of major daily newspapers like the Milanese *Corriere della Sera* as well as in the provincial *Giornale di Sicilia*. The author directed his tales to a reading public of the professional and semi-professional middle class, for whom the novelle were little mirrors of their suffering and frustrations.

In writing his novelle, Pirandello had behind him the long Italian narrative tradition of novellistic art that arose in the late thirteenth century with the *Novellino* and early attained near perfection with the *Decameron*. The novella tends to concentrate on a single central event that determines the course of the main character's life; that event serves to reveal the inner strengths or weaknesses of the tale's protagonist. In the early history of the novella the event was often no more than a practical joke (*beffa*) played on the hero, who either proved himself a *savio* by resorting to his superior intelligence or showed himself a ridiculous idiot like Boccaccio's Calandrino. In Pirandello's writings signifiers like "*beffa*" and "*savio*" will convey humoristic overtones about life's jests and the paradoxical nature of a wisdom that appears to be madness. After more than two centuries of decline, partly caused by ecclesiastical censorship, the Italian novella experienced a resurgence around 1830 through the efforts of Romanticists intent on educating the general reading public in a morality of *bontà* (social and individual goodness). Authors like Cesare Cantù, Giulio Carcano, Luigi Carrer, and Francesco Dall'Ongaro adapted the exhausted novellistic tradition to a short narrative form concentrating on depicting a specific setting (rustic or urban), exploring the plight of the lower classes, and emphasizing moral education. By the close of the nineteenth century Verga's two collections, *Vita Dei Campi* (*Life of the Fields*, 1880) and *Novelle Rusticane* (*Rustic Tales*, 1883), marked the definitive shift in stress from exterior action and verbal witticism, as in the Boccaccian novellistic tradition, to an examination of inner motivation and the influence of environment. Despite their Veristic aim to achieve objectivity, the novelle of Verga betray a fatalistic attitude that seems to be inherent in that narrative form and that distinguishes it from the regional short stories of other nations like Russia or the American South. The art of the novella lends itself to an irrationalistic presentation of life, where chance or fate strikes the protagonists.[1] Many of Pirandello's early novelle study the same insular world as is found in the tales of Verga. With his humoristic vision Pirandello saw life as a cruel practical joke, and his novelle are histories of the jests that delude his characters.

Neither in the earlier volumes nor in *Novelle per un anno* is there any attempt to place the tales in a frame story, as in the *Decameron*. Pirandello also abandoned a plan to publish his tales in volumes of thirty novelle as literary "months," thus recalling the ten "days" in Boccaccio's masterwork. Through the use of a frame story Boccaccio had succeeded in juxtaposing the licentious actions of the hundred tales in the *Decameron* against the moral restraint and refinement of the supposedly "real" characters who relate the frequently salacious novelle. But Pirandello realized only too clearly how by the twentieth century it would have been artistically false to encircle the chaotic material of life in a harmonious frame. Even in the individual tales the Sicilian author rarely resorted to that frame device of a story within a story which characterizes one fourth of Maupassant's tales and aroused Sartre's disapproval in *Situations II* for the apparent solidification of experience that the technique makes possible. In those Maupassant stories the frame introduces a gathering of the socially elite where a highly respected member of the group relates some adventure of his past or reflects on a curious confrontation of years before. Pirandello did not wish to focus on his tales from the outlook of a secure and seemingly stable social class, nor did he desire to set the throbbing pain of experience at a distance by employing the double past of the framed convention in the time of the fictitious narrator and that of the author. Incapable of affirming a connection between social hierarchy and narrative mode, Pirandello refused to people a frame story with morally positive characters, as he stated in that early tale "La Scelta" of 1895. The wretched, inane puppets in his novellistic world appear as calculating peasants, hypocritical clerics, disillusioned artists, game-playing entrepreneurs, lonely students, shrewd lawyers, disappointed Garibaldian veterans, unfulfilled teachers, exploited sulfur miners, reactionary aristocrats, neglected wives, unwanted children, the elderly longing only to die. Theirs are the masks and petty roles in a society that founds itself on mutual deception. Pirandello would not regard those dramas of deceit from the bourgeois point of view of order as affirmed by the frame convention. His novelle should be experienced as isolated moments of intense agony or brutal irony. It is true that both within the individual tales and the ensemble of the *Novelle per un anno* there is a universe: one of the submerged despairing in their anguish.

Settings of the novelle are in Sicily, with its contrasts between Greek temples, fetid peasant huts, fields blazing under an African sun, the eternal darkness of mines, the lunar madness of nighttime. Some of the novelle are set in Rome—not the city of Latin splendor, Renaissance glory, or Baroque pomp, but the overcrowded capital of united Italy. Heat, always ready to burst forth in flames of passion or violence, is a constant force throughout Pirandello's tales:

the fiery heat of the Sicilian landscape, the sultry oppressive-
ness of August afternoons on the streets or in the tenements
of Rome, the repressed emotions that finally explode with a
savage fury. Occasionally there are brief excursions to cool
mountain resorts where the characters can relax their masks
as they enjoy a holiday from the usual social pressures.
Reference is sometimes made in the novelle to the cities
of the Rhine Valley, where a few of the protagonists let
themselves be beguiled by a dream of love that eventually
eludes them. Some of the late tales take place in black Har-
lem, Jewish Brooklyn, and the loveless apartments of New
York. Quite often the scene is in a train compartment,
usually second class, or at a railroad restaurant where the
restless try to find each other. The one frame device that
does occur several times is that of an encounter, where the
narrator tells of a *recent* meeting with an individual who has
disturbed him to the very depths of his being. A large number of the characters suffer from myopia—physical myopia
and, by symbolic extension, spiritual—and are thereby
hampered in their quest for self-realization. Whatever the
social roles may be, wherever the novella is set, the characters remain separate from each other, each immured in his
own loneliness.

Even in his earliest novelle Pirandello tended toward
dramatic enactment of scene rather than pictorial presentation of events.[2] Indirect discourse is almost totally missing,
and lively dialogue takes its place. The novella "Formalità"
("A Mere Formality") of 1904 illustrates the dramatic technique of the stories written in the third person. It is structured in seven dialogue scenes that give the impression of
being staged rather than related. The opening scene very
briefly introduces the weary banker Gabriele Orsani and his
old trusted clerk Carlo Bertone. As a background effect the
sound of the surf is heard breaking against the Sicilian coast.
Scene two begins when the insurance agent Lapo Vannetti
presents his business card which, like a nameplate on a door,

acts in Pirandello's narrative as a variant of the mask and
official mirror image. A few sentences that read like stage
directions present this tale's prevailing mood of grotesque
automatism where Vannetti is described as an automatic
puppet (*"fantoccio automatico"*) made to perform ridiculous
movements as if someone were pulling marionette strings.
Vannetti's grotesqueness, emphasized by his vain attempt to
disguise a glass eye with a monocle, extends also to the
agent's speech, that has a lisp that he tries to cover with
a half-hearted laugh. Automatism and disguise emerge as
the leitmotives of the tale, where the banker as shown in the
third scene will no longer be able to mask the financial ineptitude that has wrecked his firm. In commenting on the
technique of comic unmasking or self-betrayal, Freud observed that psychical automatism results from an individual's
persistent reaction to different situations that demand flexibility but cause defeat for a person of habitual action. A
vital adaptability, an absence of automation, can rescue a
grave situation. Automatism also figures for Bergson in
Laughter as individually and socially destructive, because
mental inelasticity and inappropriate response prevent one
from facing present realities. But both for Freud and Bergson the comic mode unmasks inflexibility and corrects
society. Pirandello's humoristic art, however, does not accept
successful aggression against inelasticity. The disguised aggression behind Vannetti's speech defect and laughter as
well as Orsani's melancholy resignation to economic ruin
will not allow for a comic corrective. Three dialogue scenes
have presented a drama of psychical automatism and vain
disguise.

A language of deception, to oneself and others, characterizes this and other Pirandellian tales. For in the third
scene the conversation gives a glimpse into the banker's
past and how he permitted his father to force him into
a commercial life for which he was unsuited. Orsani mentions in what might seem a trivial remark to Vannetti that

he once played the violin, letting the reader behold him as a would-be artist who lost his opportunity for a brilliant future. Unlike Balzac or Stendhal, who genuinely imagined many alternate futures for their characters and expressed them in para-stories within conditional sentences and past contrary-to-fact clauses, Pirandello employs the past conditional tense and the imperfect subjunctive mood to uncover the ways that persons lie to themselves. Orsani thinks that his father believed that he would have succeeded in adapting himself (" . . . *sarebbe riuscito ad adattarsi . . .*") to banking. The linguistic device here is one of falsification, whereby the protagonist casts responsibility from himself to his father. Through retrospective summary the author attempts to represent the flow of thoughts in Orsani's mind as the tired banker assesses his misdirected life, the marriage without love that he contracted with an orphaned cousin just to please his father, the nine years of immobile cohabitation that built a wall of silence between the married couple, and the loss of a consoling friendship with a Dr. Sarti, whose education Orsani sponsored only to see the physician intrude in his private life as the confidant of the banker's wife. The verb *pareva* followed by a clause in the imperfect subjunctive (*dimenticasse*) indicates how in Orsani's envious eyes it seemed that Sarti was forgetting that he owed everything to the banker's generosity. During the presentation of the stream of Orsani's thoughts and memories, Pirandello avoids intervening directly into the narration; instead of commenting or analyzing in the manner of a Stendhal, the Sicilian author allows thoughts and events to occur as in a natural process.

With two knocks at the office door the drama resumes, and Orsani's wife, Flavia, makes her grand stage entrance in all her blonde radiance. As throughout Pirandello's tales, novels and plays, theirs has been a marriage founded on mutual incomprehension and finally shattered after uncontrollable circumstances necessitate a confrontation, as here when Orsani announces the collapse of his firm. Marriage, rather than being an affirmation of life in society, is a form of aggression through the inability of husband and wife to communicate with each other. Flavia's talk about a new carriage seems like a foreign language that Orsani cannot comprehend. In contrast to the tales of earlier authors like Giulio Carcano, whose protagonists reveal their inner strength of character by withstanding conflict, this typical Pirandellian couple reacts with furious resentment over the years of useless sacrifice that neither one wanted or appreciated. Unlike Carcano and his generation of writers, Pirandello was not concerned with moral education. But like his predecessors the Sicilian writer was interested in the reaction of his characters to conflict rather than in the conflicts in themselves. The drama here is one of emptiness, of vitally void persons whose futures have no more possibilities.

A violent anticlimax occurs when Orsani suddenly faints, and the "myopic" Dr. Sarti rushes in to examine his unconscious friend. Once again the author enters into a character's mind as he enables the reader to listen to the agitation and nascent hope in Sarti's thoughts as he attends to Orsani with a stethoscope. Since boyhood Sarti has loved Flavia, but only recently did the two confess their mutual affection. As dialogue resumes, Sarti informs Flavia that her husband is mortally ill and that he will never know the harm he caused the three of them. Here stress falls on social roles: those of husband, wife, physician, friend, lover—all of which involve obligations and cause conflict of interest when an individual assumes multiple parts. As the novella's sixth and truly climactic scene ensues after Orsani recovers consciousness and sends his wife away, a Pirandellian anguish prevails in the realization that all companionship is illusory and that every individual remains isolated. To his lifelong "friend," Orsani announces that he has overheard the conversation with Flavia about the banker's fatal illness. In direct dialogue the author reinforces the atmosphere of attempted deception when Sarti pauses in astonishment and then tries to deny the seriousness of the illness: *"Che . . . che hai sentito?"* ("What . . . what did you hear?"). Orsani's behavior in this scene is one of almost insane rationality characterized by a deceptive calm and a calculated control of speech, laughter, and gestures that mask an explosive desire for revenge. The menace of violent action is ever present in Pirandello's narrative writings, ready to burst through the tense language of his characters. The banker intends to do violence to the love between Sarti and Flavia by compelling the physician to declare him in perfect health to Vannetti so as to arrange for an insurance policy that will provide for Orsani's children. In his official post as the insurance company's local physician, Sarti realizes that he will never be able to marry Flavia, from fear of prosecution as an accomplice in fraud. The question arises as to why Sarti yields to Orsani's demand. Is it because the banker assails him with accusations of adultery, or is it the weight of his past friendship with Orsani? Scandal could also wreck his medical career. The future that Sarti dreamed for himself and Flavia has to vanish as the physician assumes the role of an automaton in the tale's final scene, attaching his signature to the medical statement that Vanetti calls a "mere formality." As the title indicates, persons of automatic habit are prisoners of social ceremonies, of formal procedure. Pirandello studies here the values and ceremonies of the Victorian middle class in Sicily and finds them devoid of that *"bontà"* which earlier writers felt would redeem society. Because of his Veristic desire for an objective literary method, Pirandello has given this novella a decidedly theatrical dimension. The succession of dramatic scenes pauses only for a summary of past events and a review of earlier feelings as reflected in the minds of the characters themselves and rendered in a substitutionary speech that recaptures each individual's own idiom. Narrative distance makes the story appear to happen on the page as though in a theater. When the novella ends, it is as if a final curtain were falling.

In contrast to the technique of dialogue scenes and reflective "narrated monologue" in third-person tales, Pirandello employs "interior monologue" in first-person novelle to establish a direct relationship between the fictitious narrator and the reader.[3] It is an oral mode of address to the reader. The tale "Quand'ero matto ("When I was mad," 1901) opens in this manner: "First of all, I request permission to state in advance that I am now a wise man. Oh, on account of that I'm also poor. Also bald. When I was still, in a manner of speech, the honorable Mr. Fausto Bandini, I was rich and I had a head full of the most beautiful hair—proof positive that I was mad. . . ." Here the dominant signifiers are *matto* and *savio*, placed in antithesis to each other but with humoristic overtones as to the true nature of wisdom or madness. The solitary mode of first-person narration, as also in Maupassant's tales, is suitable to stories of madness since it compels readers to behold reality from the viewpoint of the perhaps deranged narrator. Another signifier that figures importantly in this tale is *imbecile*, such a favorite Pirandellian term that it is the title of a tale and a one-act play derived from the story. Fausto Bandini is among the first of those monumental figures of madness in Pirandello's writings which include Enrico IV and Vitangelo Moscarda in the author's final novel. The term *matto*, or its equivalent in the play *Enrico IV*, *pazzo* is a label that others impose on an individual who threatens their view of reality.

From the start of his tale Bandini develops an immediate dialogue with the reader-listener, but he displays none of the frightening intensity of an Enrico IV or Vitangelo Moscarda. This technique also has a visual dimension that permits the reader to imagine the now-bald Bandini as his face changes expression during the course of his long monologue; a certain "*poétique du regard*" operates here as the narrator projects distorted images of himself as rich man, beggar, madman, and sage. The tense can shift from the narrator's present sanity to a descriptive past when he occasionally relapses into madness. Fausto relates how one evening he met a beggar girl on the street and took her home to work as a servant for his wife, Marta, who very sanely dismissed the girl and scolded Bandini for that latest relapse into extravagance. The beggar girl and the wife represent opposite poles of conduct between insanity and rational stability; as choral figures they determine different realities for the narrator. Snatches of dialogue in the encounter with the girl give the reader-listener a vivid impression of Bandini's most recent skirmish with insanity.

Through the technique of interior monologue the narrator also enters into a debate with his audience in an effort to demonstrate his position and prove his contention that to pursue wisdom and behave morally will only provide convincing evidence of a demented mind. In *Madness and Civilization* Foucault declared that the necessity of madness is bound to the possibility of history. Bandini's personal history arises out of the madness of social relationships that Pirandello's paradoxical art probes. In dichotomies like *matto / savio* or *ricco / mendicante,* the signifying terms of the story establish reflexive relations as the tale turns on itself in an examination of an individual's nocturnal nature, which the narrative method permits the reader to explore. The reader becomes an internal observer as the author eliminates the initial narrator / reader distance and reproduces the schizoid annihilation of ordinary chronological time in order to transform present and past into eternity. With its starts, interruptions, and winding back upon itself, the interior monologue serves here to represent the linguistic structures of the unconscious.

In the tale's second section Fausto describes his madness as a state of dwelling not in himself but fusing in the lives of others. He made a hotel of his being and allowed others to become the tenants of his heart. Hoping to win his first wife, Mirina, over to his views, he composed a treatise called *The Foundation of Morality*, also in the form of a dialogue with his spouse in which he defended his belief in an immanentist philosophy with its vision of a harmonious world. Mention of the dialogue treatise adds another narrative level to the tale that proceeds from the present of sanity to a past of madness and then to the pantheistic text with its debates. Bandini's longing to experience a continual empathy with the surrounding world, even to penetrating the life of plants, belongs to the same kind of mystical lunacy as that of St. Francis d'Assisi and follows an inclination studied by Freud of the conscious desire to adhere to the nonconscious. Within this tale's multiple levels the narrator wishes to show his former pantheism as an error, for when he thought he was living a divinely inspired existence, his employees were robbing him. His new wisdom consists of thinking solely of himself. The novella becomes an argument between the audience-readers and the narrator who, in the guise of asserting his present selfish attitude, is truly trying to persuade himself that he has found the one sure means of salvation. But no one, reader or narrator, remains convinced of the madman's conversion.

Fausto Bandini's tale contributes to the modern definition of madness. As Roland Barthes stated in a review of Foucault's text, madness no longer requires a substantial definition as a disease or a functional definition as antisocial behavior but a structural definition as the discourse of reason about nonreason. This last procedure is that of Pirandello's fictitious narrator, who adds to the proliferation of discourses in the world. Bandini keeps interrupting his narrative with philosophical comments and then excusing himself to his listeners in this way: "But I had promised to relate only what I did." But his discourse about nonreason is a futile one, as he came to realize shortly after the death of his sister-in-law, Amalia, who was murdered by Mirina. With what he then though was wisdom, Fausto drove his murderous and adulterous wife away from their home to her lover; all he earned was the contempt of her relatives and the hatred of his wife. The narrator's mental derangement has derived from believing that other persons perceived the identical reality that he did and from not recognizing that each individual must find truth for himself. The tale is a discourse on the languages of relative truth. This novella with its various levels of debate—between the narrator and the reader, between Bandini and other characters—displays the dialectical nature of Pirandello's writings. The story leaves the impression of being a series of disputations re-enacted for the reader, who feels almost impelled to contribute to the discourse. The more logical the arguments, the more unnatural they become, since, as the author was later to assert in *Umorismo*, logic works against the vital process to impose rational constructs. In the novella's final section, "School of Wisdom," Bandini tries to pursue his mad logic that reasonable thieves should never destroy the source of their enrichment, an argument that, regrettably for him, his rapacious employees did not accept. Only one person heeded Fausto's discourse: his conscience-stricken secretary Santi, who robbed modestly and often invited his tattered master to dinner, when debate continued between Bandini and Santi's wife, Marta. At those dinners Marta argued that when all others robbed without moderation, then any check on thievery showed not reasonableness but stupidity and cowardice. Marta understood better than Fausto or Santi the nature of "role" in society. Since Bandini declared that his role was to live for others, Marta reasoned that his wealth therefore belonged to everyone else. And those others, the thieves, must regard their voluntary victim as a madman, never a sage. Fausto Bandini, living on the charity of one of those thieves, joins those "beggars at the gate" who are among the most important of Pirandello's characters and include most of the protagonists of his novels as well as Enrico IV or Signora Frola in the play *Così è se vi pare*.

Ironically, Fausto's discourse triumphs, for thanks to Santi's virtuous wisdom the narrator eventually weds Marta after the secretary's death. Pirandello's novella presents the paradox that a madman will in time be led on the path of prudence through the foresight of a kind and grateful thief. The interior monologue and the author's use of it to awaken discourse arise from the humoristic outlook that always sees the opposite of any assertion. By relating the tale in phrases that move tortuously upon themselves, the narrator employs a psychologically designed language that is the voice of a madman rebelling against social roles.

These two novelle, both written within the first decade of the author's literary career, reveal the antithetical tendencies of the romantic world view that Pirandello shared with other writers of his generation at the turn of the century. From its beginnings after the Napoleonic wars, Italian Romanticism had advocated a program of truthfulness in art, but writers differed sharply in defining the nature of the truth that art must find—either an inner, intuited poetic truth or the truth of facts that can be documented.[4] Niccolo Tommaseo (1802–1874) illustrates the first attitude by stating in his *Diario intimo* that he hoped to write poetry imitating a piece of music, a painting, a building, a garden, a leaf, the human body, and that he wanted to describe the invisible world, an interior world, a new mythology. The emphasis on poetic intuition was one day to produce movements like Symbolism, Decadentism, and Surrealism, whereas the demand for factual representation led to Verism. In the novella "Formalità," Pirandello made a Veristic study of a bourgeois environment in Sicily; that tale could easily be considered a demonstration of the concrete art that Luigi Capuana recommended in his essay *Gli 'ismi' contemporanei* of 1898. But Pirandello also recognized that there could be no single solid reality, and "Quand'ero matto" is a dialectic between the saintly insanity of self-effacement and the practical need for self-assertion. What the author presented as an abnormal case in Bandini's story was to become the principal realm of investigation in his major writings.

The Role of Death

While love figures as an empty illusion in the lives of the novellistic characters, death is a supremely powerful force that reduces persons to playthings. Although Freud noted that in literature there still were persons who knew how to die, many of Pirandello's characters do not know when to die. The title of his second volume of novelle is *Jests of Death and Life,* with emphasis on the paradox of the flesh that lives but that one day must rot. Death's decisions are alone irrevocable. Pirandello's preoccupation with death can easily be shown by the number of times it appears in the novelle. If a reader opens any volume of tales, he or she will find out that death is a major actor in at least two-thirds of the tales.[5] The volume *La Rallegrata* exemplifies the predominance of death. Its title story, "La Rallegrata" ("Horse's Gambol"), belongs to Pirandello's series of animal fables; it presents funeral rites as viewed by talking horses. The former regimental horse Fofo fails to understand that he is working for a mortuary to help draw a hearse; instead, he believes his employers are transporting valuable cargo that has to be accompanied with all the pomp of caparisoned horses, a band, and strangely dressed men in black skirts. In "Canta l'epistola" ("He chants the epistle") a young ex-seminarian takes part in a duel although he is certain that he will be killed. Death by one's own hand is the subject of "Sole e Ombra" ("Sunlight and Shadow"), where the elderly Ciunna knows that shortly his embezzlement of a large sum will be exposed to the authorities and he goes off for a seaside outing with the determination not to return alive. Both suicide and the threat of murder obsess the protagonist of "L'Imbecile." A youth who went mad after his fiancée's death persists in gazing at her apartment window even though a year has passed and a humpbacked dwarf has moved into the apartment; the physically deformed heroine of "I Tre Pensieri della Sbiobbina" ("The Humpback's Three Thoughts") readily understands the fatal misfortune that deprived the young man of his sanity. In "Sopra e Sotto" ("Above and Below") Professor Carmelo Sabato cannot console himself for his wife's death, and while her body lies downstairs in state, he climbs up to the roof to get drunk. The heroine of "O di uno, o di nessuno" ("Either of the one or of no one") undergoes a spiritual reawakening after she becomes aware of her pregnancy, but no sooner is the baby born than she dies. Two tiny children, title characters of the story "Nené e Niní," seem to possess diabolical powers along with a considerable inheritance, and they pass from one set of parents to another as each new guardian dies from grief. In one of the few stories where Pirandello sees death as a collective experience, "Requiem aeternam dona eis, Domine," the people of a mountainside village struggle with the authorities and their feudal landlord for the right to have a cemetery of their own; in a nighttime funeral ritual the village patriarch tries to hurl himself into a grave that his devoted townspeople prepared for him. For Pirandello the moment of death and the act of love always seemed physically repulsive,[6] and in the novella "Notte" ("Night") he introduces a widow whose lustful husband died during intimacy with her. All of these tales from La Rallegrata illustrate an interest in death that Pirandello pursued during his entire literary career. Two of the stories, "L'Imbecile" and "O di uno, o di nessuno," were in fact to inspire later plays.

Even some of the most Veristic novelle reflect the author's obsession with death as life's most accomplished jester. The tale "Il Vitalizio" ("The Annuity for Life") of 1902 recounts the story of a man who avoided death. At the age of seventy-five the peasant Maràbito turned his farm over to a usurer for a lifelong annuity of two lire a day. At the time of the sale the peasant sincerely believed that death was near, and the usurer eagerly entered into the annuity agreement in the hope of making a profit in five years or less. After five years of an idle and boring life in town, Maràbito fell ill from pneumonia and almost died. Upon his recovery the old man took up basket weaving to give himself a renewed interest in existing and also to provide a dowry for his adopted daughter. Soon afterward the usurer passed away, and a notary assumed his accounts and continued to pay the annuity. Throughout the region Maràbito became known as the man who would not die, for punishment of the rich money-lenders. On the occasion of the peasant's one-hundredth birthday, the notary held a banquet to celebrate the event. At that party the notary collapsed and died. By the story's end Maràbito returned to his farm, where he continued to live in contentment with his adopted daughter and her husband who worked the land for him. In "Il Vitalizio" the author used a real-life story to show how death in its capriciousness would not always come to those who were resigned to its inevitability.

By contrast, another Sicilian novella, "La Mosca" ("The Fly"), of 1904 reveals how death cruelly strikes the young, who are the most fit to enjoy life. Because the young peasant Giurlannu Zarú decided to take a nap in a barn while his cousins Saro and Neli worked during the night with the farm women shelling almonds, he was condemned to die. For while he slept, Giurlanni was bitten by an insect that was carrying an infectious and deadly disease. Toward dawn his cousins found him feverish, bloated, and black in color. This tale presents a spectrum of death and life: the livid hue of a dying man, the blinding glare of the sun over the countryside, the cheerful moonlight by which peasants work and sing. Giurlannu and his cousin were supposed to take part that day in a double-wedding ceremony—weddings being an affirmation of the vital principle, according to Pirandello. As the dying peasant listened to the physician who was explaining the probable cause of the fatality, Giurlannu saw a fly alight on Neli's cheek and start moving toward a small cut on his chin. Giurlannu could have called out, but at that moment envy of the cousin who might live and marry and know happiness so swept over him that he waited until the fly had bitten Neli. The tale closes in silence, with Giurlannu left alone to die in the company of the satisfied fly. Instead of a double wedding there is to be a double death. But just as the adjective *cupo* (gloomy) predominates in coloristic terms, the adjective *solo* (alone) stresses the solitude of each of the cousins at death. If one considers the strength of kinship ties in Sicily and the particular closeness of cousins of the same age in that society, then one can appreciate the isolating effect of death in Pirandello's tale as it annihilates all bonds. Giurlannu's deadly silence is a primitive response to the life and joy that were to be denied him as death made him insensitive to the values of family ties. Death's violent intrusion leaves no possibility of preparing for the final moment, when that moment is expected to be one of the nuptial festivity. Although in both "Il Vitalizio" and "La Mosca" Pirandello displayed the Veristic concern for documenting details of the setting and rustic customs, with particular stress on representing social differences (landlords versus tenants, an educated physician before illiterate peasants), he also endeavored to create a sustained mood of fatality in the Sicilian landscape of despairing solitude, with desolate hills and dusty roads alongside menacing ravines. Pirandello went beyond realism by personifying death as a fly that mocks human aspirations, as in this line: "No one knew it, but death meanwhile was there, yet so small that one would scarcely have been able to notice it if he had paid attention to it." The placement of temporal adverbs like *intanto* (meanwhile) and *ancora* (yet) contributes to indicating the insect's fatal persistence. In the tiny fly the author found a symbol of that power which crushes man.

An entire series of Pirandellian novelle could be labeled as *graveyard* or *funeral* stories. None of them are nightmare excursions reminiscent of tales by Poe, Heine, or Maupassant, for their most outstanding feature is the author's everyday depiction of the rituals and environments connected with death. Even though fear of the unknown occasionally appears in these stories, it possesses little of the shiver before inexplicable forces that characterizes horror stories. In many of the tales Pirandello juxtaposes the ridiculous against the pathetic. The tale "l'Illustre Estinto" ("The Illustrious Corpse," 1909) could easily be considered an illustration of a comment in *Umorismo* that death was not particularly respectful to the human love of pomp. In the novella the illustrious corpse is that of Costanzo Ramberti, former minister of public works. As he assumed his high position, death was already upon Ramberti and soon compelled his retirement after he collapsed from a stroke. The one consoling thought of the dying man was that of a magnificent state funeral, with the eulogies, wreaths, and public honors that government deputies would provide in his memory. The living always expect to be remembered, and Pirandello follows a modernist, literary approach to death by showing discontinuity rather than commemoration. For although the mayor of the town in which the deputy died did his utmost to drape the shabby city hall with due pomp, none of the officials at the funeral reception came out of respect but merely used the occasion to get their names and pictures in the newspapers. Even Ramberti's own corpse failed to be reverent; at the funeral's most solemn moment, when the president of the House of Deputies entered, a loud rumble burst forth from the corpse's stomach—a highly humoristic occurrence of *digestio post mortem:* bodily processes noisily intrude where there should be solemnity. At the Rome train station porters negligently confused Ramberti's casket with that of a poor seminarian, so that the following day the mayor of his municipality delivered a funeral oration over the wrong casket while he named Ramberti Square. When town officials learned of the mishap, it was too late in the ceremony to correct the situation. Late that night the mayor and four gravediggers secretly transported the real corpse from the train station and buried it with the hushed furtiveness that would usually be accorded the most infamous criminals. When confronted with death, a man who has had a successful public career is but a spiritual bankrupt, and his burial turns into a farce instead of a triumph. Death reveals in Ramberti's case how inauthentic his whole life of government service was. The ill man died alone (always the Pirandellian emphasis), except for the secretary who felt it his duty to attend the former high official.

The semantics of death can readily create situations of comic misunderstanding. In the late novella "Resti Mortali" ("Mortal Remains," 1924), a relative's dying proves to be a continuation of the problems an old man had persisted in creating throughout his life. Elderly Uncle Fifo insisted on disobeying his physician's orders and traveled from Rome to Bergamo to extend his farewell to a nephew who was about to embark for America. As might have been expected, the stubborn old man could not withstand the rigors of the train trip and passed away immediately after his arrival in Bergamo. Although preoccupied with the preparations for his departure from the port of Genoa, Fifo's Bergamasque nephew found time to arrange for shipping the corpse back to Rome by rail. Out of respect for the old relative whom he had repeatedly cursed, the nephew filled out a shipment form with the label "mortal remains" instead of "corpse." At the Rome station relatives were waiting with a first-class hearse drawn by four horses, wreaths of flowers, lines of nuns and choir boys, a priest, and representatives of organizations in which Uncle Fifo had been a member. But the indignant customs officials at the station presented the stunned relatives with a bill for several thousand lire as a fine for the fraud that they accused the nephew of attempting in order to avoid paying the regular fee for transportation of a coffin. The term *mortal remains* was supposed to designate some ashes and bones in an urn, which cost a low fee for rail shipment. The officials refused to recognize a mere difference in semantics between *resti mortali* and *salma* (corpse) or *bara* (coffin), for they could only interpret as deliberate deception the designation that the nephew had meant as a final act of reverence to his uncle. While the relatives argued with the customs officials to make them understand that no one had intended fraud, the members of the funeral party were standing outside in the street under the August sun. No one on either side yielded, and the entire funeral was dismissed. It seemed that Uncle Fifi had played another trick on his family and forced them to go to a great deal of trouble for nothing. Pirandello's treatment of the obdurate customs officials who held to the letter of the law recalls Bergson's definition of the comic in *Laughter* as arising when life repeats a fully mechanical process. The officers in the Italian novella resemble the guards described in Bergson's treatise who rushed over to some survivors from a shipwreck in the English Channel and seized them for not officially entering France. Once again mental inelasticity produces a comic situation, and the relatives dressed in ceremonial mourning are almost as guilty as the officials of failing to be flexible—refusing to complete the funeral over the principle involved with the fine. The ruling perspective of the tale is a humoristic one that reduces Uncle Fifo to an inanimate object (no longer a person whose memory is to be revered) over which interested parties dispute proper designations. Uncle Fifo's death is the old man's final revenge on the relatives who never cared for his eccentricities, and bureaucratic obstructionism shows how governments never render life easy by making death a grotesque comedy.

A few of Pirandello's graveyard novelle examine the

lack of communication between husbands and wives. For although death is a final event for the dead individual, the remembrance of the departed by survivors bridges time and frequently dominates the present and future. This preoccupation with past memory is again symptomatic of mental rigidity, described by Bergson as "privileged recollection" wherein an individual fails to behold the present reality but sees the world as it was. Instead of adjusting to a present situation, the individual lives a past and truly imaginary reality. Sometimes a person comes to an awareness of what is actually before his or her eyes, but the handicap of memory can prevent this self-liberation. In the gloomy tale "Prima Notte" ("First Night," 1900) a couple spend their wedding night wandering about a cemetery. The groom is the cemetery caretaker and he has remarried a year after his first wife's death solely to have a homemaker. His bride, young Marastella, has wed out of economic necessity and not love, for seven years before, her father and fiancé were killed in a shipwreck. After the bride falls to the ground and begins to weep at her fiancé's grave, the caretaker leaves her and goes over to his first wife's tomb to call out her name. With their attachment to the ghosts of the past, the couple will make a living reality of death and never establish any conjugal affection. Theirs is a nocturnal passion for the shadows of the past that privileged recollection summons before their eyes.

A breakthrough to redeeming self-awareness occurs in the tale "La Corona" ("The Wreath," 1914). After seven months of marriage the middle-aged Dr. Cima has received from his youthful bride only respect, tepid affection, and occasionally gratitude but never love, which she reserves for the memory of a student who died some years before. By accident the physician learns that his wife has ordered a wreath that she wants to place on the student's grave to honor the anniversary of his death. Momentarily enraged by this sentimental betrayal, Dr. Cima at first plans to send his wife back to her parents so she can spend the rest of her life mourning for the student. Overcoming his emotions, the physician himself takes her to the cemetery and places the wreath on the grave. For the first time the girl's eyes open to present reality as she comes to recognize her husband's capacity for compassion and understanding. Her plea for forgiveness marks the start of a genuine marital relationship. The physician's generosity permits the wife to surrender privileged recollection and begin a new relationship. Here Dr. Cima breaks into the walled circle of his wife's love for the phantom student. For both this tale and "Prima Notte," Pirandello used a minimum of pictorial detail to create an appropriate mood for the barriers between married couples: lugubrious moonlight and shadow for the hopeless mourners; new green, songbirds, butterflies, and blossoms for the renascent springtime of "La Corona." To make a new life for themselves after death has deprived them of the ones they loved, the novellistic characters have to learn to live with the past and not in it.

Funerary inscriptions can attest in stone to the tender regard a husband and wife once felt for each other. In the novella "Due Letti a Due" ("Double Tombs for Two," 1908) Pirandello studies the falseness behind the communication code of many inscriptions. Death, like any other human event, requires its own system of signs to convey messages of heartfelt regard or enduring esteem. As the poet Ugo Foscolo affirms in "Dei Sepolcri" ("Of Tombs"), tombs are of service to the living and future generations rather than the dead. In Pirandello's tale a Signor Zorzi requested that upon his death his attorney Gàttica-Mei construct a tomb for two in a Roman cemtery so that one day Signora Zorzi might rest beside her husband. Three years earlier the lawyer had built a similar double tomb after his wife's death. Gàttica-Mei not only carried out his client's request but added the inscription that Zorzi was waiting for his "faithful companion" to join him. The inscription's hypocrisy angered the widow Zorzi, who for three years had been carrying on an adulterous affair with the attorney. The widow was eager to legitimize the relationship, and she understood from the inscription that Gàttica-Mei had no intention of marrying her. Here the attorney's reluctance to alter reality illustrates a literally petrified example of privileged recollection, for along with a desire not to alter his way of life Gàttica-Mei hesitated before remarriage mainly because he did not wish to disturb the perfect symmetry of the double tomb. The attorney is such an egotist that he finds it difficult to affirm a sense of community with the living that remarriage would achieve. In this tale that pair of tombs for two was actually another of those human constructions which, according to Pirandello, served to impose artificial constraints on the vital force. In time the widow Zorzi won her way with the lawyer after she nursed him back to health from a serious illness. The thought of the two twin tombs continued to torment Gàttica-Mei, who expected to die before his second wife and feared for the harmony of the tombs. After the lawyer's death his widow made what she thought was a respectable decision, since she desired above all to be considered a respectable lady; throughout the novella she insisted on the idea of "*onestà*", the social respectability that became a category of existence in one of Pirandello's most important social plays. The widow Zorzi-Gàttica-Mei decided to bury the lawyer in the double tomb with her first husband, and she reserved for herself the right to be entombed with Gàttica-Mei's first wife. In that manner a new symmetry was created. Those double tombs did not bear witness to eternal marital loyalty and consoling remembrances but became monuments to death.

For some of the novellistic characters a grave can offer comfort and an appealing sense of permanence. Nonno Bauer, an elderly retired bank clerk in "Il Giardinetto Lassù" ("The Little Garden Up There," 1897), treasured plants more than anything else in life. Once he moved away from an apartment house rather than watch a tree die in the build-ing's courtyard.[7] Since he lacked the funds to acquire an apartment with a garden plot, he determined to provide for his death and find space for a little garden at one and the same time. He purchased a cemetery plot and lavished on it all his loving care so that it brought joy and bright color into the somber Roman graveyard. Whenever persons saw old Bauer working over his blossoms, they wondered if he were a ghost risen from the grave to see that it was properly tended. During the old man's final illness he offered to share his burial plot with a little boy who was dying of typhoid fever. Nonno Bauer's generosity appears quite unique in Pirandello's novelle, where the characters usually guard their burial rights with a fierce selfishness. In the tale of the kindly old Alsatian Bauer, death loses some of its grimness.

A direct invitation from death generally arouses conster-nation and immediate resentment. Scalabrino, the lazy hearse driver of "Distrazione" ("An Oversight," 1909), re-verted to old habits one blistering August afternoon while he was transporting the first corpse of his new job to a Roman cemetery. As the miserable third-class hearse climbed slowly up a steep hill, the driver began to doze. On awakening, Scalabrino momentarily forgot the nature of his job, and he hailed a pedestrian to mount the hearse. To the driver's total astonishment the pedestrian threw a package at him and then climbed up on the hearse to strike him until passersby and the police restrained the man. Scalabrino's oversight in inviting the pedestrian to get on the hearse occurred because up until the day before he had worked as a cabbie and he was accustomed to signalling to pedestrians that his cab was free. Naturally the man on the street did not welcome a ride to the cemetery; he was pre-pared to fight against an appointment with death. A similar battle against death is the subject of "L'Uccello Impagliato" ("The Straw Bird," 1910), where the brothers Marco and Annibale Picotti resort to every extreme health stricture to

survive past the early age at which most members of their
family died of tuberculosis. After they have passed the age
limit, Annibale starts to relent on the rigid regimen of diet
and sleep. When Annibale marries, Marco breaks with him
and divides all their belongings. As a talisman of good luck
Marco takes a bird of straw, which in the novella serves as
the concrete symbol of his determination to defeat death.
When three years later Annibale dies, life closes around
Marco in all his solitary contempt for youth, love, and springtime. After his devoted housekeeper falls fatally ill, he sends
her away to perish in a hospital all alone. Marco would agree
with the narrator of Maupassant's tale "The Mad Woman"
in this view of fatality: "When death has once entered a
house, it almost always returns immediately as if it knew
the door." For, as in Maupassant's story, death here is
personified as a crushing force that paralyzes its victims.
In encountering the unseen, incomprehensible might of
death, Marco is determined that fatality will never overtake
him. After scoring a partial victory by surviving to sixty, he
slashes the bird to shreds and shoots himself. Knowing that
no mortal illness will ever claim him, Marco chooses death
on his own terms. This attitude toward death is that of a
suicidal mind in a state of torpid annihilation. Fear of dying
incapacitates his rational faculties until he falls into the trap
that death sets for everyone.

For Pirandello death is far more a psychical state than a
physical condition. Matteo Sinagra, the protagonist of "Da
Sè" ("By Himself," 1913), realizes one day that he has been
dead for three years. Fortune had always favored him until
all of a sudden his business collapsed, and he is now reduced
to working as a messenger for a rural bank. Three years
later (note how Pirandello prefers this symbolical interval)
he meets an old acquaintance, and in his friend's eyes he
sees the almost unrecognizable mirror image of himself:
faded suit, weather-worn hat, torn shoes—the picture of a
run-down failure lacking the moral resiliency to recover from

the shock of his commercial losses. Sinagra is a psychic suicide who has already retired from life. Seeing that he is no more than a walking and breathing zombie, Matteo takes it upon himself to spare his relatives the expenses of a second-class funeral. He determines to arrange everything "by himself" and to stroll leisurely to the cemetery, where he will shoot himself. Now that the agony of dragging out a physically and psychologically depressed existence is behind him, Sinagra can look at the world with the vision of one who has found liberation in death. Trees, mountains, clouds, the sea, the very air enrapture him as they could never do in life. As the living dead, he is able to enjoy "eternity, vivid, present, trembling," which people fail to notice because of their preoccupation with trivial, everyday affairs. The tremendous effort of will required to make this fatal decision, following the mirror analogue of his acquaintance's eyes, briefly brings him out of the syndrome of the walking corpse. Entering the graveyard, Sinagra resolves to walk around the grounds and marvel at the funereal scenery until the moon (the usual Pirandellian signal for death) rises. True death is that of the personality and its sense of reality. As an individual Matteo Sinagra died along with his business ventures, and suicide in the world of time proves no more than the cutting off of a meaningless physical existence. The second shock of the mirror experience momentarily awakens the dulled consciousness of the psychic suicide who, by deciding to confront death, comes to rejoice in the timelessness of a liberating encounter with outward nature that he will join through his fatal gesture. Whereas Marco Picotti's suicide results from a stagnant nihilism, Sinagra's self-destruction springs from a realization of the need to participate again in the source of life.

One of the situations that recur frequently throughout Pirandello's writings is that of the death watch, where friends and relatives perform the ritual routine of waiting out a person's final moments. A society performing such a routine is one that has become encapsulated in habit, as in the novella "Visitare Gl'infermi" ("Visiting the Sick," 1896) where the author exposes the hypocrisy behind the convention of the wake. While riding across the countryside on a typically Pirandellian August afternoon, Gaspare Naldi was stricken by a cerebral embolism that paralzyed his right side. Ironically he had ridden out that day to pay condolences to a friend who had recently lost a son. As it proceeds the tale serves to degrade the tradition of the death watch. The entire story is built on the conversations of the visitors, physicians, and immediate members of the family during the hours of Naldi's death agony. Everyone there seems to be playing a part. Some of the friends who came supposedly to express their sorrow appear relieved to learn that Naldi is preceding them in death. The cynical physicians show themselves more interested in prolonging Naldi's suffering with injections of stimulants than in saving his life or at least making his dying as painless as possible. Genuine sentiment is equally lacking in the official representative of institutional faith: the night-duty priest takes pleasure in the fact that this case requires little more of him than merely placing a crucifix beside Naldi's pillow. The high point of the evening arrives with the entrance of a government deputy in the company of a prefecture counselor and the acting mayor; the deputy's coming causes the conversation to shift from family gossip and pseudo-medical diagnoses to the current political issues. While the scene of insincere concern is played out by the visitors enjoying the cool of the night on the balcony, the only true drama takes place in the death chamber. Naldi is not striking a pose. After a bout with pneumonia some years before, he began to wear a rabbit's hair shirt under his dress blouse, like a cuirass against death. Pirandello depicts Naldi's dying with the scientific precision of a Verist but also with the compassion of a humorist. As he was later to state in *Umorismo*, death does not possess romantic splendor. A humoristic author must show how the dead soil their sheets. Naldi's agonizing is not lessened by sentimentality or a romantic aura of decay. The body's final twisting and the darkening of its color are reported without any attempt at sugar coating or sensationalism. By dawn Naldi dies, and the visitors scatter on the slowly brightening streets to return to their own problems. Something significant may have happened during the night of the death watch, but everyone remains too preoccupied and too concerned with conventional attitudes to reflect on the ritual that has been performed in the name of good manners.

Death in the novelle likes to tease. It will steal into a home and leave its calling card with a note that it will come back at its own convenience. Once death played a cruel joke on Saverio, the talented puppet maker of "La Paura del Sonno" ("The Fear of Sleep," 1901). Saverio's greatest despair used to be that his wife Fana was continually falling asleep and never had enough waking time to finish sewing clothes for their puppets. A day came when Fana did not awaken from her sleep, and her husband reproached himself for not seeking medical advice about her condition. But as her body was being conveyed on an open litter to the cemetery, Fana's dress caught on the branches of a fig tree and she awakened. Her return to the land of the living began Saverio's torment as he struggled for months to keep her from falling asleep, spending whole nights reenacting puppet plays about Roland and Charlemagne. After her second apparent death, the puppet maker begged the pall-bearers to stay clear of the fig tree on their way to the place of burial. A second awakening would have proved too excruciating for Saverio. Often when death pays its friendly visits, it takes delight in deforming its hosts without completely killing them off. In "La Toccatina" ("The Gentle Touch of Death," 1906) Cristoforo Golisch declares that he will have the courage to shoot himself rather than drag on his life as a half-dead human caricature like his old friend

Beniamino Lenzi, who remained paralyzed on one side after a stroke and used to pull himself along on a cane to appointments with a physical therapist. Lenzi succeded only in mumbling words, unable to pronounce *l*'s and *r*'s. Death had an even more grotesque deformation in store for Golisch, for after a similar stroke and paralysis on the opposite side of the body from that of Lenzi's, Cristoforo Golisch became a foreigner to his native country. Born in Italy of German parents, he had always spoken Italian; but on first recovering from his stroke he could speak only German. With patient coaxing his sister taught him to speak Italian again, but with a German accent. Instead of shooting himself, Golisch requested to join Lenzi in physical therapy sessions. Despite his earlier resolve, he accepted partial dying almost sanguinely. As he and Lenzi hobbled to the therapist's, they resembled a pair of matching book ends. As its gift to those two former companions in romantic escapades, death fixed a mask of childish incomprehension on their faces. Pirandello as humorist did not need to distort his characters as had Valle-Inclán; life and death carried out the grotesque deformation that he as writer recorded and as humorist pitied.

When a person dies, those who have been close to the deceased wonder if he would still be interested in what is happening in the world of the living. Signor Aversa in "Notizie del Mondo" ("World News," 1901) decides to write down his observations on current events for his friend Momo, who has just passed away. Momo's new address is the Roman cemetery Campo Verano, which Aversa feels was made for the living as well as the dead. Aversa regards cemeteries as miniature cities, with the usual distinction along class lines in the quality of dwellings. He especially resents that Momo's widow has had to lodge her husband in a rented tomb until a vacancy should occur at a regular tomb, as sometimes happens when a family moves away from Rome and decides to take the remains of a relative with them. Aversa so dislikes the idea of a secondhand tomb that he finally has a new gravesite constructed for Momo. In his correspondence with his dead friend, Aversa repeats Nietzsche's theory of eternal returns; perhaps in thirty thousand years, he suggests, one might repeat "this fine puppet show of our existence." After Momo's widow makes plans to marry again, Aversa realizes that it is a crime to continue to tell the departed about life on earth. Death is a release from the painful situations of life, and no one should remind the dead of the torment they have escaped.

Not every character wishes the escape offered by death, for the realization of death's nearness makes life precious. A long lament for life that is denied occupies almost all of the novella "La Morte Addosso" ("Death Upon Them," 1918), a dialogue tale that the author later recast as the one-act play *L'Uomo dal fiore in bocca* (*The Man with a Flower in his Mouth*), with no significant changes except for brief stage directions. The dialogues take place at an all-night café (the original title of the story was "Caffè Notturno")—a scene of fatigue, bewilderment, and a feeling of oppression. A traveler who has missed his train sits in the café waiting for time to pass until the next train arrives so that he can return to his vacation home and bring his wife and daughters the parcels they asked him to fetch from town. The tone of his words conveys a sense of weariness and even exasperation with his middle-class family responsibilities, but he does not appear to hold a fierce rancor against his destiny. By contrast, another café customer, who strikes up a conversation with the traveler, soon reveals his bitterness toward fate; his comments become increasingly vehement and drawn out to the point of turning the novella into a long monologue. First the customer displays a strange attention to commonplace activities, as when he describes in almost ecstatic terms the care that store clerks take in wrapping gift parcels. His chief desire seems to be to lose himself, even to letting his being fuse with the silk ribbon on store packages. That need for evasion causes him to stand for hours outside shop windows to watch the clerks at work and to follow the shoppers with his eyes as they carry their packages away. His imagination must be forever occupied away from himself and the persons he knows well, into the lives of complete strangers, where he can exercise his powers of fantasy to the utmost. When the somewhat-puzzled traveler remarks in words broken by astonished pauses that the customer must derive a certain degree of curious pleasure from the workings of his imagination, the other emphatically denies that he has experienced any intellectual satisfaction. Again he takes flight into the inanimate world by comparing his disinterested attitude to the indifference that the chairs in a physician's waiting room hold toward the patients who sit in them. Through observing the slightest details of vital activity and reflecting on them, the customer desperately desires to convince himself that life is so stupid that he need not worry about ending it.

What might seem to be another suicidal longing by a typically depressed Pirandellian character acquires a new dimension of hopelessness and utter moral destitution with the introduction of a third figure as a silently mourning choral character: the customer's wife, who stands in the shadows and never speaks. For him she is the shadow of death, stirring an agitation in his heart like the earthquakes that destroyed Messina and Avezzano in 1908. The silence between husband and wife derives from the tragicomic inability of most Pirandellian characters, even an eloquent one like this customer, to communicate their agony. Knowledge of imminent death has sometimes brought members of a family close together; in Pirandello's novellistic world the awareness of fatality separates. These moments of tense encounter at the railroad restaurant betray a quality of kinetic temporality within instants of apparent stasis between train journeys.

The customer is one of those persons to whom death has paid an advance visit, for he is dying of a cancerous tumor over his lip—the flower in his mouth, which like many of the flowers in Pirandellian titles symbolizes death and ultimate separation. The flower image with its delicacy veils the painful destruction of the disease. As this story shows, Pirandello joins those modern writers who represent the pathology of life in the twentieth century. Yet, the reality of this dreadful illness sometimes eludes the man as he admires the tumor's flowerlike violet color and takes a sensual delight in its mellifluous Greek name, *epithelioma:* how can such a pleasant sound cluster signify death? The customer realizes that death is man's most individual act and that no one can die for him or offer him the consolation of company. Consequently he rejects his wife's attempt to join him in death by scratching her lip and kissing his tumor. Death is making him an intransigent stranger, an existent in time that is drawing short. All he can attempt is to seek distraction in other persons' affairs, hoping to quiet the inner violence he might turn against someone like the traveler or against himself. His way of dying is that of the humorist, transforming his ferocious anger into melancholy laughter and into a verbal performance to demonstrate the moral superiority of his observations and deliberations. The man's one consolation is that death has released him from the daily tribulations that prevent vitally involved persons from appreciating the world's beauty. His last words to the traveler evoke an idyllic vision of sweet apricots, green meadows, and little girls dressed in white and blue—all the colors and fragrances of life in its loveliest moments.[8]

Neither the diseased customer nor his wife possesses the solace of belief in an afterlife. Pirandello's portrait of death reflects a post-Christian ethic, where dying no longer provides passage to a higher existence but merely proves that life's natural conclusion is in nothingness. In that early essay on contemporary art and conscience, the author admitted that once there was a time when death led to the true life, since earthly existence was only a pilgrimage toward a genuine world. The Christian world view granted to every individual a meaningful role in society's structure—whether as king, rich man, beggar, or peasant—which offered the opportunity for them to work out their own salvation. But for Pirandello social life in our times is imposed, artificial, and mendacious. The effort of the imagination to seek significance in both the moral and physical worlds so as to construct a coherent whole for life at the moment of death is doomed to a disillusioning failure. All the ties that should bind men together in living and dying are falsely contrived and sentimentally hypocritical. As an artist the Sicilian author was unable to view death as a romantic appointment with destiny, even as represented ironically by a writer like Thomas Mann in *Death in Venice*, as a revelation of inner moral and aesthetic decadence. Pirandello's novellistic art works to uncover the progressive dissociation of individuals from an absurd world; the concentration of his tales' structure falls upon a decisive incident of mirrored insight, which forces the protagonists to behold their emptiness and impels them to death. Like Sartre after him, Pirandello would agree that only the dead are truly free; yet he differs from the existentialist philosopher in judging the release of death, not as liberation from the necessity of forging new essences out of life's crucial situations, but as a definitive freedom from the need to construct the social mask and puppet figure. Despite Pirandello's materialistic conception of death as total physical annihilation, there was another side to his humoristic view of life: a mystical, pantheistic vision of a universal existence beyond the limits of earth's imprisonment. In his late mythical play *Lazzaro* (*Lazarus*), he was to explore the possibility of transcending the agony of living and the nothingness of dying.[9]

The Pain of Living

Life for the novellistic characters resembles a wearisome journey that many of them are only too eager to end. No matter what the circumstances of their birth, education, and social status, they are mostly misfits in the art of living. During the feverish pace of their working hours those lonely characters behold each other again and again without recognizing their common distress. And after their suffering has grown so intense that they at last reach out to each other, they quickly become ashamed of their momentary weakness and withdraw behind their logical masks of impassivity. Pirandello looks upon his inept characters with a humorist's capacity for compassion. He represents them as born to lose in life, victims of injustices that they commit upon each other because life makes them cruel. For many of the characters, existence holds no moral implications, since it punishes them even when they are without guilt. Life closes upon the novellistic characters with its painful reality, and, as Jacques Lacan has observed, "there is nothing at the final limit of existence except the pain of existing." [10]

An entire group of tales deals with unwanted children who would have fared better if they had never been born. They are resented as living reminders of their parents' moments of weakness. In "Uno di Più" ("One too Many," 1931) Abele Nora angrily declares before his little daughter Dreina that if she had not been born, his mother could have continued to live with him and his wife. After Dreina saw the tiny, miserable, rented room to which her grandmother was forced to move, the girl understood the grief she had caused. Out of the sad realization of being an extra, unwanted person—one too many—Dreina died; but her dying was in vain, since her grandmother had to stay on in the rented room. The child's death merely deprived Abele of an excuse for turning his mother away. Another little girl proves to be one too many in "l 'Ombrello" ("The Umbrella," 1909) for a widow with limited finances who wishes to remarry but hesitates, fearing that a new husband would dislike her pensive, school-age daughter Dinuccia. One night the mother sends Dinuccia to bed without supper for fighting with her very likable baby sister, Mimì, over a new umbrella, a costly item that had to be shared in turn by the children since the mother could not afford to buy two new umbrellas. Within six days Dinuccia dies from pneumonia, leaving her mother free to marry again and enjoy the financial luxury of not having to worry about the price of a second umbrella. Neither Dreina nor Dinuccia intentionally sought to hurt others. It was solely the fact of their presense that irritated their parents and reminded them of their own shortcomings, forcing them to conclude that life would have been more comfortable if they had never given birth to the girls.

Pirandellian children suffer not just the lack of parental love but actual physical abuse and criminal neglect. Little Nenè of "Servitù" ("Servitude," 1914) receives only cast-off clothes from the wealthy children her mother attends as a nurse. Beauty and magic enter into Nenè's shabby life with the gift of an expensive doll called the Marquess, who becomes, in the bright sanctuary of the child's rich imagination, a real person whom she must serve humbly as a rare privilege. But when Nenè's father sees the doll, he rips it to pieces because he does not want an aristocratic lady in his impoverished home. While the story of Nenè does betray a definite maudlin sentimentality on Pirandello's part, his account of society's mistreatment of orphans in "Il Libretto Rosso" ("The Little Red Book," 1911) is a pitiless condemnation of merchandise in human life. Whenever a baby dies in the Sicilian town of Nisia, the mother adopts a foundling and cares for the child at the expense of the municipality, which allots a monthly stipend that is registered in a little red book, that becomes in this tale a terrifying symbol of dehumanizing traffic in human life. What the law originally intended as a humanitarian procedure is transformed into an instrument of greed, for the local Maltese cloth merchants become the effective foster "mothers" by trading garments for those booklets, with the understanding that the foundlings will continue to be fed by the official foster parents. Through the commerce in red books the Nisian girls are enabled to assemble trousseaus. Occasionally one of the foster mothers does not have sufficient milk and the foundling perishes; but the death is made to appear accidental so that the municipality will furnish a new baby. Children in Pirandello's novelle are rendered less than human: objects of barter for greedy brides or scapegoats for their parents' failings. Frequently in literature babies represent an affirmation of the fictitious society, in which adults are prepared to make sacrifices for their children's future. But a community that values Maltese cloth over the lives of foundlings does not merit reinforcement or futurity. That society lacks the potentiality for encouraging love and mutual concern for the welfare of its members. To save a baby's life is to preserve the community.

Italian writers of short fiction between 1830 and 1850 stressed moral education in the parent-child relationship as necessary to develop the inherent sense of *"bontà"* and teach children to withstand life's temptations and conflicts. But in Pirandello's fictional world no age group escapes the inequities that life metes out to its victims, who are vitiated through existing itself. The author delighted in examining adolescence as a middle world of suspended experience between childish fantasy and adult reason, a momentary stage between childhood's fabled visions and the disenchantment of maturity. A train ride from Palermo to Zùnica— note the frequence of the journey theme in Pirandello's works—destroys in the tale "La Veste Lunga" ("The Long Dress," 1913) all the childhood dreams and trust of sixteen-year-old Didì Brilla. To prepare the girl for the purpose of that journey Didì's father told her to put on a long dress for the first time in her life—the outward sign that she must join the world of adult responsibilities. For Didì the town of Zùnica was always a mythical and wondrous realm from which her father brought her delicious fruits. Now during the trip she learns from her elder brother that she is to marry the eccentric heir of an estate that their father has administered over the past twenty years. Slowly realizing that her father is sacrificing her to safeguard his own economic security, the girl moves from being an uncommitted spectator of adult life to an object of exchange and instrument of her father's financial schemes. Her father has perverted the parent-child relationship and exploited her dependence on his authority. He destroys every claim to his daughter's affection and respect. The fantasy land of Didì's early dreams turns into a nightmare of a gloomy palace where she will have to suffer the envy of relatives-in-law and her husband's mistresses. With this forced awakening to dreadful reality, the girl has to abandon all privileged recollections, seeing how domestic warmth vanished *three* years before with her mother's death. As fond memories of a sweet childhood vanish, the girl reverts to psychic automatism by acting with robotlike gestures as she gulps down her father's heart medicine, which becomes lethal in large doses: hysteria is a child's reaction to the corruption demanded by the adult world. Once again a Pirandellian character chooses death as the only means to avoid a trap, as here in being initiated into adulthood with its shameful accommodations. The long dress, emblematic of that initiation into a world that the girl rejects as vile, becomes a shroud, in the usual Pirandellian association of sexuality and annihilation. This case of an adolescent recoiling before her womanhood and acting violently is not isolated in the novelle, where infantile dreams and awakening sensations clash so intensely that only self-destruction can result.[11] Having to leave home is recognition of a fall from innocence, a farewell to the privileged recollections of childhood.

An arid sense of being betrayed without hope in the future caused Didì's suicide. As opposed to her negativism, eighteen-year-old Cesarino Brei of "In Silenzio" (1905) courageously accepts the challenges of an unexpected reality that befalls him when his mother dies giving birth to an illegitimate child. In this tale as well as throughout his novelle Pirandello creates a literature of silence. Here the predominating terms are *lontano* (distant) for the gulf of incommunicability separating persons like Cesarino and his mother (who died alone in the secret torture of guilt); *silenzio* that pervades a comfortable middle-class home as well as the impoverished apartment where Cesarino attempts to make a new life with the baby; *sordo* (deaf) for the insensitivity the stunned youth shows to persons like his school director and the devoted family maid who aid him in structuring a new life as a clerk in the Ministry of Public Education while continuing studies to enter the university; *muto* (mute) for the impentrable silence of death, which cuts off all discourse. Although silence can sometimes offer the promise of discourse or even express a deep-felt nonverbal communication with a touch of the hand or a nod of the head, as in many of Pirandello's stories, here silence for Cesarino is language's zero degree of withdrawal from others; scorn and bewilderment before an identity as an illegitimate child that alone unites him to his half-brother. Silence works as a self-protecting shelter wherein Cesarino seeks to find a refuge for himself and the baby. At best, silence is a comforting sensation that sweeps over a Roman balcony in the evening when persons are down in the gardens watering the dry land. But less than a year after the youth has begun to put his life in order, a disquieting invader comes in the person of the baby's father, asserting his legal rights to take the child away from Cesarino. Silence then becomes not only resignation before life's injustices but also the violent breaking off of all discourse as Cesarino gets ready a brazier to kill himself and the baby by asphyxiation. Rather than surrender the only hope he has known in the company of his half-brother, the youth prefers to leave "in silenzio." Neither he nor the baby can be blamed for the circumstance of illegitimate birth, but they are unable to establish communication with social authorities in order to be permitted to lead their own lives. Under life's relentless assaults the firmest resolve yields to an almost serene longing for the quiet of death.

Even those who survive the painful transition from adolescence to adulthood are never exempt from the unequal struggle against an unjust destiny. Like many writers of short fiction, Pirandello uses the novella as a narrative form that expresses the inequities of fate. Most of the adult characters in his tales believe that some evil spirit is pursuing them to deprive them of any satisfaction, and they are rarely able to transcend the void (*vuoto*) of silence to communicate their apprehensions to others in an effort to demonstrate their sincere desire to be understood and appreciated. No matter how honest and kind, the intentions of Carlo Nocia in the tale "Lo Spirito Maligno" ("The Malign Spirit," 1910) are always interpreted by others as acts of betrayal. Marriage to a lovely and wealthy girl came to Nocia only because his future father-in-law mistakenly believed that Carlo had supported him in defrauding the heir to a sulfur fortune. When on a trip to Rome Carlo Nocia attempts to bestow some charity on an old woman, he ends by being arrested for the theft of her purse. He can never remove the label of *thief* that an evil destiny has assigned to him. The novellistic character becomes the victim of a misunderstanding, and language will never succeed in rescuing him.

A profoundly humoristic case of poor requital for individual probity concerns the naively devout mason Spatolino, protagonist in the novella "Il Tabernacolo" ("The Shrine") of 1903. After the Quixotic Spatolino refused to join the socialist union and became president of the Catholic Society of Mutual Aid among the Unworthy Sons of Our Lady of Sorrows, his business suffered so much that his wife was reduced to sewing and washing for others. Pirandello plays ironically with the name of Spatolino's union, whose members never come to his aid. The impossibility of there ever being an effective brotherhood is evidenced after fate at first seems to relent as the mason receives a commission from a notoriously anticlerical notary to build a roadside shrine. But the notary dies just before the shrine's completion, and his heirs refuse to honor the oral contract. Twice Spatolino takes the case to court and loses both times, having to pay court costs. Convinced that divine justice does not exist, he stations himself at the shrine, wearing all the attributes of the martyred Christ. Seeing himself as the martyr of an empty faith, he remains in that pose for the rest of his life, surviving on donations. Instead of committing suicide, Spatolino assumes the immobility of a statue as a protest against the unmerited punishment he has suffered. The mason's plight reminds one of Frank O'Connor's interpretation of the situation of the protagonist in Gogol's "The Overcoat": ". . . to take the mock-heroic character, the absurd little copying clerk, and impose his image over that of the crucified Jesus, so that even while we laugh we are filled with horror at the resemblance (*The Lonely Voice* [Cleveland, 1965], pp. 15–16)." Spatolino's pose as the crucified Savior is fully humoristic in being both a ridiculously futile gesture of protest and pathetic because of his innocence and good faith: an agonizing mirror image of submerged humanity, whose sufferings find articulation in the stories of writers like Pirandello and Gogol.

Some of the heroines in the Sicilian's novelle recall the love-starved feminine figures in Chekhov's plays. These Pirandellian characters and those of the Russian dramatist similarly wear black as if they were in mourning for life or lost youth. The identity of these figures in black is that of persons suffering from the sense of deprivation that has haunted their lives. Although two of these novelle, "La Maestrina Boccarmè" ("Schoolmistress Boccarmè," 1899) and "Scialle Nero" ("The Black Shawl," 1900), are narrated in the third person, the narrator's sympathy for the heroines is apparent in presenting the ancillary characters who exploited the unfortunate women. For twenty years Schoolmistress

Boccarmè was able to endure the dreary routine of classes because of the comfort she felt in the memory of a single night of love she had spent with her cousin Giorgio, whose portrait she has kept in her apartment as a treasured reminder of affection. The portrait is a sacred item that evokes a solitary experience of total happiness. That precious memory becomes threatened with violation when a spiteful former schoolmate invades the sanctuary of Boccarmè's apartment and derides her for a lifetime devotion to a worthless and financially ruined man who not only abandoned his cousin but gave his portrait to all of his mistresses. The schoolmistress's mode of living and reacting to situations follows that of privileged recollection, but here the narrator does not view the protagonist with irony or seek a comic corrective for her excesses. For in order to redeem the treasured image of her past Boccarmè sends all her savings to Giorgio in remembrance of the good and evil he caused her. Reared as an orphan charity case in a boarding school for well-to-do girls, and afterwards accustomed to the loneliness of being a spinster teacher and principal, Mirina Boccarmè saw her life open once for her—like a flower that a thoughtless creature plucks in a moment of distraction. To critics who have judged her gesture of generosity as ringing false, it is imperative to view her actions as measures to preserve the privileged recollection.

Another heroine in black, Eleonora Bandi of "Scialle Nero," never enjoyed a bittersweet memory from her youth to sustain her across the years. The lyrical quality of the story of the schoolmistress, who delights in strolls by the harbor of her town, is lacking in this tale of a bleak existence. That *bontà* which should result from proper moral education is absent here, even though Eleonora sacrificed her youth by turning down marriage proposals in order to educate her brother, Giorgio, and his orphaned friend, Carlo. Pirandello shows the selfish Carlo and Giorgio as moral doubles, looking like matching bookends, who understand each other so completely that they communicate without words as they respond to Eleonora's kindness with ingratitude and compel her to stop giving music lessons once they have established professional careers of their own. All the fierce contrast between Civilization and Nature emerges after the friends banish Eleonora to the family farm, where she begins to tutor a stolid peasant boy named Gerlando. In the language of the characters, Pirandello contrasts the refined restraint of Eleonora's elegant phrases with Gerlando's obtuse and brutish demands. Refinement yields to savage temptation one night when Gerlando assaults Eleonora, and she surrenders to the erotic force that she had earlier always avoided. Throughout the scenes between Gerlando and Eleonora there is a frequency of bodily contact words like *mano, bocca, braccio,* and *labbra,* which stress the agitation within the thirty-nine-year-old woman as she attempts to elude a physical contact that she considers repulsive. But forced by Giorgio and Carlo to wed the youth, Eleonora finds herself a prisoner within a place of privation and harassment as Gerlando's family goads him to assert his conjugal rights to assure his having an heir and thereby retaining his dowry from Eleonora. The author contrasts the woman's defenselessness with the venal calculation of the peasants. Not only does she lose the baby in a miscarriage following one of Gerlando's assaults, but also, in a desperate effort to escape outrage, she hurls herself from a cliff. At the moment of suicidal frenzy the Pirandellian moon shines down on the peasant youth in accusation. Eleonora never comes to know the kind surrender that Mirina Boccarmè experienced. A sensitive person born to give love but not *eros,* Eleonora passes a life without ever receiving another's affection. Although part of her failure derives from refusing to accept her sexual nature,[12] the narrator presents Eleonora as a victim of injustice and would have agreed with this observation by a Maupassant character about an unhappy woman: "I felt weighing upon this human creature the eternal injustice of implacable nature!" Never once does a spark of goodness from another person illumine Eleonora's dark life.

Earthly existence for many of the novellistic characters resembles a prison, a confining situation that they can neither escape nor improve. The characters from the middle and upper classes know the imprisonment of living without experience of tenderness from others, while the impoverished are economically entrapped in a social situation that they are powerless to change. For Pirandello, Sicily's sulfur mines symbolized the imprisonment of an underprivileged class who were exploited by bankers and entrepreneurs to gain a quick profit from an industry that succeded only in destroying the island's agricultural economy. In novelle like "Il Fumo" ("Fumes," 1901) and "Ciàula scopre la luna" ("Ciàula discovers the moon," 1912) the author denounced the enslavement of children as beasts of burden in the mines to haul the ore that the regular pick-axe miners dug from the depths of the earth. Parents used to release their rights to their sons, sometimes as early as the age of eight, for a compensation from the mining companies, which then employed the children as *carusi* (helpers) for the miners. Even when helpers came of age, their servitude continued, since most of them knew nowhere else to turn for employment. Pirandello saw the miners and their helpers alike as creatures who were already dead and entombed but compelled to toil throughout their living death.

Humanitarian social protest becomes a poetry of desperation in "Ciàula scopre la luna," the story of a miner's helper who in an astonishing moment briefly escapes the oppressive environment of the sulfur industry. The novella presents a descending hierarchy of abuse: the theatrically irate supervisor Cacciagallina exercises his authority over the mining prisoners with curses and a pistol. Yet, the only worker that Cacciagallina can fully dominate is old Zi' Scarda, who lost an eye and his only son four years before in a mine explosion. Although Zi' Scarda performs as well as any young pick-axe worker, the company keeps him on as a charity case because he is the sole support of his daughter-in-law and seven grandchildren. Resigned to hardship, the old man enjoys a single vice and consolation—that of savoring the salty bitterness of the tears that he sheds from his only eye for the lost son. In his turn the old man may also exercise tyrannical control over his imbecilic helper Ciàula, who at thirty years of age seems wholly dehumanized by his labor as a *caruso*. The name *Ciàula* means "crow," and the youth caws like a crow and answers to bird-call commands from Zi' Scarda. Pirandello's portrait of Ciàula's stupid, toothless smile of satisfaction with his grime-hardened shirt might appear so grotesque as to rob the figure of any poetic sympathy, but once again the author is thrusting responsibility for his characters' grotesqueness not on his artistic method but on life itself, which reduces creatures like Ciàula to a subhuman condition. The deformation is not a product of literary manner but that of a bestial situation.

The tomb where Zi' Scarda and Ciàula are immured is like the earth's womb, a subterranean prison of perpetual darkness that is brightened only by flickering terra-cotta lamps and the shining eye of the tunnel's exit. The outside landscape is that of fields stripped of every blade of grass and pitted with mine shafts that look like anthills. Ciàula adapts himself to the world of monstrous shadows cast by oil lamps on cavern walls, where he crawls like an animal to transport sacks of sulfur ore. For years his life has remained divided between the dark tunnels and the brilliant sunlight over the barren landscape. On the night of the explosion that killed Zi' Scarda's son, Ciàula suffered the most frightening experience of his life: that of emerging from the mines into the blackness of nighttime. After that encounter with nocturnal gloom the youth wished only to fall asleep before sunset and to be kicked awake at dawn. Ciàula could find his way through the caverns but not

through the night-darkened landscape. One evening, however, he and Zi' Scarda have to toil overtime—without pay,
of course—to fill the ore wagons. As Ciàula drags his heavy
load of material to the tunnel exist, he gradually grows
aware of a strange silvery glow from outside. At last the
youth discovers the moon, which he has never seen before,
although he knew of its existence as of some inconsequential
fact. Now he need not fear the dark night, since the moon
will light the way for him. Whereas the moon may serve
in Pirandello's novelle as a symbol of death, madness, or
violence, it can also represent a spiritual reawakening. Ciàula
becomes a human again as he weeps in ecstatic rapture at
the moonlight that liberates him from a realm of darkness
and inhuman labor. Beneath the mask of subnormal intelligence there is a sensitive creature who responds to the
moon's splendor and thereby flees his psychic prison.[13]

The enchantment of moonlight offers the mine helper a
way out of his entrapment, and other Pirandellian characters also turn to the heavens to forget their distress. The
novella "Pallottoline" ("Juggler's Balls," ca. 1895) explores
a profoundly humoristic situation in the household of
the astronomer-meterologist Jacopo Maraventano, who
attempts to elude life's trivial problems through the joys of
astronomy. Dwelling in a former monastery that has been
converted into a summertime hotel, Maraventano occupies
an apartment with his wife and two children while operating
a year-round weather station from his mountaintop observa-
tory. He never allows domestic or terrestrial concerns to
distract him from his telescope or readings in astronomy.
Whether his daughter needs warm clothes to ward off the
winter cold or his own teeth are aching from decaying
cavities, the astronomer loses himself in observing and commenting upon the immensities of outer space. The earth
seems petty when compared to the almost numberless stars
and the many other possible planetary systems. Humor
arises in the contrast between Maraventano's flight of imag-

ination through the stellar distances as opposed to the
pathetic reality of his shabby home. As he lectures about
the wonders of Alpha Centaurus to his family, the astronomer may still be performing the commonplace task of fan-
ning the fire under the kitchen kettle for the night's supper.
A man's soul may roam through the stars, but his feet must
remain stuck to the ground. When the wintry fog settles
on the mountain, Maraventano's wife dreams of city comforts and tries to find solace in static objects like the kitchen
utensils hanging on the wall. Their daughter longs for the
summer in the hope that some vacationer will take her
away to a new and better life. In the meantime Maraventano, oblivious of family and personal needs, plays with the
solar system and constellations the way a juggler tosses his
balls about. He founds his serenity on telescopic alienation
from mediocre reality.

Geography provides still another artificial method of
evasion. Three novelle in particular examine the relief that
a knowledge of geography can bring to troubled persons.
Valeriano Balicci of "Mondo di Carta" ("Paper World," 1909)
lived only for the books he could collect and read, until he
ended by taking on the complexion of paper and losing his
sight. Condemned to an outer world of darkness, Balicci
wished to preserve his universe of books, and he hired a
youth to catalogue his collection so that he could locate any
desired volume and caress the pages as he summoned back
cherished memories. He especially liked travel books, and
when a lady reader dared to inform him that from her own
travels she knew a certain text had made erroneous statements about customs in a Norwegian town, Balicci fired her
on the spot. Through reading geography texts Balicci had
constructed his own reality, which he could not permit anyone else to threaten with a report of actual experience.
While geography served as an abiding consolation for Balicci, it appeared as an unexpected and at first maddening
revelation for Belluca, the bookkeeper protagonist in "Il

Treno ha Fischiato" ("The Train Whistled") of 1914. For years Belluca stoically resigned himself to supporting twelve depenedents (three of them blind and helpless) on his meager salary from his daytime position and from extra jobs. All of a sudden one day he furiously rebelled against his office director, and his astonished fellow workers had to commit him to an asylum for mental observation. The mathematically prosaic bookkeeper surprised everyone by uttering poetic phrases about snowy mountains, blue horizons, and dense forests. Belluca's illness assailed him as he lay half asleep on his tattered parlor couch and chanced to hear the whistle of a distant train. That whistle lifted him out of an existence of domestic stress and claustration, reminding him that persons in Florence, Bologna, Venice, and Turin were leading exciting and meaningful lives. The responsibilities that had arrested the dynamic flow of his life momentarily vanished as Belluca recognized an unsuspected and poetic facet of his personality, a totally new self. Although he realized that he would have to abandon the complete liberty of spirit that others felt was insanity, the bookkeeper came to possess a new source of strength. For whenever the death mask of everyday life oppressed him, Belluca could fly away in his imagination to the frozen lands of Siberia or the steaming jungles of the Congo. Those visions of other places and different forms of life would enable him to experience vicariously the thrilling freedom of the vital force.

Full elaboration of a system of liberation through geography appears in the story "Rimedio, la Geografia" ("Remedy: Geography," ca. 1921). In the style of the interior monologue, the novella presents a guide for life that makes possible a certain spiritual elasticity. The narrator relates how he survived the agony of a deathwatch at his mother's bedside by absorbing himself in his daughter's geography textbook and its descriptions of Jamaica. Now he has assigned a particular part of the world to each member of his family; his wife, for instance, is Lapland. Whenever insurmountable problems occur, he concentrates on some foreign scene and abstracts himself from the present affliction. The absolute certainty of life somewhere else in the world dispels the anxieties and constant doubts that plague the narrator's daily existence. Like the astronomer of "Pallottoline," he seeks to dismiss personal misfortunes as insignificant events in a multiform universe. Hypnotic images of distant climes furnish a remedy to relieve the torment of characters like the argumentative narrator, Belluca, and Balicci.

Generally Pirandello's female characters do not resort to subtle intellectual schemes of escapism, but rely on their instincts. Often when the conditions of life grow impossible for them to sustain, the women of the novelle take the path of dishonor as their only way out of an intolerable situation. For young Tuta of "Il Ventaglino" ("The Little Fan," 1903) death by drowning in the Tiber seemed at first the only means to avoid the homelessness and starvation that threaten her and her seven-month-old baby. That naive girl from the Roman Ciociaro countryside has been the victim of a cruel deception by a man who married her in church at a moment in Italian history when the strife between the government and the Vatican was so fierce that ecclesiastical weddings had no legal validity. Sent to Rome by her false husband to find work as a wet nurse, Tuta loses her lodgings, her earrings, and her suitcase when she refuses to accept the landlady's indecent proposals. Sitting on a bench in a Roman park on one of those sultry August afternoons when violence usually occurs in Pirandellian novelle, the girl at last decides to survive, and with the few cents that a well-to-do lady gave her as charity, she purchases a cheap paper fan. As she begins to uncover her breasts and fan herself, Tuta casts provocative glances at the passing soldiers. In a moment of desperation Tuto has willed life with the optimistic phrase, expressed in Ciociaro dialect (a linguistic refuge for the bewildered girl): *God provides.* In the story of Tuta the author's mood is one of detachment where he passes no judgment and wishes only to present a drama of a choice between suicide or survival, but in another tale of the same year, "La Balia" ("The Wet Nurse") Pirandello's tone is vitriolic as he indicts the affluent liberals for their hypocritical manipulation of the poor and helpless. A wealthy Roman family exploits a penniless girl from the South, persuading her to leave her home and child to work as a wet nurse in their mansion with the promise of a large salary that would suffice for her family needs while her husband serves a prison term for revolutionary activities. The girl's employer is a socialist politician who delivers eloquent addresses on equality of opportunity but remains utterly indifferent to the wet nurse's plight. Language serves as an effective force of contrast in this tale, not only in the gap between the socialist's empty rhetoric and the wet nurse's pleas for understanding and assistance, but also in the cultural gulf that has opened between the girl, who speaks only her native southern dialect, and her employer's wife, who once was the nurse's schoolmate in the South but who now speaks only standard Roman and fears that her child will be contaminated by the girl's speech. During the nurse's absence from home her baby dies, and her husband swears vengeance if she ever returns to the town. Once the politician's child has been weaned, he agrees to the demands of his pathologically jealous wife and turns the wet nurse out of his home. Too terrified to go back to the South, and lost in the Roman metropolis, the girl becomes the servant of the socialist's corrupt secretary, who will make her his mistress for as long as it pleases him. For those who choose to hold onto life, even though society offers them no honest means to support themselves, the sole recourse is to sell the one capital that nature provides.[14]

The drama of the two wet nurses is that of derelicts cast completely alone in the world with no one to protect them.

Pirandello differs from writers of an earlier generation like
Dall'Ongaro, who while depicting the plight of peasants in
a hostile urban environment believed that moral integrity
should always be safeguarded in spite of all pressures. The
Sicilian writer also did not intend his stories of exploitation
as moral education for the upper classes to bring about
change. Pirandello's focus is upon helplessness and the fear
of loneliness rather than social reform.

It is this dread of solitude and the need for the shelter of
another's affection that impels many of the female protagonists in the novelle to the illusory search for love. Pirandello
began his novellistic career with a volume entitled *Amori
senza Amore* (*Loves without Love*), which exposed the
selfishness and longings to possess others that wrecked the
chance for persons to experience genuine love. One of the
tales, "l'Onda" ("The Wave"), shows how love is a wave that
crests and falls away as passion and jealousy alternately
work on the protagonist's emotions. Originally love was a
game of flirtation for Giulio Accurzi in "l'Onda": from the
commanding position of his balcony or from his own garden
he flirted with the young ladies who rented the first-floor
apartment of the building he owned. But eventually a girl
came who paid no attention to her amorous landlord, so
absorbed was she in a fiancé who had gone to study philology at Heidelberg. Agata Sarni's indifference was a novel experience for Accurzi, who felt powerfully attracted to her.
In time he succeeded in marrying her, although she admitted she held no affection for him. Ironically, the moment
Agata started to reciprocate Giulio's love, he lost interest in
her. Only after her former fiancé returned and made clear his
regret for deserting Agata, did Accurzi again begin to appreciate his wife. Accurzi (and, to a less examined extent,
the fiancé) is what Lacan terms a *"sujet vide,"* a subject
who requires the mediation of his desire through the desires
of the other, first Agata and later her former fiancé. Giulio,

while posing as a master figure, will always remain enslaved to the desires of another person. Agata's fate was to find herself beloved when she did not return love, and to remain unloved when she extended her affection. Pirandello viewed love basically as a counterfeit sentiment that persons used to conceal vanity and the frustrated yearning to dominate others.

In the empty attempt to obtain love and the inner security it might bring, some of the novellistic characters are prepared to make dishonest and even degrading compromises. Their acts can end only in failure, largely because of the mutual incomprehension that prevents two individuals from properly appreciating each other's values. Candelora, the title character in a novella of 1917, resented poverty and the lack of recognition from art critics for the productions of her husband the painter Nane Papa. Through her own initiative she convinced a prominent critic that her husband had something new and excitingly different to say to the world. A favorable review from that critic brought Nane fame and financial success, although Candelora was forced to repay the critic and wealthy clients with her own attentions. Nane Papa remained equally indifferent to critical acclaim, luxury, and his wife's infidelity. His career was an exercise in self-absorption; he wished only to pursue his art. All he ever expected of his wife was to have a companion who would accept and share his poverty without complaint. Nane's absolute devotion to painting and his inability to display jealousy so grieved Candelora that one sweltering August afternoon she bit his arm after he failed to express a feeling of shame for her adultery. Her act of animal ferocity was the one means of communication the woman hoped would reach her husband, since words—the great enemies of reality, as Joseph Conrad called them—made no impression on him. Yet nothing she did succeeded in provoking anger or shame in her husband—signs that would have proved that he cared for Candelora. There exists in Pirandello's narrative writing an entire language of nonverbal communication made up of silent gestures and expressions of the eyes as well as voice inflection, which convey far more unequivocal messages than words ever could; in his plays this same attention to nonverbal expression is reflected in minute stage directions that detail even subtle eye movements that the audience could never observe. After Candelora's first recourse to animal communication failed, she resorted to a still more desperate measure: poisoning and shooting herself. What she wanted from Nane Papa was for them to express their love to the full once they had succeeded in attaining a level of economic independence. Only her suicide succeeded in shocking Nane out of his indifference as he wept over her dead body. Candelora and her husband had each asked for something quite unalike from life. The intention of this tale is to illustrate the suicidal wastefulness of self-delusion where two individuals share nothing in common.

At times it seems that the silent requests of the novellistic characters for recognition of their longing for happiness will be answered, but either circumstances beyond control or social pressures force them to renounce forever the opportunity to know contentment. The novella "La Rosa" of 1914 could be classed with Maupassant's finest stories, especially "The Necklace" in its masterful treatment of a person's enjoying a supreme moment of sheer mad delight and then having to pay for it all the rest of her life. A young widow, Lucietta Nespi, resolutely faces adversity after the murder of her journalist husband by training for and winning a position as municipal telegraph operator in a small town, whose backwardness and remoteness from the main centers of Italian society seem to offer a shelter from the treachery of large cities. The mother of two small children, Lucietta brings a quality of feminine loveliness long lacking in that dull community, and a delegation led by the mayor invites her to the one important social event of the year: the grand ball at the local club. Hesitating about whether or not to attend, Signora Nespi makes the decision to go to the ball on finding outside her home a rose that has blossomed way ahead of season. The rose serves as a concrete novellistic symbol of Lucietta's youthful eagerness to experience an evening of intense pleasure. With the rose in her hair, she triumphs as she dances with a seemingly endless round of partners. The rose becomes transformed from a symbol of victory to one of irrevocable defeat after an argument over the choice of a partner for the final dance. A scuffle occurs as several men fight to retrieve the rose, which has fallen to the floor. After the mayor hands Lucietta the rose, she at once, as a gesture of reconciliation, presents the flower to a man who has not danced with her all during the evening: Fausto Silvagni, the first person to befriend her in the town. They had met on the train that brought her from Genoa after her husband's death. Instead of placating the rivalry in the ballroom, the offer of the rose to Silvagni is at once interpreted as a declaration of love, and the sympathy of the townsmen for the widow immediately turns to resentment. Lucietta at last perceives that pettiness is not the sole prerogative of a metropolis. Embarrassed by the sudden change in the now menacing crowd, she denies the seriousness of the gesture. To rescue her from their anger, Silvagni returns the rose and she tosses it away to prove how little she cares for the man. Yet earlier that evening Silvagni, the town secretary, had decided to propose to Lucietta, who would gladly have accepted that chance to know again the happiness and security she had shared with her first husband. That innocent gift of the rose and the crowd's spiteful jealousy compelled her and Silvagni to lose forever a dream of love. For the exhilaration of the ball, Lucietta Nespi was prevented from gaining the protection of a man who adored her not just for her outward loveliness but also for the courage with which she had faced life. If it had not been for the rose, Silvagni and the widow would have overcome the painful isolation of existence in that wearisome community. Society instead showed itself a source of oppressive irresponsibility.

Through a moment of embarrassment, Lucietta Nespi fails to take hold of all the beauty that life promises. Another widow, Adriana Braggi of "Il Viaggio" ("The Journey," 1910) suffers a pitiless fate after she finally awakens to her instinctual longing for life and love at the very time she receives the sentence of death from cancer of the lung. As the tale's title suggests, Adriana will make a journey of self-knowledge, away from the drought-ridden town of Sicily's interior, where she had always dwelt, not understanding that the vital flow had long dried up in that community. Her earlier life had been a silent and voluntary martyrdom of fidelity without love for a tyrannically jealous husband. After her husband's death Adriana lived an unconscious charade of absolutely proper behavior as she stayed on in the same house with her two sons, her mother, and her brother-in-law Cesare. Life in all its confusing whirl of new sights and strange sounds rushes in upon the widow after she has to leave the town's stagnant atmosphere to travel with her brother-in-law to Palermo in order to have a medical consultation. Nothing except the necessity of that trip would ever have disturbed the routine of her life, which conformed to the rigid code of traditional village customs in Sicily. But with the trip comes a change in apparel and coiffure, as if Adriana were beginning a new life. Despite the melancholy that oppresses her after a specialist pronounces a fatal diagnosis, Adriana undergoes a mystical experience when a voluptuous sensation of eternity passes over her as she stands by the Fountain of Hercules in Palermo's public garden. The joy of a seemingly endless moment permits the widow to dominate the dread of death as, for the first time in her life, she opens her being to all the elusive magic of rich sensations.

The tale of Adriana Braggi is one of passing barriers.

That arid village where life withers away is left behind as the widow takes her first train journey. Then, after the diagnosis, Cesare refuses to permit Adriana to return to the slow death of living in the village, and he takes her with him to Naples. Crossing the sea to reach the continent is the passing of the second barrier, for with the primitive insular mentality of Sicilians the widow feels that the journey across water must signify a change in her life. At Naples she and Cesare confess that they have always loved each other; a mere gesture like touching each other's arm as they promenade on the street one evening suffices to reveal to them the affection to which they never admitted earlier. The certainty of death makes possible the violation of a traditional way of life, and Adriana can cross the barrier of social taboos to experience the freedom of surrender to rapture. With the collapse of moral structures, she and Cesare start out on what will be a journey of both Eros and Thanatos for the widow. Through Rome, Florence, and Milan their trip follows a frenzied delirium of passionate love where every moment becomes more precious than the one before, since it may be the last they will share together. At Venice, perhaps the city most symbolic of decay and death, Adriana spends a day of velvet voluptuousness: the velvet of gondolas which, however, reminds her of the velvet lining of coffins. No longer able to elude the mirror image of death upon her face, Adriana passes the ultimate barrier by poisoning herself. Her love for Cesare could never know the disenchantment that usually follows the rapture of passion in Pirandellian tales. From the imprisonment of life in a Sicilian village she has moved to the final confinement of death to end the journey into life. The tale's structure is based on the principle of water as the source of life and death that Gaston Bachelard traces in *Water and Dreams:* the arid villege, mystical rebirth at the Palermo fountain, the liberation of the first steamer trip, and the gentle cradle-rocking of the Venetian gondola. The image of water dominates with its dream of Eros and Thanatos.

According to Pirandello, an enduring happiness can never grow from the sensual and sentimental relationship between a man and a woman. He felt that one of the few sources of lasting contentment was maternal love when it was allowed to blossom. The novella "Felicità" (1911) shows how the satisfaction of the maternal instinct can enable a woman to withstand social humiliation and poverty. The tale illustrates Pirandello's art of contrasting spaces of sadness with spaces of warmth and intimacy. It too is a story of barriers, ones that the charcters raise to isolate themselves from each other. All her childhood Elisabetta Grisanti lived in the dreary shadows of her family's ducal palace, knowing her father did not love her because her lack of beauty would not attract a rich match to restore the family fortune. She felt no regret at being banished from the palace after her father consented to her wedding a tutor— a man from a far inferior social rank who would afterward be permitted to enter the palace only by the servants' staircase in order to collect the meager checks that were granted him in place of a dowry. Since the duke never intended to look at Elisabetta again, he arranged for his wife to meet her in a rented carriage. Pirandello's emphasis here is on the distances that persons establish in order to be apart from each other.

After Elisabetta's husband deserts her and flees Sicily to avoid prosecution for theft, the young woman rises above misery through the radiant joy she has found by giving birth to a boy. She does not have to become reconciled with the duke, who continues to make a pompous daily appearance in public, riding through the streets in a coach attended by footmen in perukes and livery. What need does Elisabetta have to return to the melancholy darkness of the palace when she can live in her humble home near a countryside of cheerful sunlight and fragrant jasmines? She has created her own corner of happy retreat, such as those Bachelard studies in *The Poetics of Space*. With a strength of will that Pirandello considered unique to mothers, Elisabetta can bear exclusion from her aristocratic heritage because she discovers in maternity a truly vital identity that permits her to construct a zone of private contentment.

As an affirmation of life as a creative principle, motherhood can offer a release from the anguish of existence. But, as has already been illustrated by the case of Eleonora Bandi in "Scialle Nero," not all women are physically or emotionally capable of becoming wives and mothers. Although Pirandello could represent pregnancy as a glorious condition, he also showed how some persons would view that state as an obscenity. As a humorist the author felt the need to state the other side of a situation. While recognizing that paternal love could be a strong instinct in some men,[15] he usually portrayed the male attitude toward marriage and procreation as horror before a trap, as in the tale "La Trappola" of 1912, where Signor Fabrizio despises women for the way they excite men and trick them into generating children who will become as dead as their parents. For Fabrizio, life is an illness that kills persons by fixing them into definite forms. Illusions freeze the personality into an unchanging mask. Fabrizio tries to avoid a living death by forever standing in front of a mirror so as to alter his appearance by shaving his hair or cutting off his moustache. Yet even he succumbs to a seductress, who uses Fabrizio to become pregnant and then returns to her sterile husband. Fabrizio would like to strangle the woman before she gives birth, for by murdering a pregnant woman—a key temptation for some Pirandellian characters—he could save a child from the death of assuming a form; but she flees to Sardinia. For the past seven years the narrator's paralytic father has been reduced to a vegetable state except for eating and weeping, and Fabrizio dreams of escaping from their entrapment by setting fire to the house so that he and the invalid may perish. But when the sun begins to shine, he puts aside his homicidal thoughts and takes his father out to enjoy the splendor of the day. Although Fabrizio succeeds in avoiding the violence that might free him from the trap of the senses, other Pirandellian figures will not hesitate to make a ferocious attack on life.

This nihilistic attitude toward the continuance of life through procreation found particularly bitter expression in novelle like"Il Professor Terremoto" (1910) and "Niente" (1922), in which neither heroism nor artistic talent suffices to redeem life from its misery. Professor Earthquake received his nickname after he rescued six persons during a quake at Reggio, Calabria. From being a bachelor with a promising future as teacher and author, he ended by marrying the mother of the family he saved in the quake, and in the space of a few years he became the sole support of fifteen persons. Not coming to know the pleasures of geography, which provided relief for characters like Belluca in "Il treno ha fischiato," Professor Earthquake could give vent to his feelings of burdened responsibility in no way other than writing cynical books of philosophy that caused his superiors to reprimand him for his disappointing literary performance. For an unselfish act of heroism he saw his own life turned into a constant earthquake. The professor's cynicism, however, seems almost sanguine when compared to the bleak outlook of Dr. Mangoni in "Niente," a physician who declares he has voluntarily resigned from life by avoiding intimate relationships and refusing to establish a true home for himself. Most nights he sleeps on a couch in a pharmacy while awaiting emergency calls. On one of those moonlit nights when Pirandello's characters can no longer meet the challenge of living, Mangoni is called to a poor tenement to attend a youth who tried to asphyxiate himself on failing to be hired as a reporter for a Rome newspaper. Arriving too late to resuscitate the youth, Mangoni comments that suicide is the best way out of life's wretchedness.

Although the young man had already given proof of undeniable poetic talent with a volume of verse, his life
would not have been one of literary glory but of everyday
tribulation, since he might have married the daughter of the
man who provided him lodging. The youth's future would
have been one of wife, babies, home, and unceasing problems. Dr. Mangoni asserts that the more fiercely one
struggles to be great, the more tormented he becomes.
Greater sensitivity is a sure sign of a larger capacity for
unhappiness. The young poet's actual suicide has its parallel
in the physician's living suicide.

None of the preceding three protagonists takes action
against life. But Nicola Petix, the central character of "La
Distruzione dell'Uomo" ("The Destruction of Man," 1921)
translates thought into violent action. In his longing to stay
outside of life, to be nothing, Nicola Petix anticipates that
stranger to life as imagined by Camus in *Le Mythe de
Sisyphe* and *l'Étranger*. Petix's act of violence—although
accomplished with astonishing calm—does not display, however, the absurd casualness with which Meursault shoots the
Arab in Camus's novel. Like Elizabetta in "Felicità," Petix
was always excluded from his father's affections, but he
could not transcend his failure to enter into another's life
except by harboring an explosively increasing resentment.[16]
The way he persisted in changing his major at the university
(trying out medicine, law, mathematics, and humanities)
without ever taking a degree recalls the ineptitude of Italo
Svevo's anti-hero in *La Coscienza di Zeno* (*The Confessions
of Zeno*, 1923), who also shifts between chemistry and law.
Whereas the figure in Svevo's novel smiles self-indulgently
at his failures and plans new resolutions for a healthy life
of activity even though he may not succeed, Petix retreats
farther and farther into a pathologetical alienation that can
result only in a savage outburst. Ironically, the father who
rejected his son as a shamefully idle individual made it
possible for Petix to persevere in his potentially dangerous

idleness by leaving him a small trust fund. Free from the responsibility of earning his livelihood, Petix has all the time in the world to brood on the bestiality of life.

As in the tales of the two derelict wetnurses, the city of Rome becomes a major actor in determining events and attitudes here. The tale is narrated in the first person by someone who is apparently well acquainted with the neighborhood in which Petix's crime takes place. The narrator, who attempts to appear dispassionate and objective during Petix's trial, devotes seven paragraphs to describing the environment of the murder: near one of the decrepit and overcrowded tenement buildings that were hastily erected after Rome became Italy's capital. When the expected population boom did not immediately follow construction, most of those tenements were left to crumble until by the end of the nineteenth century a housing shortage did develop, and great numbers of persons were squeezed into narrow and dilapidated quarters. The human element predominates in the narrator's urban description. For ten years Petix has had to dwell in one of those tenements where from all sides —in the other apartments, on the stairs, and in the courtyard—he suffers from the ceaseless noise, the nauseating odor and the loathsome sight of filthy children. Persons confined in city apartments exhibit the same characteristics as animals in the captivity of cages: a fierce irritation that can end in violence. In his barren aloneness Petix feels a profound disgust at the sickening proliferation of humankind. To him copulation becomes a profanation. He wants to strike out against the very source of life, to destroy the vital instinct which makes possible the birth of nasty children. Certain sights in particular offend Petix because they symbolize the eternal rhythm of sexual attraction, marriage and birth: an engaged couple in the early glow of love, a pregnant woman. During all the time of his stay at the tenement, Nicola has had to face the repulsive spectacle of Signora Porrella, who in eighteen years of marriage has undergone fifteen miscarriages. After she enters another pregnancy, Petix begins a tacit wager against her to see whether or not she can successfully give birth. The whole apartment house around Petix reminds him of the woman's misshapen abdomen—a gigantic womb working to the pain of gestation. Language in Pirandello's tales, as even in an avowedly naturalistic writer like Zola, is never truly referential. Here the language situation is that of explosive violence, such as Artaud was later to define as the exercise of consciousness in conferring a color of blood or a cruel note to any vital act. Terms like *"bestia"*, *"cenci sporci"* (dirty rags), *"ozio"* (idleness), *"tedio"* (boredom), *"fracasso"* (noise) all contribute to forming a symbolic field which expresses the tension around the tale's center which is *"nulla"*—the existential *néant* or nothingness that propels Petix against those who live merely to live. For on an October day when chill winds sweep leaves off the plane trees and the Tiber floods its banks (note how visual details of the cityscape intensify the mood of a season of death), Nicola commits his crime of radical annihilation of life by pushing Signora Porrella into the river. The murder is not a Gidian gratuitous act that one performs spontaneously out of a superabundance of vital energy without thought of profit or satisfying individual passions. His rancor against life does not compel him to prevent merely the birth of Porrella's child, as he does not wish to destroy any particular baby but *man* as incarnated by the unborn child. The crime by its very judicial consequences also represents an act of suicide since Petix will be tried for premeditated murder. The dimensions of the story are almost metaphysical, because its nihilism elevates it from being the case record of an individual murder but makes of it an assault upon the well-springs of life itself.

Extreme measures like homicide and suicide, along with the joys of maternity, geography, and astronomy enable the novellistic characters to arrive at an accommodation with existence. In the extreme cases there is no hope for individual or societal redemption as Pirandello's narrative art does not always work in the manner of comedy for the renewal of the world but for its destruction. But reliance on the instinct of motherhood or distraction in the stars or faraway lands are a choice for survival. Life in Pirandello's novelle is an experience which one must constantly dread. An early novella, "Se . . ." ("If . . .") of 1898, expresses an ever-present anxiety about the fortuitous events and encounters that lead to disaster not because of some malign destiny but because of the character weaknesses inherent in man. The very title of one novella, "Paura d'esser felice" ("The Fear of Being Happy," 1910), clearly indicates the terror that life will crush man's fondest hopes. To live in society implies that one must bear responsibilities toward others, as the protagonist of "Leviamoci questo pensiero" ("Let's get rid of this worry," 1910) acknowledges by the mad haste with which he tries to carry out duties and important tasks even to the point of alienating everyone who benefits from his pathological promptness. Also, in social relationships an individual's security and happiness must often be built on another's misfortune, and in order to evade recognition of selfish motives some of the novellistic characters, like Lydia Venturi in "Una Voce" ("A Voice," 1904), unconsciously attempt to mask their intentions as altruistic acts until an inevitable confrontation forces them to admit to their exclusive self-interest. Once underlying motives are exposed and the mask of self-deception is discarded, a gnawing sense of guilt remains to torment the characters who merely sought to find contentment without consciously intending to harm anyone else. One of Pirandello's favorite novelle, "La Pena di Vivere Così" ("The Pain of Living That Way," published in 1920 and partially revised in 1936), proceeds according to a series of mirror-image revelations wherein the myopic heroine perceives the falseness of her orderly and exemplary life. The tranquillity and the almost antiseptic cleanliness of the heroine's home conceal the inner hypocrisy of a woman whose apparent revulsion for physical contact hides an attraction to sin. After the heroine fails to yield to her erotic passions, she is left spiritually naked, since the brush with life's violence has divested her of all illusions about being a charitable, self-effacing individual. In the moral emptiness of disillusionment only the throbbing pain of existence persists on to remind the protagonist how life clashes within itself.[17] In their dread of living, many of the novellistic characters manufacture a logical order, but in so doing they betray life, which eventually takes its revenge. That consoling moral code of *bontà* which sustained the protagonists in the tales of Pirandello's predecessors is either absent or figures as part of the language of deception of oneself and others. Although the characters of Pirandello's novellistic world constitute a community of the submerged, they never form a brotherhood of the suffering to rescue each other from mechanical and meaningless lives. The Pirandellian universe appears as one of a retreat into the automatism of privileged recollection.

Escape toward a Higher Reality

Several of Pirandello's final novelle—written during the years of his most intense theatrical activity—reveal a desire to evade everyday reality in a higher plane of experience. What was examined in earlier tales like "Quand'ero matto" of 1901 as an escape into insanity became a mythic realm that the novellistic characters longed to enter. The dream world of these later tales recalls the higher reality that the contemporary school of French surrealists wished to explore. Like the poet Paul Eluard, the Italian author endeavored to recreate the death of the ego in a mirror (Eluard's *"mirroir sans tain"*), which absorbs the conventional personality image.[18] Along with the surrealisti school Pirandello accepted the coexistence of contradictory entities within the human psyche. Just as the surrealists turned to the clinical research of Charcot on hysteria, Pirandello had earlier found confirmation in the theories of Marchesini and Binet on the contradictions and multiplicity of the individual personality. Pirandello's preoccupation with fortuitous events resembles the "objective hazard" of surrealists like André Breton, who probed the apparently inexplicable forces that determine a certain course of events. The Italian writer shared with the surrealists a total distrust for logical order, which tried to arrest the vital flux. Pirandello wished to investigate how the secret life of the instincts could invade consciousness and produce a dreamlike state while destroying the ordinary perceptions of time and space. The writer hoped to re-create that marvelous movement when the psyche would be displaced in opposite directions at once. Through the instantaneous spasm of the marvelous, Pirandello aimed at reaching those moments of lapse when persons were restored to possession of an authentic inner life. Although the titles of his late tales deceptively relate to his earlier stories of conventional reality by referring to concrete objects like a commonplace flower or to everyday occurrences like a visit, the Sicilian writer was pursuing a journey across strange vistas that could not be predicated on the structures of chronological time and where the psyche had to undergo a constant experience of disintegration. The frightening realm of the late novelle is one in which the public self becomes submerged in the struggle between the waking ego and the no longer suppressed instincts. But in his effort to create a mythic representation of the conflict between the marionette of Culture and the anarchical beast of Nature that is fought in the mind of every person, Pirandello differed fundamentally from the surrealists in that he never practiced automatic writing. Conscious rational control is evident in almost every line he ever wrote. The oneiric visions of his later novelle are captured in a style over which the author exercised full mastery.

Pirandello's desire to fashion myths for modern times reflected the mood of Italian writers during the Fascist era, when political reality was so oppressive and demoralizing that a literature of fantasy alone could effectively elude government censorship. Surrealism in Italy possessed a political dimension that was unnecessary in France, where writers rebelled against bourgeois values but did not have to seek refuge from the agents of a dictatorship. Political necessity compelled many Italian writers to veil sense with non-sense, to cross that literary frontier which, as Freud observed, would arrive at "wit": a frontier where, as Lacan was later to mention, "man tempts his very destiny when he derides the signifier." Among the authors of this special wit between the two world wars was Pirandello's friend Massimo Bontempelli (1878–1960), editor of the cosmopolitan review '900. In tales like "La Scacchiera davanti allo Specchio" ("The Chessboard before the Mirror," 1922) Bontempelli experimented with a style that he called "realismo magico"; in that work persons become objects and objects take on human personality during a journey through the mystery world behind a looking glass. Magic realism begins with a situation of conventional reality that is steadily demolished as the fictitious characters carry their absolutely logical designs to absurd outcomes. Bontempelli aimed at creating fables of persons imprisoned by time and death. The atmosphere of miracle that suffused the semi-realistic, semi-fantastic universe of Bontempelli's writings also came to characterize the borderland between daily reality and hallucination in the later Pirandellian tales.

The discovery of a terrifying power removes the protagonist of "Soffio" ("A Breath," 1931) from the everyday world and transforms him into a fatal instrument, perhaps Fate itself. The tale has all the disturbing force of Kafka's *Metamorphosis* as it recounts the protagonist's shocked awareness of his ability to cause death merely by joining his thumb and index finger and blowing lightly on them.

This novella is in the first person, and the astonished narrator relates his initial lack of comprehension on discovering his death-dealing might after he first made the fatal gesture and blew the lethal breath upon an acquaintance who had just told him about the sudden death of a mutual friend. Again and again the protagonist repeated the identical gesture, with the same deadly results, until the newspapers declared that a mysterious epidemic was raging through the city and decimating the population. Afraid for his sanity, the protagonist stopped his experiments, and the city returned to normal. After two weeks the narrator decided to conduct a crucial test. With the detachment of a scientist practicing eugenics, he chose as the subject of his experiment a deformed child, who died with a smile on his face after the fatal breath touched him. By then the narrator understood that he had become Death, impartiality killing persons without any feeling of hatred. The situation of this tale seems a logical conclusion to Pirandello's preoccupation with the relationship between life and death. Death figures as the force of negation because it is the persistent negative power residing in being itself. To demonstrate his fairness, the protagonist performed the gesture on himself by standing before a store mirror. Here the motif of the mirror portends self-annihilation, for the narrator's image vanished forever after the mortal breath blew across the glass surface. The individual consciousness, on mirroring itself, has passed through reflection to complete dissolution. This novella, which began in the matter-of-fact tone of realistic narration, moves from relating the protagonist's uneasy recognition of his deadly gift to a nightmare atmosphere when he became pure disembodied spirit. His frantic distress, rendered all the more effective by the first-person technique with at times anguished repetitions of forms of verbs of urgency like *scappare* (to run away), diminished only after his spirit floated away to the countryside where he could introduce Death as a gentle force. While the physical self has crossed the line to disintegration, outer nature remains. Arrival at cosmic unity must result in total dispersion. A yearning for annihilation dwells at the center of Pirandellian art. Its paradox is that absorption into the cosmos acts as a form of re-creation, and absolute indetermination appears not a menace but a temptation. In this tale as in most of the mythic novelle, a language of shock predominates, especially as expressed by adjectival past participles like *sbalordito* (astonished), *alterato* (changed), *annichilito* (annihilated), *respinto* (pushed back), which delineate the changes that suddenly overcome the protagonist. Despite his ever-increasing anxiety, the narrator kept seeking rational explanations for the epidemic he seemed to cause; like most Pirandellian characters, he resisted becoming an excluded one. Here the signifying function of language undergoes a deliberate crisis that parallels the physical disintegration as language moves toward non-sense in the narrator's bewildered voice. Like Poe and Maupassant in their epidemic tales, Pirandello searches here the mystery between life and death.

Death as a floating away into nothingness is the message of the novella "Di Sera, un geranio" ("At Evening, a Geranium") of 1934, which so transcends the conventional sense of narrative as to acquire an evanescence of style as the disembodied spirit wanders across a familiar realm that is rapidly becoming remote.[19] A man who feared a dangerous operation has died. To die is exactly to lose contact with the material objects that go into the construction of life. The bewilderment of the spirit floating around the death chamber is shown in the adverbs of place like *qua* (here), *giù* (down), *là* (there), which establish a staccato rhythm for the forcible flight of the consciousness. As a sentient form it used to find identification in thought and in the outer world but never with the body, toward which it feels rancor in death. Living consists in the immaterial flash of the thinking process and in the images that others project upon an individual. Dying is a dissolution into formlessness, the fading away of all constructs. The structures of life that the mind and the senses try to grasp—like a clock, a picture hanging on the wall, the rose color of a lamp—were all illusions that must vanish into death's nothingness. Pirandellian characters do not experience that alienation from physical objects which forms the illness of Antoine Roquentin in Sartre's *La Nausée* (1938) and the painter Dino in Alberto Moravia's novel *La Noia* (1960). The Pirandellian aspiration is to escape the condition of the conscious *être-pour-soi* to acquire the inertness of *être-en-soi* in the object's resistance to the *néant* that death threatens. Whereas Sartre's protagonist recoils before pebbles and tree roots, and Moravia's anti-hero confesses to an object-malady that has plagued him since childhood, the dying spirit in the novella wishes—before it completely disappears—to reside in something like a stone or a flower. Instead of being superfluous, objects in their thingness possess a formal structure that is denied to the thinking spirit. Just as in the story of the man with a flower in his mouth, in this novella a flower serves as the symbol of death but also as a blazing moment of eternity. For a second the spirit enters into the life of a geranium, which suddenly catches fire and flames brilliantly until the spirit has faded altogether away. The momentary flickering of mortality ends. Language and poetic image capture death's phenomenology and psychology. Although this novella points out how death is the horrifying chasm of nothingness, it shows the act of dying as holding no terror, but only a melancholy sense of separation from the objects that impart a transient meaning to life.

Time and death are both conquered through the dream vision of the tale "Visita" of 1935, where the waking world merges with the irreality of an hallucination. The novella opens with an extremely brief interchange between the narrator and his butler, who has announced the visit of a Signora Anna Wheil. But the narrator knows from an obituary notice that Anna Wheil died the day before in Florence. In a parenthetical paragraph the narrator admits that he may never have held that interchange with the butler, that the scene may well have been a dream caused by reading the obituary notice. All that he recalls for certain is that he saw Anna Wheil in a dream, in which she appeared clothed in the chaste whiteness of a cloud that started to dissolve, exposing the rose-toned nudity of her body. Anna Wheil was indeed the object of the narrator's erotic desires, which could be satisfied only in dreaming; the very Germanic form of her name makes of her an exotic figure who remains forever elusive. When the narrator discovers her waiting for him in his study, he at once understands the appearance of the white cloud, because she is wearing the same white summer dress from three years before at the time of their sole meeting during a garden reception. Pirandello here reproduces the way dreams transform objects of conventional reality, almost magically remaking the world and investing it with the seductive attractiveness of desire. This dreamlike mood of voluptuous confusion is self-generating as a complex of sensations of color that annihilate the ordinary sense of temporal incompleteness by merging past and present. The fusion of past and present appears in what the narrator calls an "eternal present" when he makes a grammatical play between the present tense "La conosco appena" ("I scarcely know her") and the imperfect "La conoscevo appena" ("I scarcely knew her"), as he succeeds in recapturing with all the vividness of present time the enchantment of that garden party on an afternoon in late springtime. That garden served as his terrestrial paradise, the *locus amoenus* where the narrator represented Man and Anna became the supreme Lady, the object of adoration who can never be attained. As he was introduced to Anna, she was bent over, playing with some children, and he glimpsed the white beauty of her breasts. With their eyes alone he and Anna exchanged a silent communication that

bound them together for eternity. The language of the
narrator's worshipful appreciation of Anna's feminine loveliness adds an erotic refinement to the religious devotion
for a sacred lady that medieval poets of the Italian Sweet
New Style like Dante and Petrarch used to address to the
donna angelicata of their sonnets and canzoni. Anna is the
"ewig weibliche" that no man will ever truly possess to the
depths of her being. Her breasts were like the promise of a
gift that Heaven granted man to console him for his sufferings on earth. Yet, in the atmosphere of the tale, where the
levels between dream and reality are blurred, Anna remained a woman of everyday society who had a husband,
and the narrator understood that he would have to have
been twenty years younger to take her away from her husband. Thus the respectful distance that separated him from
Anna resembles the detachment of the medieval love poets,
who always chose another man's wife as the object of their
affections.

As he emerges from the splendid dream of the past, the
narrator hears Anna speaking to him with the familiar
pronoun. At that present moment, following the notice of
her death, he seems to discover her there in the green-
tinged light that filters into the study through the trees
outside his home and gives the objects in the room the harmonious color of hope. But Anna now reveals to him how
cancer has deprived her of those breasts which he admired
at the reception. When he looks, however, the narrator sees
only the whiteness of the newspaper which included the
obituary, for his Anna has disappeared. That whiteness
becomes the color of annihilation. To some critics Anna's
breasts have appeared as those of a mother figure, and the
cancer which ravaged them is interpreted as an incest
prohibition.[20] Pirandello's mythic novella may be seen apart
from a Freudian interpretation. The cancer which mutilated
and eventually killed Anna is another of death's preliminary
visits. Her beauty will, nevertheless, be everlasting because

it has entered the narrator's unconscious from which it can
be summoned for a dream visit. The haunting image of the
lovely female at the garden party represents in the novella
the erotic transformation of creative visual energy from a
supremely transitory experience. Anna's breasts are the gifts
of ripe abundance, with a complex of effete impulse, desire
and aspiration that they arouse in the narrator, only to
vanish in the disintegration of the dream vision. As often
in Pirandello the tale is constructed around an absence
revealed through the narrator's consciousness that remains
"opened" to discourse. The chaos of elements such as the
swirling colors works upon the narrator, who stays a passive
figure through whom the dream transformation takes place.
In the art of this mythic narration death and the ravages of
disease are defeated as a mortal creature like Anna Wheil is
elevated to an atemporal sphere, which corresponds to the
crystaline life aspired to by Breton and that concrete universe closed to casual passersby which Aragon sees as the
surrealistic state of grace.

The gloomily obsessive atmosphere of a nightmare
haunts the tale "*C'è qualcuno che ride*" ("There's Someone
Who Is Laughing") of 1934. This novella may very well
represent a political satire of the spirit of conformity that
characterized life in Italy under the Fascist regime.[21] It
bears a striking similarity to the allegorical satires of Musso-
linian Italy in Moravia's *Racconti surrealistici e satirici*,
where the self-satisfied adherents of the dictatorship appear
as greedy monsters intent only on gratifying their many
lusts. In a deliberately unnamed city an official proclamation
has invited (commanded) the people to attend a reception
(rally) at a ballroom. Not even the brilliance of chandeliers
nor the liveliness of dance tunes could succeed in dispelling
the feeling of uneasy apprehension at that evening's ball.
The restlessness that pervaded the gathering derived from
the fact that no one knew the reason for the invitation.
Like the defendant in Kafka's *The Trial*, the guests were

left perplexed by the machinations of a superior power who made all the decisions for them. At the orders of official photographers some of them were dancing to create the impression of a festive occasion; they were merely performing the dutiful obligation of pleasing the authorities who had invited them to the ball. From time to time a guest had to disappear into a secret chamber where everyone supposed a serious decision was being reached. The door to that chamber recalls the heavenly gate in *The Trial:* symbol of frustration for those forbidden to enter it an emblem of the aspiration toward a nonexistent meaning. All that most of the guests could do was perform a funereal masquerade where the dancers resembled old toys that had been stored away for years and were then unpacked for the event. While they awaited a public announcement that might bring clarification, the passive guests appeared to share a tacit agreement to maintain the grave decorum that alone would be appropriate under the weighty circumstances. In the ballroom's claustrophobic atmosphere, oppressed by seventeenth-century frescoes of menacing nocturnal scenes, the guests were reduced to dancing automata.

All the counterfeit solidarity of the crowd—founded as it was on fear and ignorance—was threatened by three persons who broke from the norm of automatic gestures and openly laughed aloud. The laughter of a father, his university-age son, and his adolescent daughter seemed an affront to the event's solemnity, and all the other guests soon became convinced that the act of nonconformity was the result of a conspiracy to create embarrassment. While everywhere else the ballroom's mirrored walls reflected the "emperor's-clothes" ignorance and paranoia of the crowd, the laughing expression of those three insouciant guests alone disturbed the mindless harmony of the reflections. To punish the three for their defiance, the entire crowd arose in perfect robot unanimity and started to hem them into a corner. Three official figures who were robed in domino hood and mask appeared from the secret chamber and took the lead of the crowd. With their hands burlesquely shackled together by napkins, the dominoes stood before the terrified family in the sarcastic attitude of criminals begging for mercy—the dominoes thus became the mirror reflection of the posture that the laughing trio had to be intimidated into assuming. After a loud sardonic laugh burst from the crowd intent on teaching the family a lesson for their bad manners, the father barely managed to take hold of his children and escape. The whole tale is structured on a series of repetitions and imagery to convey a nightmare experience. Here the narrative must turn upon itself to distort and exhaust discourse until it is reduced to the insignificant communication code of totalitarianism.

Public derision and banishment from the communal assembly of the ballroom were the only penalties that the nonconformists suffered, but the crowd's aggressiveness betrayed a ruthless desire to suppress all dissent. The laughing trio made the supreme mistake of enjoying the reception without fearing the consequences of their conduct, which must have seemed normal to them but to the majority that laughter could be viewed only as overt disrespect. Bergson observes that laughter indicates a slight revolt on the surface of social life, which in Pirandello's tale is choreographed as a robots' ball. Laughter works to convert rigidity into plasticity, but it can also repress any separatist tendency, as in the laugh that the crowd returns to the family. Under a dictatorship the normal becomes abnormal and suspect. In the climate of a totalitarian state, the most natural act could be interpreted as a challenge to official policy.[22] Pirandello's novella anticipates studies of conformism like Ionesco's play *Rhinoceros*. In every dictatorial regime "spontaneous" emotions must be the result of careful planning and orchestrating; otherwise the chaos of genuine feelings might disturb the public's submission. If this novella is to be regarded outside the traumatic context of the Fascist era, it should be classified along with the nightmare novelle of the Italian writer Dino Buzzati (b. 1906) for its representation of the vague fear that has obsessed individuals in the mass societies of the twentieth century.

A few months before Pirandello's death, the *Corriere della Sera* published the novella "Una Giornata" ("A Day"), which proved to be the author's farewell to the world. The "day" of the title is the symbolic day of an entire life-span, from birth to death. Through first-person technique the narrator surveys the confusing panorma of his life. At nighttime he is tossed from a train coach into a strange station; he must have been asleep for some time because he cannot recall boarding the train. Nocturnal darkness here is that of birth and childhood. The choice of a train station as the bewildering point of arrival for life is of course typical of the author, who saw in such a setting all the agony of life's puzzling activities. In the darkness the narrator becomes aware of a light, which moves, seemingly of its own volition, to the train that leaves without him: from infancy every individual recognizes certain forces that operate beyond human control. Before he ventures into the unknown city, the narrator examines himself just as an infant will explore the unknown territory of his own being. After dawn, on the busy downtown streets, he observes how other persons rush frenetically about as if they were absolutely certain about the seriousness of what they are doing. The narrator resolves to act like others and appear to be fully convinced about the significance of his acts. Here conformity is not acquiescence to a dictatorial society but the simulation of life. The narrator will let others be the mediators of his actions and goals, imitating the patterns of behavior that he observes to be acceptable to others.

To his astonishment persons seem to recognize the narrator. He wonders if they are greeting him or his suit. Is it only the social mask that others acknowledge? In the breast pocket of his jacket he finds an old wallet that must have fallen once in a puddle since he cannot make out the blurred name on the water-stained identification cards. The narrator also discovers the photograph of a lovely girl in a bathing suit; somehow he thinks that the girl in the photo is throwing a greeting meant especially for him. The position of the photo next to a religious Sunday-School card would seem to indicate his fiancée. The wallet also contains a large bank note—perhaps an inheritance or his first earnings; since the time is already past noon, more than half of life has passed. In a restaurant, in a bank, the narrator continues to be recognized, and he plays his part in the comedy of life by taking directions from others in the hope that they are in the know and possess the vital secret. A car drives up, and the chauffeur takes him to an elegant older house where the same family must have dwelt for several genera-tions. Yet he still feels an intruder in that traditional setting. In the bedroom the beautiful girl of the photograph is waiting for him to join her. At dawn of the following day she is gone, and the bed feels as cold as a tomb, since the death that has already overtaken her draws close at hand for the narrator. The mirror on the wall—always the Piran-dellian mirror, which shatters any illusions—tells him that he is an old man. The vital cycle completes itself when his children and grandchildren invade the silence of the dusty old room where he once enjoyed the warmth of love. And while the elderly narrator still has the strength, he watches his grandchildren standing near his armchair. Before he even realizes it, they too have grown old.

In that final novella Pirandello traced the allegorical journey of life, using the modern machines of alienation like the locomotive and the automobile. The protagonist passes through life like an amnesiac who never emerges from his hypnotic trance. Time is never arrested in the tale, for it moves away like the light from the train. Brief clauses re-create the staccato, panting thoughts of the bewildered narrator. Short periods of restoration along the journey produce illusions of order that quickly vanish. Life attains its fullest moment in the consummation of the love-death in the bed that becomes a grave: here the acts of love and dying are free of the physical repulsiveness that torments many of the author's protagonists, and the lovers almost seem to be taking part in the ritual of a medieval romance. But much of life is a sequence of ritualistic gestures whose significance eludes the pilgrim. Rather than stressing the nihilistic conviction of life's futility, however, this novella of leave-taking emphasizes the bewilderment of the human pilgrimage in a post-Christian universe. The vital quest for understanding closes with a recognition of the confusing nature of earthly existence. Humankind must forever pursue a journey for which there is no close except in death.

With the final mythic novelle, Pirandello left behind the Veristic preoccupation with factual reality to create an art form that demolishes the physical barriers of the exterior world to undertake a voyage of exploration through the inner landscape of the mind. Escape from life's entrapment characterizes both the Veristic and mythic tales, which respectively display the contradictory conclusions of Romanticism in Naturalism and Surrealism. With those last tales Pirandello actually succeeded in fashioning the new mythology that Tommaseo hoped to be the goal of his writings. Pirandello's novelle create a discourse about nothingness as they define the edges of the void menacing modern life. The novellistic language seeks to go beyond the confines of realistic reference to open new dimensions of psychic and social signification. Through his novelle the author had been able to examine individual cases of the failure or success of his fictional characters to reach an accord with life. Each tale traced the absurd, circular pattern of social existence or the brutalizing conformism with stifling codes and customs. But by the very limitations of its condensed form, the novella could merely suggest the relationship of the individual character to the social environment in which he or she thought himself or herself to be a prisoner or outcast. It was to the expansive technique of the novel that Luigi Pirandello turned when he sought to study in depth the conflict between personal aspirations and societal constraints.

Early Novels of Sicily

The Emergence of an Italian Novel

Although the tradition of the novella in Italy went back to
the late thirteenth century, the novel was still a rather recent
and highly suspect literary genre for Italian authors when
Pirandello wrote his first novel, *L'Esclusa*, in 1893. The
emergence of the novel in Italy had coincided with the
awakening of a sense of national identity. It was indignation
at Napoleon's betrayal of the Venetian realm to the Aus-
trians in exchange for Lombardy that inspired Ugo Foscolo
(1778–1827) to write the earliest Italian novel *Ultime Lettere di Jacopo Ortis* (*Last Letters of Jacopo Ortis*), which
was first published in complete form in 1802. Turning to the

foreign model of the epistolary novel as in the works of
Richardson and Rousseau, the young Foscolo sought to
represent the tormented states of mind of his suicidal protagonist almost in the very act, for the various letters of
the novel were intended to constitute a psychological portrait of the alternation between hope and despair at crucial
moments in the final months of the hero's life. In an attempt
to confront the problems of his generation, Foscolo also set
his novel in the contemporary period of the Napoleonic
wars in Italy. Yet, despite the favorable critical reaction that
Foscolo's novel received outside of Italy, his innovative
example failed to establish a vital tradition for other Italian
writers to emulate.[1]

In the repressive atmosphere of the authoritarian governments that were restored to power throughout the Italian
regions after Napoleon's fall, authors turned to their nation's
past in an effort to elude official censorship. It was Alessandro Manzoni—one of the few Italian writers whom
Pirandello was to consider a genuine humorist—who succeeded in creating the form of the novel that dominated in
nineteenth-century Italy: the historical novel, with his *I
Promessi Sposi,* first published in 1827 and then revised
between 1840 and 1842. By placing his novel in the seventeenth century, Manzoni was able to expose the moral decay
and injustice that prevailed in Italy under foreign enslavement. Along with an emphasis on a reality of historical
facts, which could be verified by documentation, Manzoni
also introduced an entirely new human world to Italian
literature: the realm of humble peasants and tradesmen.
By constantly revising his novel according to contemporary
Tuscan usage, the Lombard Manzoni offered a solution to
the problem of a standard literary language for all of Italy.
Throughout the nineteenth century more than a hundred
historical novels were written by Italian authors imitating
Manzoni, and even Pirandello produced a historical novel
with his *I Vecchi e i Giovani* of 1909.

Once Italy had achieved national unity, novelists turned increasingly to the investigation of their native regions and the exploration of that world of the humble which Manzoni had first presented. The Verists Capuana, Verga, and Pirandello after them, of course studied the shepherds, peasantry, miners, nobles, and rising bourgeoisie of Sicily. In novels like *Giacinta* (1879) and *Il Marchese di Roccaverdiana* (1901) Capuana examined the force of sensual passion and the inescapable recognition of personal guilt. Verga projected a cyclic series of five novels to be called *I Vinti* (*The Defeated*) to give a panoramic view of struggle and failure across the different levels of Italian society. Although he completed only two novels in the series, Verga succeeded in representing the dignity and noble sense of resignation to a life of toil and privation among Sicilian fishermen, peasants, and artisans. An almost religious cult of the family inspires the title characters of his novel *I Malavoglia* (1881) as they battle to regain their homestead and preserve their honor. A patriarchal love of land and not greed motivates the eponymous protagonist of *Mastro Don Gesualdo* (1888) in his futile attempt to acquire immortality through his vast material possessions. Verga compassionately identified himself with his Sicilian characters and joined in their sufferings. Even though he wrote his novels in standard Italian, he introduced the proverbs and rhythmic phrasing of the Sicilian dialect into the dialogue and indirect discourse of his works. Truth for the Verists was not that of historical documentation but that uncovered by the scrupulous analysis of man's basic instincts and passions.

Regionalism in Italian literature permitted authors to interpret the desires and traditions of their own people. Antonio Fogazzaro (1842–1911) placed the principal action of his novels, like *Piccolo Mondo Antico* (*Little World of Earlier Times,* 1896), in his native province of the Valsolda between Vicenza and the Lake of Lugano in northern Italy. Fogazzaro excelled at the creation of *macchiette,* comical pictures of eccentric local characters; and he did not hesitate to use dialect to evoke an authentic atmosphere of provincial life. His novels also served to express the longing of the educated middle class in the new Kingdom of Italy for lay reform within the Roman Catholic Church.[2] Close observation of life in the slums of Naples characterizes the novels of Matilde Serao (1856–1927), who in her voluminous and uneven writings wished to portray the moral shortcomings of the Neapolitan people and their spirited accommodation to poverty and its misfortunes. Sardinia and its primitive inhabitants provided the background for the novels of Grazia Deledda (1871–1936), such as *Anime Oneste* (*Honest Souls*, 1896), *Il Vecchio della Montagna* (*The Old Man of the Mountain*, 1900) and *La Madre* (*The Mother*, 1920), where the author treated the themes of carnal desire, religious duty, and renunciation. The emphasis on regional realism sometimes led to an excessive reliance on the picturesque presentation of folklore, because the novelists delighted in describing local processions, tribal practices, and traditions, often to the exclusion of studying the inner life of the fictional characters. Pirandello's own novels were to mark a constant moving away from the regionalist's interest in exteriority toward a total preoccupation with exploring the interior landscape of the human personality.

During the same period that the regionalists were excitedly discovering the charms of the provinces, the novelistic form also mirrored the ultra-refined tastes of the sophisticated urban classes of Rome, Florence, and Milan. Verga himself had written novels like *Tigre Reale* (*Royal Tigress*, 1873) and *Eros* (1875) on the vain search for pleasure among the debased members of the smart set in central and northern Italy; his earlier novels were melodramatic studies of strong and remorseless *femmes fatales* who led their weak-willed lovers to destruction. In contrast to Verga's critical attitude toward moral corruption that resulted from the material progress in the commercial and industrial centers of the new Italy, Gabriele D'Annunzio (1863–1938) asserted that life became meaningful only in the attainment of sensual joy. Although the protagonists of his novels never truly attain the height of erotic pleasure, each novel like *Il Piacere* (*Pleasure,* 1889) or *Il Fuoco* (*The Flame of Life,* 1900) celebrates the quest for deliriously ecstatic experiences. Sensation may be aroused innocently by the color, texture, and fragrance of a rose, or sadistically through murder, rape, and incest. The very failure to know the supreme gratification of desire propels the heroes of each successive D'Annunzian novel to more and more extreme measures in order to reach the most complete possession of voluptuous rapture. In the preface to the novel *Il Trionfo della Morte* (*The Triumph of Death,* 1894) D'Annunzio best expressed his aestheticist program: the mimetic re-creation of natural sensations through a musical language that would be orchestrated like a Wagnerian opera. There would be a single protagonist: a Nietzschean Superman proclaiming the morality of a master race. Plot structure and psychological individuation found no place in D'Annunzio's novels with the exaltation of the hero who has no limitations. The novels are set both in the urban scenes of Sybaritic pursuits and in the author's native province of the Abruzzi, for D'Annunzio acquired from the Verists an attention to the details of peasant life, which he viewed as essentially depraved. With his typically decadentist interest in fragmented experience, D'Annunzio succeeded only in recapturing scattered intense moments through the descriptive beauty and alchemy of language.[3]

Resistance to the seductive splendor of D'Annunzio's rhetoric came from the two most important novelists to appear during the last decade of the nineteenth century: Luigi Pirandello and Italo Svevo. Pirandello despised the rose-scented and blood-stained pages of the Abruzzese writer, and many years later he incurred the wrath of D'Annunzio's Fascist admirers when he contrasted the empty literature of words in D'Annunzio to the literature of substance in Verga. As opposed to the musicality of

D'Annunzian prose style, the Triestine Svevo wrote in a style that might be called "tone deaf" for its deliberate avoidance of sonorities. To D'Annunzio's romantic myth of the self-sufficient individual both Svevo and Pirandello opposed a novelistic truth about modern man's inherent limitations and dependence on others to mediate his desires.[4] The original title of Svevo's first novel, *Una Vita* (*A Life*, 1893), had been *Un Inetto* (*An Inept Man*), but his publisher persuaded him to change the title. The Triestine writer saw contemporary man as a diseased creature longing for the health that would permit him to cope with life's challenges. Across his three novels Svevo moved from a Schopenhauerian pessimism to a recognition of disease as an acceptable part of life. While the anti-hero of Svevo's first novel ended in suicide, admitting he was no longer capable of living, the protagonist of his second novel, *Senilità* (*As a Man Grows Older*, 1898), merely withdraws to a sterile loneliness. Finally, in *La Coscienza di Zeno*, written after the holocaust of the First World War and the author's acquaintance with Freudian psychoanalysis, the inept anti-hero triumphs over his seemingly healthy rivals. Whereas in Svevo's novels the pathological protagonists are forever weaving new fictions to create an illusory sense of order in their lives and the surrounding world, Pirandello as humorist leads his characters to the mirror confrontation where every self-deception is exposed for its vanity. Even in his earliest novels Pirandello saw in the provincial world that regional writers before him accepted as a firm reality, the absence of an objective existence that his characters attempt to mask with the conventional forms of social life.

Banishment from Life: l'Esclusa

Banishment from the lives of others is one of the most recurrent themes in Pirandello's writings. The heroine in

"Felicità" and Nicola Petix of "La Distruzione dell'Uomo" were both cut off from a father's love. In the Sicilian author's first novel, *l'Esclusa* (*The Outcast*), the protagonist, Marta Ayala, comes to suffer ostracism from her husband, her father, and almost the entire community of a town in Sicily for an offense she never committed. At first Pirandello thought of giving the title *Marta Ayala* to the novel after the protagonist, but the definitive choice of *l'Esclusa* underlines the pathetic state of isolation that the heroine must suffer. It is not character but situation that the writer studies. Marta's tyrannically jealous husband, Rocco Pentagora, merely caught her reading a letter from an ardent admirer of hers, the lawyer Gregorio Alvignani and, acting only on suspicion, he has turned her out of their home. The accusation of adultery alone suffices to convince everyone, including Marta's father, of her guilt. On the very day that Marta gives birth to a still-born child, her father dies of an apoplectic stroke. Soon the family's tannery business collapses, and Marta, along with her mother and younger sister, faces total destitution in that hostile community. Unlike Ibsen's feminist heroine Nora, who leaves home on her own initiative, Marta became an *"esclusa"* through unjust banishment. Although forcibly estranged from society, the Ayala woman did not react to victimization by renouncing the world. In the illusion that her abilities can win back honor for her, Marta successfully passes the government examination for a teaching position, but local opposition prevents her from receiving an appointment until Alvignani, recently elected to the Chamber of Deputies in Rome, secretly intercedes on her behalf. Encouraged by their parents to defy their new teacher, Marta's students create so much havoc in the classroom that the district school superintendent has to place her on temporary suspension. Again with Alvignani's support, Marta receives a transfer to a school in Palermo. In the provincial capital the young woman and her family begin a new life full of hope that they can leave the suffering of the past behind them. Yet, even though Marta demonstrates her ability to conduct her classes successfully, she encounters new problems as a woman alone in society without the protection of a husband when her male colleagues begin to make advances to her. In her loneliness she seeks the consolation of Gregorio Alvignani, and soon they transform the false accusation of adultery into reality. Shortly afterward her husband, recently recovered from typhoid fever, begs for a reconciliation and acknowledges Marta's innocence. When they at last meet by the bedside of Rocco's dying mother, Marta confesses her transgression but then yields to her husband's pleas for them to start over again. The novel follows a vicious and ironic circle: when innocent, Marta suffered exclusion; when guilty, she is restored to social respectability. The irony is the more devastating in that Rocco's legitimate heir has died, and in time he will accept Gregorio Alvignani's child as his own.

Written in 1893, *L'Esclusa* was first published in serial form by the *Tribuna* in 1901. It thus belongs to the same creative period as the first published volume of novelle, *Amori senza Amore* of 1894. The marriage between Marta Ayala and Rocco Pentagora would constitute just one more case of love without love, a relationship built on easily injured vanity. True to the principles of Verism, Pirandello avoided direct intervention into the narrative, which seems to create itself. Following a third-person narration, the novel continues in linear fashion from the moment of Marta's initial disgrace up to her readmittance to honorable society. Part One of the novel closes with the departure of Marta and her family from their home town, while the second part is concerned with their efforts to construct another life in Palermo. As always in Pirandello's writings, numerous dialogues abound in which the characters attempt to convince each other and themselves of the sincerity of their motives; in this novel as in many novelle, the author sought to represent the almost instinctive need felt by Sicilians for dialectic demonstration of their points of view. Even with his efforts to preserve a Veristic impersonality, the writer expressed his own polemical attitude by the manner with which he structured certain key scenes. The sixth chapter in Part One illustrates the author's anger over the injustice that fate and social prejudice inflicted upon the heroine. Three events occur simultaneously: the agonizing birth of Marta's dead baby, her father's prolonged death agony, and, outside on the street, the triumphal cries of a crowd proclaiming Alvignani's election. The reader is thrust into the scene of death, where the writer does not hesitate to mention details about blood and odor; death, as Pirandello later declared in *Umorismo*, is not beautiful or even particularly clean. For some critics the unrelieved intensity and graphic realism of the sixth chapter are the result of the author's artistic immaturity.[5] Understanding of such a "dense" scene is gained, however, not from attributing its excesses to Pirandello's lack of narrative mastery, but from considering his pitiless vision of life and constricting human society. This first novel may appear somewhat heavy-handed in its execution because of the author's refusal to compromise his art by lightly dismissing the cruelty that he felt to be an intrinsic part of human existence.

Pirandello's desire to probe man's savagery is evident in the chapter where he describes the procession of the twin Saints Cosimo and Damiano on their feast day in Marta's town. He captures the mad excitement of the crowd as the images of the saints are conveyed through the streets: the crushing of bodies; children trampled; porters drunk from wine and from being almost divinely possessed by the saints that they are carrying in a race through the town; black bread raining down from balconies where ladies wait to show their devotion to the twin martyrs. This picture of the pagan adoration paid to the patron saints of fishermen anticipates two later Pirandellian works: the novella "Il Signore della Nave" (1915) and the play derived from the tale *Sagra del Signore della Nave* (*Sanctuary of Our Lord of the Ship*) of 1924. It also recalls similar descriptions of saints' festivals in Verga's novelle and in some of D'Annunzio's *Novelle di San Pantaleone*.[6] All three writers share the same regionalist interest in representing the typical customs and ceremonies of still primitive communities; each author, however, studies the scene in an individual manner. Verga uses the festive background of the Fair of St. John in the Sicilian village of Vizzini as a contrast to the sadness of the title character in the novella "Ieli Pastore" ("Ieli the Shepherd") after he accidentally causes the death of a colt on the way to the fair; in other tales, like "Libertà," Verga seems to recoil with fear from the menace of an angry crowd. With his usual taste for blood sacrifice, D'Annunzio participates directly in scenes of sadistic enjoyment as when a character in "L'Eroe" cuts off his hand after a heavy image of a saint has crushed it, and then makes an offering of the shattered limb to the saint. As he does throughout his first novel, Pirandello here maintains an ironical detachment, for although he recognizes the masochistic pleasure that some of the porters derive from being crushed under the weight of the saint's bier, he wishes to stand apart as he accurately records the mob's exaggerated frenzy. That ironical detachment also permits him to point out the commercial exploitation of the saints' devotees by the directors of the festival, who set up shop in church to receive votive offerings of grain, lambs, and ewes. Out on the street vendors put up stalls to hawk their saints' images and toys. Verga mentions the same commercialism at the fairs, but he accepts them as a routine business occasion for peasants to sell their livestock and grain. Pirandello in addition reveals that not all the brutality of the procession arises from the worshipers' spontaneous enthusiasm, since he shows how Antonio Pentagora, Marta's unrelenting and unforgiving father-in-law, signals the porters to chase Marta and her family away from their observation perch on a balcony by hurling the iron heads of the saints against the balcony railing. The author has integrated the episode of the saints' procession into the novel's main narrative as an insult against the outcast and her family.

Inclusion of episodes such as the saints' festival clearly indicates Pirandello's ties to Verism. When the novel first appeared in book form in 1908, the author prefaced it with a dedicatory letter to Capuana in which he confessed to the artistic difficulty of fitting life's disorder into the harmonious scheme of a work of literature. The very plot of *L'Esclusa* strikingly recalls Capuana's tale "Ribrezzo ("Disgust," 1885), which was also the story of an innocent woman accused of an infidelity that she eventually commits after her father and everyone else have condemned her as an adulteress.[7] Perhaps the chief difference between Pirandello and Verists like Capuana and Verga is the younger writer's attitude to the traditional Sicilian honor code. While Verga and Capuana deplore the code and portray its tragic results—like the duel to the death between the lover and the betrayed husband in Verga's novella "Cavalleria Rusticana"—they accept it as a necessary principle for preserving one's dignity and purity in social relationships. Pirandello exposes the absurdity and stupid cruelty of the code. The enraged husband in *L'Esclusa* insists on fighting a duel with Alvignani, and as a result of the ridiculous ceremony he ends with a scar across his left cheek. With his humoristic penchant for analysis, Pirandello demolishes the fundamental constructs of the provincial Sicilian world, whose validity earlier writers never questioned. He rejects the positivistic belief in an absolute and verifiable truth such as Rocco Pentagora attempts to establish by proving his wife's faithlessness with the documentary evidence of the letters she exchanged with Alvignani. Instead of firm codes and concrete truths, the writer views narrow-minded prejudices.

In his effort to represent the spiritual limitations of that closed society with its provisional life forms, the author studies the interior distance of the homes where the main characters enact their dramas of suspicion and resentment. The novel opens in the gloomy dining room of Antonio Pentagora's house, with its oppressively low ceiling and yellowed walls, where embarrassed silences alternate with the explosive outbursts of Father Pentagora against the treachery of wives. The lack of domestic harmony is emphasized by the long lines of chairs that do not even match each other. A moldy odor pervades the house that never knows happiness. Yet Rocco Pentagora feels in that home a sense of freedom from the marital responsibilities that he abandoned when he cast Marta out of their new house with its luxurious furnishings. By returning to his father's house Rocco surrenders to the weight of the past, which reclaims him with the family curse of conjugal infidelity. Antonio Pentagora built his house like a tower, story by story to the fourth floor, with the intention of renting apartments, but the rooms remained empty except for the mice that invaded them. Only the old man's sister Sidora manages to escape the home's dreary confinement, by communicating with the spirit world of the "Maidens," who speak to her on windy nights. Madness, superstition, and distrust emanate from the poisonous atmosphere of the Pentagora home.

Love was also a stranger at the house of Francesco Ayala. Whenever someone in the family accidentally broke a small and inexpensive item like a bottle or a picture frame, Father Ayala flew into a violent rage at what he considered an affront to him as the person who originally purchased the object. Greed never fired his vulcanic temper; rather, a feeling of insecurity toward others motivated his desire to win and hold onto their respect. His house and its possessions had no intrinsic value for him except for the admiration that others would express for them; therefore the destruction of a single trifling object seemed to him an attack aimed at undermining his prestige as head of the household and a man of authority in the town.

Francesco Ayala's true indifference to material possessions was evidenced by his withdrawal to a single room that he made his prison because of the scandal over Marta's alleged infidelity. The house had become one of public shame, and Ayala declared himself a stranger in it as he retreated to the total darkness of his room to await death as a release from his dishonor. It did not matter to him that his voluntary seclusion served for the whole community as an admission of his daughter's guilt. Once his precarious dignity had been put to question publicly, Ayala was prepared for the ruin of his home and family, which he well knew would occur if he neglected the operations of his tannery. His wife, Signora Agata, always endured the role of a beggar in that house for Francesco's affections; she had to play guardian over its possessions and see that no one disturbed them. The younger daughter, Maria, forever lived in the shadow of Marta; and even after her sister's wedding Maria did not add a single object of her own when she moved into Marta's old room, which she immediately gave back to her elder sister upon the break-up of the marriage. Never having been a place of harmony, any more than Pentagora's house despite the apparent togetherness of the family, the Ayala home became a house divided against itself, with the father secluded at one dark corner and his wife and daughters dwelling at the opposite side of the building. For the first time in her life Maria felt a sense of self-importance as she assumed the task of go-between for her father and the rest of the family; once, to her amazement, the old man embraced her with a tenderness he had never shown before; the shock of the family disgrace had forced him to look at his younger daughter as a person in her own right and to recognize her capacity for love. Actually, the only member of the family that experienced a genuine sense of security and ease in the house was Marta, who would spend hours staring at familiar objects like armchairs, both to understand the feeling of identity they gave her and to appreciate the meaning of their own separate inanimate existence. Sainte-Beuve's verse "Naître, vivre et mourir dans la même maison" would express the longing for continuity that living in the house of one's father might provide. A conventional arranged marriage, typical of that insular community, first separated Marta from her familiar attachment for and affinity with the objects in her father's house. Then the scandal brought her again in constant contact with the beloved objects. Within the novel's ironical structure it fell to Marta alone to assist the process-server who came to make an inventory of the house and its belongings for the auction to settle the debts of her deceased father. Pirandello throughout his writings creates a language and situation of patricide. In the Sicilian society for this novel's time period the father was a feared authority figure, and the auction of the Ayala house as a consequence of Marta's supposed offense completes the murder of the father. The house which old Ayala established as a visible symbol of his pride could not survive the disgrace to his family name.

Buildings are thus another example of the ideal constructions that persons erect to give meaning to their lives and to command the respect of others. A home functions as a public mask; its façade reveals what the owner wishes to show the world. The construct of the home also collapses from life's chaotic pressures. Throughout l'Esclusa, various buildings represent the attempts of characters to patch the crumbling structure of their existence. The three bright rooms of the apartment where Marta and her family seek shelter after the auction witness the death of the heroine's hope to triumph over the force of local prejudice through a teaching career. Once Marta visits the town church with the intention of finding some inner peace in the confessional, but all she can experience beneath the heavy pillars and wide arches of the edifice is a "sense of oppression" (Mondadori ed. [1945], p. 41) and she flees the building. The nave, with its uneven floor on which worshipers kneel before going to confession, seems expressive of a fanatical religion that requires suffering. The heroine, who is innocent of the offense everyone attributes to her, cannot confess and discover tranquillity in the cold stillness of the church. After Marta and her family move to Palermo upon her transfer to the new school, they rent an apartment on Via del Papireto, the street on which Francesco Ayala once fought as a Garibaldian volunteer. In the cheerful rooms of the new apartment, with its floors of Valencian tiles, both Signora Agata and Maria succeed in restoring a semblance of orderliness to their lives: the mother sews and attends to her domestic duties while the younger daughter resumes her piano playing; only Marta continues to feel herself the excluded one, forever in exile from the happiness her family has regained thanks to her labor. Although the Palermo school building pleases her with its almost luxurious classrooms, she comes to regard the teachers' reading-room as a place of ambush where her amorous colleagues compete for her attention. Only one building in Palermo appears to welcome Marta and call her to itself: the charming villa on Via Cuba at the outskirts of the provincial capital, where Alvignani has gone to escape the exhausting battles of the Roman parliament. The villa's eight elegantly furnished rooms and spacious courtyard where flocks of doves alight make of the building an earthly paradise where death and unhappiness dare not enter. Yet Marta experiences the disenchantment of a purely sensual relationship there in the villa. In his treatment of buildings and interior distance Pirandello differs immeasurably from Verga, who viewed home and land as hallowed sanctuaries for all that is precious and worth defending in life. Pirandellian characters do not possess the firm ideal of home that protects and inspires against life's onslaughts.[8]

Along with the author's study of interior distance, he also desires to depict the sympathetic response of his novelistic characters to outer Nature. He makes a point of mentioning the balconies and terraces of the buildings where Marta, her family, and even Alvignani briefly flee the confinement of a claustrophic existence. The characters find in Nature the reflection of their own emotions; at times Pirandello verges on the pathetic fallacy in establishing parallels between natural phenomena and the characters' states of mind in the alternation between turbulence and gentleness. Moonlit nights for the author usually represent sacrifice, potential violence, and abandonment, as on the night when Rocco broke with his wife and Signora Agata tried in vain to convince her husband to effect a reconciliation before a public scandal resulted; the scene of the deserted streets mirrored the desolation in the heart of the mother hurrying from her home to plead with Francesco Ayala at his tannery: "The suburb's main street, which was rather animated during the day, remained as silent and lonely at night as a street in a dream, with its tall houses lined up in a row where the windows here and there reflected the green glitter of moonlight. From time to time a heavy, uneven stretch of vaporous clouds veiled the moon's pale and cool serenity and cast gloomy shadows on the humid street" (Pt. 1, chap. 3). Nighttime and its quiet create an impression of dreamlike unreality and a dread sense of deprivation when all hope dies. The moon does not bring solace to the novel's tormented characters.

After her arrival in Palermo, Marta wishes to believe that she has truly conquered her past and achieved a position of social respectability on her own initiative. Winter has passed, and the renewal of earth in springtime appears to offer her the opportunity for an inner renascence: "How gently the new leaves rustled at sunrise when she passed under the trees of Piazza Vittorio in front of the Norman Palace and then under those of Corso Calatafimi beyond the New Gate. Against the sky's tender azure the circle of mountains seemed to be breathing, almost as if they were not made of hard stone. . . . Truly, the mournful days had passed; spring was also coming back for her. The earth was not alone in shaking off wintry shadows; she too succeeded in shaking off the nightmare of sad memories" (Pt. 2, chap. 1). The protagonist self-consciously recognizes her own desire for a new life in the loveliness of reawakening Nature. Through use of adjectives of color the author seeks a picturesque effect, like a painter at his canvas, and with descriptive terms like "tender azure" (*"tenero azzuro"*) he attempts to convey the heroine's longing to rediscover sweetness and kindness in a world where she has had to endure daily hostility and exclusion.

Pirandello goes beyond the conventional lyricism and picturesque effect of landscape description when he sets the scene in the eighth chapter of Part Two for Marta's yielding to the temptation of the love offered by Alvignani. The panoramic view from Alvignani's balcony provides more than a highly aesthetic pleasure for the troubled heroine, who hesitates before succumbing to the lawyer's invitation for her to live again:

Up there Marta felt her heart opening wide.
The spectacle was truly magnificent. The great circle of mountains lay dark and majestic under the brilliant sky; the powerful ridges were sharply delineated by the clear-cut shadows. And Morreale looked like a white flock pasturing half-way up the slope, and down below the countryside stretched out under a veil of shadows that were broken up by tiny white houses.
"And now look at this side," he said.
Just as the first spectacle seemed near-at-hand and somber, the view on the opposite side opened wide and resplendent. Marta could see the entire city with its vast expanse of roofs, cupolas and bell-towers and the gigantic form of the Teatro Massimo. Further beyond she could make out the endless sea sparkling in the sun whose rays cast a reddish glow on the happily recumbent mass of Monte Pellegrino.

This whole passage is built on a series of contrasts: between gloomy mountain shadows and sunny vistas, between sharply cut physical limitations and seemingly boundless expanses

of sea and sky. The massive natural and man-made structures impose their weightiness in dark, heavy-sounding
words like *oscurata* with its shadowy *u* as opposed to the
bright vowels of *sole* and *mare*. That disturbing darkness is
further reinforced by the repetition of the adjective *fosca*,
fosco in both genders to include all of nature. The natural
spectacle thus functions as an analogue of the conflict in
Marta's heart, which is torn between desire for affection and
the fear of destroying the precarious harmony that she has
reestablished for her mother and sister. Here the landscape
ceases to be a static picture and instead participates directly
in the heroine's inner drama.[9]

As an added device to bring natural phenomena into the
novel's events, the author uses rain as a parallel to the
characters' tempestuous emotions. Pounding rainfall, with
the visual element of lightning and the auditory element of
wind, serves to express the violence that finally overcomes
the novel's anguished misfits. It was under a pelting rain
that the grotesquely deformed art teacher, Matteo Falcone,
confessed to Marta the intense love he felt for her; he had
contrived to accompany her home that afternoon by hiding
her umbrella and afterward offering her the shelter of his
own. On their way they were observed by Rocco Pentagora,
in town to determine if his estranged wife had taken a lover.
The sight of her husband and the shock of Falcone's confession left Marta in a state of feverish confusion as she
stood stunned and almost immobilized by the heavy rainfall.
That storm prepared the scene for the explosion of a powerful, pent-up passion. Pirandello shared with authors like
Fogazzaro and Svevo the rather mechanical technique of
letting rain forewarn a tragic event like a death. In *l'Esclusa*
Rocco's mother, herself an outcast, dies in her miserable
Palermo apartment after a furious thunderstorm has struck
the city and broken all the windowpanes in her bedroom.
The wind and rain seem like a divine scourge, and the after-
math of the storm and the old woman's death will be the

resolution between Rocco and Marta to forget the turbulent memories of the past and renew their marriage. The characters must face the fury of the storm within their own souls.

Both landscape and interior distance contribute to an understanding of character as well as situation. Many of the figures of the work are realized on the level of *macchiette,* especially as caricatures of typical provincial figures, who appear more as selfish reactors to the novel's situation rather than as actors. Counselor Breganze, Knight of the Crown, is the strutting incarnation of pompous self-importance: obese, with short legs and arms, he tries to swagger and gives commands like a general to the school superintendent as he demands Marta's dismissal from her teaching post in the name of public morality. Yet, according to local gossip, that corpulent defender of morality is a cuckold. Signora Popónica, scarcely more than a servant in Antonio Pentagora's household, appears only once in the novel, but she leaves behind a melancholy, humoristic picture of a lady fallen on evil days; she tints her hair and dreams of passionate embraces that she is too old and feeble ever to experience. Some of the characters are mere sketches that the author could have developed far more fully than he did. Bill Madden, the Irish tutor in foreign languages and a fencing master, is barely realized as a psychological figure; his sometimes mournful, sometimes derisive eyes give another glimpse into a complex person who has chosen exile and poverty in Sicily, for reasons that are never explained. In Professor Luca Blandino the author presents a character type that he treats more completely in the novel *I Vecchi e i Giovani* and in the novella "La Marsina Stretta": the abstract scholar who wishes to retreat from life's noisy affairs but who can quite surprisingly rise up in indignation against injustice. It is in fact through Blandino's initiative that Alvignani lends the heroine the moral support of his political office. Of all the secondary characters, Marta's fellow tenants at Via del Papireto, Don Fifo Jué and his bride Donna Maria

Rosa, are the most thoroughly delineated *macchiette:* the long, lank Don Fifo in his tight trousers and his blonde, fat wife of only three months are like two puppets rigidly decked out in black as a sign of common mourning for Donna Maria's first husband, who was Fifo's elder brother. Often when Pirandello introduces his personages, he stops the narrative, constructs an outward physical portrait that hints at inner character, and then elaborates the figures no further. This technique, which suits the compact structure of novelle, tends to break up the synthetic harmony of a novel's form.[10]

One character portrayal in the work emerges as more than an anecdotal comic-pathetic sketch: that of Matteo Falcone, the tortured instructor who tries to compensate for his great ugliness with the dream of beauty and youth that he sees made real in Marta's person. His name of course means "the falcon," a creature of acute intelligence and a predatory nature, although his appearance causes one colleague to refer to him as the "hedgehog." As a teacher of design, Falcone is sensitive to beautiful form; crippled by club feet and compelled to wear corrective shoes, he persists in climbing the mountains near Palermo. Like many of Pirandello's tormented characters, Falcone bears his anguish in a gloomy silence; but his wild eyes, like those of some unknown animal, have a mad glint that reveals his repressed agitation. That man's domestic life would easily suffice to drive an Adonis to raving insanity, for he shared his home with his senile mother and aunt who refuse to recognize him as their relative. The two women think they are no older than twenty-eight; they keep waiting for one of them to die so that a purely fictitious suitor can marry the survivor. The neighborhood women mock them by dressing them in the fashions of a past age, selecting the most garish colors and inviting the women to admire themselves in the mirror. That masquerade of youth and beauty with its attempt to stop time and ignore the passing of the years anticipates the central situation of the later play *Enrico* (*Henry IV*) of 1922. The torture of a sensitive person's living under the same roof with insane females and his accommodation to their mad logic would at first seem to suggest autobiographical influence, but Pirandello was still a bachelor when he wrote his first novel. The house where Falcone dwells with his mother and aunt is cluttered with odd pieces of furniture that are stacked along the walls and never used. That mad accumulation of material objects which crowd out present life brings to mind the much later absurdist dramas of Eugène Ionesco like *The Chairs* and especially *The New Tenant*. Falcone is torn between a violent desire to kill the two sick women and a sense of guilt over his lack of compassion. For them he is neither a son nor a nephew, but a stranger who obstinately refuses to put his feet on straight. Although the entire episode of Falcone's private life might appear extraneous to the novel of the outcast, it explains the vehemence of the art instructor's attraction to Marta Ayala. Matteo Falcone sees in her everything that has been denied to him.. Marta's rejection of his entreaty for them to take vengeance on the hateful world pushes him over the brink into madness.

Caricatural distortion is absent in the sympathetic portrait of old Anna Veronica, the only person to come publicly to the aid of the outcast Ayala family. Anna herself had known exclusion for surrendering to a promise of love. Unlike Schoolmistress Boccarmè, whom she resembles in the sweetness of her character,[11] Anna Veronica was not able to keep to herself the memory of the fiancé who deserted her after she had tried to prove to him the full extent of her devotion. Like so many other feminine figures in Pirandello's writings, Anna always wore black—in mourning not just for the two amorous misadventures of her youth but also for her illegitimate child, who died shortly after birth. Dismissed from a teaching post in a primary school and awarded only a meager charity pension because of the scandal, she accepted her fate and showed no resentment toward the former friends—Agata Ayala among them—who shunned her. In the structure of the novel Anna Veronica's resignation serves as a foil to Marta Ayala's rebelliousness. Anna was of course guilty of violating the honor code, and she could bear the shame of being a fallen woman with the fervent religious faith of repentance. It was she who persuaded Marta to go to confession, but the serenity that the remorseful old woman could discover in the church was unattainable for the blameless heroine. Anna and Marta shared a common awareness of loss, both for their place in society and the children to whom they were never able to give their love. With the consciousness of her transgression, the Veronica woman succeeded in making a life for herself at the periphery of society, for although she could never enjoy the respectability of marriage, Anna ironically played a role in the town's major weddings by preparing the trousseaux. Unlike the novel's heroine, Anna could assume the mask of the outcast and wear it in humility.

Refusal to recognize guilt characterizes Gregorio Alvignani, and even the motto that he has printed in red on his personal stationery declares his independence: *Nihil-mihi-conscio*, the Horatian phrase *I am conscious of no guilt in myself*. With his superior insight into the game patterns of social behavior, which he manipulates to advance his political career, Alvignani understands the relationship between the self and others as one of individual submission to the opinion of many, as he asserts to Marta in attempting to justify their liaison: ". . . when I say, 'My conscience does not permit me to do a thing,' I am saying, 'Others will not allow me to do that.' My conscience! . . . It is people in me. . . . It keeps repeating to me what others tell it . . ." (Pt. II, chap. 10). Yet, despite his bold protestations and the glibness with which he expresses them, Alvignani knows that there are limits to his self-sufficiency; indeed, he has only to look at a mirror and realize how life is passing him by in his loneliness. Pirandello demonstrates in the figure of the aging lawyer that even the most professionally successful individuals can feel excluded from life. Parliamentary triumphs have not brought Alvignani close to anyone, and his turning to Marta after she has moved to Palermo represents, not the deliberate act of a cynical seducer—as some critics see him—but a desperate effort to snatch hold of life while he can still do so.[12] Even the failure of their love affair is not entirely Alvignani's fault. Although his motives may have been selfish, the deputy is capable of giving himself fully to another at the risk of his political career, and he is prepared to take Marta and her family with him to Rome. His disillusionment arises from realizing that Marta came to him not in love but in despondency over her inability to rebuild her life. In his advice to Marta to accept the reconciliation with her husband, Alvignani does more than seek an advantageous way out of his involvement since he is returning to his central idea of the others as individual conscience, for he perceives clearly the irony of Marta's exclusion from society when innocent and her readmittance when guilty. The fate that awaits Alvignani is the treachery of politics and the indifferent solitude of victory or defeat.

Of all the characters, the one who has the least personal consistency is Rocco Pentagora, who constantly adapts himself to the standards of others. Primarily he reflects his father's obsession that all the Pentagora husbands must end as cuckolds. He is a slave to everything that is accidental and circumstantial in his uninspired performance as the traditionally jealous and domineering Sicilian husband. After he sends his wife away, Rocco plays the part of a cuckold to the full by bringing a prostitute into his home and making her wear Marta's clothes for their appearances in public. Whereas Alvignani is consciously aware that social life is a masquerade and counterfeit, Rocco remains a witless counterfeit in his blind subjection to the conventional signs of the Sicilian honor code. Even when he expresses a willingness to rescue Marta and her family from destitution, he insists that his "charity" must be carried out in secret or otherwise persons would consider it weakness on his part. Rather than from genuine kindness, his charitable motivation stems from a fear that his wife might achieve economic independence as a teacher. When Rocco takes Madden with him and follows Marta to Palermo in order to spy on her, he is again assuming the role of the suspicious husband. Although he could carry out the spying mission on his own, Rocco needs Madden as a witness to his socially proper vigilance, for this counterfeit is forever posing. Only after his close brush with death from typhoid fever does he start to understand the damage he has caused. Even then Rocco's "conversion" from a vengeful to a forgiving husband is caused less by remorse than by a realization of his own loneliness and need for the love that he once received from Marta and rejected so lightly. His final, convincing appeal to win back his wife comes as Rocco beholds the death-mask face of his mother, who for the identical alleged sin of adultery suffered a life of exile and poverty in Palermo's slums. In begging for his wife's return Rocco Pentagora has to accept humiliation for his earlier imposture of respectable indignation, since he is bringing back to social recognition a woman that he was mainly responsible for driving to adultery.

It was to the temptation of a moment that Marta Ayala had yielded, induced by the flattering terms of the first letters that Alvignani threw down to her from his terrace. She made the grievous error of answering them. Feminine vanity permitted her to take the perilous, though innocent, course that wrecked her marriage as well as the security of her family. Like Didì Brilla of "La Veste Lunga," Marta had also resented how her parents removed her from school at the age of sixteen to marry her to a man she did not even know. From her studies she had expected to make a life of her own, but she was forced to comply with the desires of her parents, who saw in Rocco an advantageous match. Marta's constant longing for autonomy was always suppressed by others: parents, husband, father-in-law, neighbors, school authorities, colleagues. The author does produce in this work a feminist investigation into the restrictions that society imposes on women and how the community nearly renders it impossible for a woman to survive on her own resources. But with this first novelistic protagonist, Pirandello transcends the question of sexist entrapment within a male-dominated social order to illustrate fully the emptiness of the romantic legend of individual self-sufficiency. The individual, female or male, does not possess the freedom to forge an identity independent of the pressures exerted by others.

This is a novel about the violence that society forces upon its victims. Sicilian society appears here as a community of "habit, ritual bondage, and arbitrary law." Since others obeyed the island's honor code without question, Marta had to become its victim. Hers was a society that had impatiently closed itself to the individual woman's imaginative vision of a different kind of life from the customary roles of obedient daughter and wife. That same society was to impose upon Marta the mask of adulteress; the realization of her absolute isolation compelled her to accept that mask and take Alvignani as a lover. Again society, as represented by her husband, could arbitrarily remove that mask and restore the original mask of respectability. The experience of witnessing the death agony of Rocco's mother warned Marta Ayala of the future that awaited a woman rejected by her husband. Personal courage, integrity, and even righteous scorn proved powerless to make possible the individual freedom that the heroine sought to win from society. On becoming aware of her pregnancy and feeling that life with Alvignani would be degrading, Marta resolved to commit suicide after persuading Rocco to marry Maria.

But in this novel, unlike many of the novelle, death could not provide the proper and permanent solution to outer and inner distress. Suicide by the heroine would have appeared as the outward equivalent of a death that had been already experienced from within, but Marta was a fighter for life. Renunciation of others would have been a course of flight by a merely pathetic victim of exclusion, and this novel instead treats Marta's efforts to become reintegrated into the social group on her own terms—an impossible goal. But by confessing her adultery to Rocco and affirming how she was driven to that act by the will of others, Marta exacted revenge against the man who was originally to blame for her family's ruin. When she consented to join with her husband in the death watch by his mother's bed, the heroine was admitting to her own limitations in living in society. Forced out of life by her husband's jealousy, Marta regained social acceptability not through her own initiative but through Rocco's desire to win back her affection. The individual, especially a woman, has no independence.[13]

The heroine's return to her traditional role as wife represents the surrender of her youthful dreams for a life of her own making. As the mother-to-be of an illegitimate child, Marta reveals her final willingness to play the counterfeit part that others assign to her. In *l'Esclusa* the order and meaning that the institutions of home and family created for the characters in Verga's works are shown to be substanceless shadows, the empty forms that the humorist Pirandello must expose. In the human community the externality of conventional bonds has to triumph over the chance for a true inner relationship between free individuals. Marta, Rocco, and Alvignani form far more than the old-fashioned triangle of adultery, for the heroine in her relationship with both husband and lover comes to experience the impossibility of persons' communicating to each other their innermost thoughts and sentiments. In this first novel, as in the volume of tales *Amori senza Amore*, the primarily social feelings of vanity, resentment, and ambition prevail over love and tenderness. Sicilian society in this novel is an uncorrected "humorous" community adhering to arbitrary standards, which in his succeeding novel Pirandello exposes to the castigation of ridicule.

The Round of Frustration: Il Turno

Pirandello's second novel, *Il Turno* (*The Turn*), which he composed in 1895 and published in 1902, moves at a dizzy pace as it follows the workings of the "infernal little machine" of logic that compels the characters to take part in a round of unsuccessful marriages and frustrated ambitions. Because of the work's Sicilian setting and its almost documentary attention to local traditions of marriage rules and family structure, *Il Turno* has often been classed as a Veristic composition.[14] But this novel with its choreographic treatment of time as an endless dance-carol of frustrations should be considered as an example of late-nineteenth-century European decadentism, in exactly the same vein as Arthur Schnitzler's *Reigen* (*La Ronde*) of 1896–97. Just as the Viennese dramatist sought to present life's futile acts as frenetic moments in a round dance of mortality, with one obsession bringing on more obsessions, so the Sicilian novelist similarly structured his work on the recurrence of meaningless events that fail to attain any form of redemptive unity.[15] Thirteen years before publishing *Umorismo*, Pirandello created in his second novel a supremely humoristic work that unmasks society and its inane routines. The mere reptition of vain actions serves to reveal the absurdity of the seemingly solid constructions of the world that had figured in the novels of the Verists. As humorist, the author of *Il Turno* is initiating a task of structural decomposition that was to be fully accomplished only with his final novel, *Uno, Nessuno e Centomila*.

Even Pirandello himself was unsure about the appropriate classification for *Il Turno*, hesitating whether to label it a novel (*romanzo*) or simply a long novella. Compared to *l'Esclusa*, this work displays a streamlined economy of means to demonstrate the humoristic situation where life appears as a jester who scoffs at man's most artful and apparently rational plans to determine his own destiny. The emphasis on interior distance, outer Nature, and oppressive environment that characterizes *l'Esclusa* is deliberately absent in *Il Turno*, with its rapid rhythm. External Nature plays a part only in the mechanically contrived episode where elderly Don Diego Alcozer is drenched by a sudden shower during a picnic party and consequently contracts pneumonia. Pirandello also avoids in this work the tendency of the naturalist novelist to explain character motivation through description of the environment. The author very superficially contrasts the ancient glory of the Greek city Akragas, preserved by the temples on the outskirts of town, with the mediocrity of modern Agrigento, where neither the most energetic nor the most talented of *Il Turno*'s characters could realize the full potential of their abilities. It is only in Pirandello's fourth novel, *I Vecchi e i Giovani*, that the contrast between ancient possibilities and modern provincial limitations becomes a major theme for the author. In its structure *Il Turno* is not suited to a Veristic investigation of the deprived Sicilian environment.

Basically, *Il Turno* is a *tour de force* that in approximately eighty pages exposes the inherently irrational machinations of humans trying to live by logical constructions. In the typical style of many of Pirandello's novelle, large sections of the work are in dialogue form or interior monologue, where the characters are either arguing with each other or attempting to convince themselves of the justness of their course of action.[16] Although the work is rendered in the third person, the author seems to have disappeared completely from the narration to give the impression that his characters are enacting the scenes of their personal dramas; in this objectivity of method *Il Turno* does truly belong in the Veristic tradition, except that as a humorist Pirandello subjects his characters to a pitiless examination to uncover the self-deceit expressed in their dialogues and monologues. Despite the apparent reasonableness of the arguments raised by the work's fictional characters, the forces of life and death chaotically prove to be indifferent to human logic. Whereas in *l'Esclusa* society is felt to be the opponent who prevents the heroine from rightfully asserting her authentic personality, in *Il Turno* the general community serves as a critical conscience that condemns the Agrigentine broker Marcantonio Ravì for his attempt to compel his daughter Stellina to assume an absurd and repulsive conjugal role as the wife of Diego Alcozer. At most, the neighbors appear as an anonymous mass, taking part in the grotesque wedding between Stellina and Alcozer and paying half-hearted compliments to the ill-matched couple. The presence of the disapproving community is constantly felt in the work by the repeated efforts of Ravì, Alcozer, and the lawyer Ciro Coppa to justify their acts with long and specious explanations. It would then be in the extended social dimension that *Il Turno* could be considered a novel.

In the structure of the plot the author returns to the situation of the death watch, which here in *Il Turno* occurs twice with an ironical contrast. The first death watch takes place around Don Diego's bed when everyone believes the old man is dying of pneumonia. Ravì initially declares that the hand of God is directly intervening to further his design to have Stellina inherit Alcozer's wealth as his widow so that she can marry the penniless young aristocrat Pepè Alletto. But after Alcozer goes into a fever crisis, the broker's eagerness begins to yield to remorse before the enormity of his guilt for desiring to profit from another's death. Ravì, Stellina, and Alletto all compete in nursing the old man back to life; yet, within their souls they experience a struggle between an impatient longing to be rid of that living obstacle to future happiness and the tormenting consciousness of the blame they share in wishing for Alcozer's death. The typical Pirandellian humoristic association of opposites is made here in the juxtaposition of Thanatos with Eros as Stellina and Alletto discover their love for each other at the bedside of the seemingly moribund Don Diego. Death, however, shows himself to be a jester, mocking Marcantonio for his frenetic efforts to arrange for his daughter's security and causing the young couple to postpone their love; for the feeble and elderly Don Diego Alcozer recovers from his nearly fatal illness. As frequently in Pirandello's novelle, death here has merely paid a premature visit, in this case to taunt the opportunistic trio.

Those same three persons are to gather again at the novel's close for a death watch by the bedside of Stellina's second husband, Ciro Coppa. As Ravì looks at Coppa's deceptively powerful torso. he comments on the trick that death has once again played: "This one who seemed a lion, here he is: dead! And that horrible old man [Alcozer], healthy and full of life. In two days he gets married. . . ." The broker, who thought he could foresee and forestall every eventuality, has come to realize that one must make an accommodation to life's capriciousness. The occurence of parallel death watches, one early in the novel and the second at its end, results from the work's circular structure, which makes of the narrative not a merry-go-round of love but one of frustration. In both of these death watches, as also in the novella "Visitare Gl'Infermi," Pirandello is interested in the social circumstances of death. In contrast, Verga emphasizes the utter isolation of death. Whereas Verga's characters like old Padre 'Ntoni of I Malavoglia and Mastro Don Gesualdo die alone, Pirandellian characters usually die surrounded by hypocritical mourners. Even when Pirandello's characters manage to expire in solitude, the author places his focus not on the death scene but the subsequent ceremony of a funeral. The two death watches of *Il Turno* represent the false ritual that the living perform at the sordid spectacle of death.

Throughout this second novel the characters remain on the level of *macchiette* since they are no more than the playthings of fate. There is none of the tension between a form-conscious self and an impulsive, spontaneous self, such as is to be found in *l'Esclusa* and as will provide the central situation of the author's third novel, *Il fu Mattia Pascal* of 1904. The work's protagonist is Marcantonio Ravì, with his stubborn determination to make all others conform to the logical pattern of his plans. He is described as a stout figure with a full paunch and short legs, rather resembling a turkey; often in Pirandello's narrative writings characters with birdlike features are the ones who wish to construct the lives of others. The key word in Ravì's monologues and conversations is the forever insistent "Ragioniamo," with the double meaning of "let's talk things over" and "let's reason things out." Ravì is a methodical man who places the reason for his limited finances on the backwardness of united Italy. He coolly considers every alternative action to marrying his daughter advantageously until he finally decides that marriage to Alcozer is the only reasonable choice. Despite his love for Stellina, or perhaps because of his love, as Ravì asserts, this father behaves like a familial tyrant by placing Stellina in solitary confinement on bread and water to compel her to agree to the wedding. Ravì's whole plan for the marriage and his daughter's future well-being represents still another of man's ideal constructions that life demolishes with a chance occurrence: Ciro Coppa's visit to Alcozer's home to safeguard the timid Alletto from a jealous rival for Stellina's affections. By chance Coppa overhears Stellina complaining about the way she was "persuaded" to marry Don Diego, and immediately the lawyer offers the girl his legal services to have the marriage annulled. Although Ravì has never acted for personal profit, he finds himself labeled by the community as "Marcantonio Mammon" after his defeat in court when the marriage is annulled. Upon Stellina's subsequent marriage to Coppa, the broker cuts off all relations with his daughter; but this rupture has none of the tragic gulf of noncommunication that characterizes the alienation of Marta Ayala from her father. Francesco Ayala is a deeply moving figure whose vulnerability to the judgement of others would be incongruous in a comic manipulator like Ravì, who aspires to be the puppet master controlling the actions of those around him but ends as *Il Turno's* grand dupe. The broker's obstinate attitude illustrates that the most logical design will lead to an utterly absurd conclusion when pursued without regard to the feelings and thoughts of the persons who are directly affected by an inhumanly perfect plan. The man of reason proves himself to be irrationally inflexible.[17]

Adaptability to life's surprises is one of the principal reasons for Alcozer's longevity. This old man appears as a crepuscular figure, representing lateness and the fear of vital disintegration, since Don Diego almost feverishly clings to precious objects and young persons in an attempt to arrest time and death. The way others count on profiting by his death brings to mind the old peasant in "Il Vitalizio," who outlived the usurer that had granted him an annuity for life. Although Acozer is a tiny shriveled-up old man who tries to disguise his baldness and advanced age by carefully combing and dyeing the one lock of hair left on his head, he is not the repugnant figure of a senile predatory roué that appears in novelle like "Volare" taking advantage of lonely girls from the lower classes. Don Diego never succumbs to a senescent oblivion, forever preferring to relive the past in the present moment. At one time one of the great lovers in the court of the last Bourbon ruler of the Two Sicilies, in the novel's time span Alcozer appears as a rather sad philosopher who understands "this stupid puppet show which we call life." An elderly hedonist with a literary predilection for Catullus and Horace, he wishes to marry Stellina because he knows she will attract young persons to their home. Through the presence of his wife's guests the old man hopes to recapture vicariously the intense joys of youth. He recognizes that to succeed in society one must observe the proper spheres of transaction, and he is willing to pay his way with gifts. Don Diego continually sends Stellina golden bracelets and rings. The fact that the presents once belonged to his late wives does not indicate that Alcozer is a miser. Pirandello employs the refrain "non per avarizia" to describe Diego's frugality in using up the treasures he has accumulated over a long lifetime and several marriages. Consequently he has the gifts freshly polished by a jeweler and packaged in new cases. Don Diego realizes that he is too old to communicate with a young woman except through the gifts that he can bestow on her.

Alcozer's desire to hold onto the past is also reflected by his attire. He goes on wearing the same old clothes, which seem new to him since he has preserved them in camphor. Although he understands, like Lamberto Laudisi in the play *Così è se vi pare* of 1916, that yesterday's realities are today's illusions, he refuses to relinquish those illusions. Unable to participate fully in life, he still wishes to remain a spectator. After his wedding he invites all his wife's friends to attend soirées at his home, where he can enjoy the pleasure of looking at and listening to the young. Realizing the danger that Stellina might take a lover, Alcozer astutely manipulates the rivals for her attention so that they will prevent each other from conquering the girl's affections. But after Don Diego's recovery from pneumonia he grows increasingly bitter as he loses ground first to Alletto and then to Coppa. The old man's philosophical resignation returns only after Stellina runs away, and he lends full cooperation in the litigation brought to annul the marriage because he is eager to extricate himself from an impossible domestic situation. Unable to live alone, Don Diego eventually de-

cides to marry again, and for his sixth wife he chooses the
very neighbor who denounced his marriage to Stellina as a
mortal sin and testified in court against Ravì. Alcozer intentionally lives situations of paradox, humoristically endeavoring to reverse circumstances so that he can continue
to hold his place in life's bewildering round. Despite his
great age, he affirms self-possession against existence's con-
verging void.

Of all the novel's characters, perhaps the one who has
least reality in her own right is Stellina, another example of
the *sujet vide*. Her whole being consists in her appearance
for others. Try as she may to resist her father's authority,
Stellina cannot evade her first identity as a daughter and has
to render to Marcantonio the proper filial obedience. Although the girl feigns scorn for Alcozer's gifts, in the privacy
of her room she tries on the jewels and admires herself in
the mirror, for she is already beginning to assume her second
identity as Don Diego's fiancée. The only major instance of
her resisting the will of her father and first husband occurs
at the wedding reception, when Stellina faints, but her
gesture is so conventional as to deprive it of any authentic-
ity. During the course of her first marriage the girl takes on a
rather ambiguous identity as she adapts herself to the various
would-be lovers. Her decision to leave Dom Diego results
from Coppa's convincing argument and not truly from her
own initiative. During the period of litigation Stellina takes
refuge in a convent directed by the lawyer's sister, and for a
brief period she considers becoming a nun. But once again
Stellina shows no profound conviction, and she allows Coppa
and his sister to dissuade her from a religious vocation. Although it may be argued that Stellina can make no other
choice than to marry Coppa since her father disowned her
and the mother superior took the lawyer's part, Stellina
never reveals the resistance to her isolation that Marta Ayala
exerted during her banishment from respectable society.
The torment that Stellina suffers during her second marriage

arises from her inability to create a mask that will calm Coppa's fierce temperament and jealous nature. First she attempts to accept the life of seclusion in the countryside, where the lawyer takes her after their wedding to be away from the sight of Don Diego and Pepè Alletto. Then her husband brings her back to his townhouse and thrusts her into Alletto's presence. Lacking an autonomous will of her own, Stellina must turn to others to determine the course of her behavior; but the demon of experimentation in Ciro Coppa makes it impossible for her to establish an identity as a dutiful wife. As Stellina sits weeping during the death vigil for Coppa, Pepè looks at her and thinks of the new role she will assume as his wife and the stepmother of Ciro's orphaned sons. Significantly, Pirandello did not give Stellina a detailed physical portrait, for she is a malleable creature that the other, strong-willed characters mold according to their own desires.[18]

Pepè Alletto proves La Rochefoucauld's maxim that some persons would never fall in love unless others planted the idea of love in their minds. This youth was never seriously interested in Stellina until Marcantonio Ravì approached him one day and begged him to exercise prudence up to the time when his turn would come. Pepè is basically a frivolous fop, spending hours before the mirror to groom himself. At home he lives under the thumb of his impoverished but proud widow mother, who encourages him to avoid vulgar pursuits like a position as clerk in the civil service. He constantly throws the blame for his indolence on the lethargy of his home town and declares that his abilities as dancer and pianist would be appreciated in a cosmopolitan center. But when Pepè has an opportunity to display his talents by entertaining at Stellina's wedding, he shows how ridiculous his attainments are as he tries to impress his guests by informing them that besides playing the piano he also speaks French. He too is a nonentity in himself, waiting for someone else to give him a life form. Because of the accord he reached with Ravì, Alletto feels obligated to act as Stellina's public protector. As the guests leave the wedding party, one of them makes a slightly disparaging remark and Pepè insults him. After receiving an abusive letter from the man he attacked, Alletto does not know how to react until Coppa dictates a note of challenge for him. Once again the duel has none of the primitive savagery of the Sicilian honor code, as in Verga's novelle, but turns out to be a comic affair where Pepè looks like a "puppet in a children's playhouse" before he falls from a sabre blow. Thus the youth almost loses his life to defend the honor of a girl for whom he felt no particular affection until another person mistakenly attributed the sentiment of love to the casual attention Pepè used to show Stellina. Throughout the novel Alletto continually lends himself to other persons' designs in the naive expectation that he may derive some personal advantage, but he always ends as the plaything of others, like Alcozer and Coppa. As much as the youth desires to convince others of his superiority and to ascribe his lack of success to a stifling provincial environment, he remains an empty being incapable of masking his puppetlike impotence. Although Pepè does come to take his turn as Stellina's husband, he owes his triumph solely to the accidental course of events rather than to his own efforts.

On first examination Ciro Coppa would appear the one truly indpendent character who can assert his autonomy against other persons. Physically he resembles Francesco Ayala in his muscular frame and explosive nature. Although he has the brute force to win his way in society, he usually employs his intelligence and education to demolish his adversaries. As a lawyer Coppa represents the new Sicilian middle class that Verga merely alludes to in the pastoral world of his novels and tales; the law for Coppa is not so much a defense of family honor as an instrument of conflict in a highly complex society. The public image that Coppa creates is that of a formidable fighter as he walks about town carrying a riding whip, wearing hunting boots, and sporting two large pistols. Although the author presents Coppa as the stereotype of the jealous and tyrannical Sicilian husband, he shows how the lawyer's marital mistrust is founded on a fear that another person, such as his wife, could in any way be independent of him. His is an interior tendency—toward what Gerard Manly Hopkins called *inscape*—fashioning an artificial world where he might remain unchallenged lord. Coppa seeks inner security through complete domination over those near him. He so terrorized his first wife, Filomena, Alletto's sister, that she became afraid to stand by the window because her husband might suspect she was flirting with someone or signaling a lover. Even after consulting physicians made the prognosis that Filomena was dying of an undetermined illness, Coppa unrealistically refused to accept their opinion and tried to match his strength of will against the power of death as he fought to revive his wife. When Filomena entreated him to send for a confessor, he instructed his servant to bring back an elderly priest, for even at that moment of loss he could not escape the feeling of jealousy born of doubt about his ability to capture and hold another's affections. The lawyer constantly attempts to gain full control over every situation and other persons.

Upon Filomena's death starts a period of Spartan discipline for Coppa and his sons. Every morning he makes the boys run naked around the grounds of his estate, swim in the icy pool, and dry themselves in the sun. A compulsive desire to dominate obsesses him. When he pays his first social visit to Stellina, Coppa makes his confession about his need to be free: "Hear me out, madame: I do not have the advantage of knowing what opinion you hold about me, about my character. The reputation that I have made for myself, believe me, does not at all correspond to my true nature: to everyone I appear an arrogant person because I refuse to suffer arrogance from my fellow citizens or in local prejudices . . . consequently I seem rather strange, but only because *I want to be free* in the midst of so many persons who are slaves either of themselves or of others . . ." (chap. 19, italics added). Yet Coppa is indeed a slave, lacking faith in himself and resenting the separate existence of others as a threat to his supremacy. It is precisely from his determination to dominate himself and conquer his jealousy that the lawyer brings about his own death. He makes Alletto his secretary and deliberately creates situations for the youth to be alone with Stellina. To vanquish jealousy would signify genuine liberation and self-mastery. But the tension required to restrain himself finally causes death by apoplexy, a typical Pirandellian close for a life that was sustained by the repression of violent energies.

Although Pirandello's second novel exposes tyrannical acts of violence by irrational parents and husbands, it emphasizes life's capriciousness. The human aspiration for certitude is shown to be the result of insufficiency and a lack of self-confidence. The novel's grotesque puppet play presents the ceaseless round of man's quests after fond illusions: Ravì's desire to assure his daughter's financial security; Alcozer's nostalgia for the joyousness of his vanished youth; Stellina's need for the social identity that a stable marriage can provide; Pepè's longing for the motherlike love of an affectionate wife; and Coppa's determination to assert his independence before the world. With his decadentist vision of the world, Pirandello saw his characters as caught in situations of isolation where the attempt to grasp the other never quite succeeds; theirs is a hopeless, routine repetition that fails to bring an inner awareness of the unchangeable and the ineluctable. This second novel illustrates that one cannot speak of a Veristic and Sicilian Pirandello on the one hand, and a humoristic and European writer on the other. From his earliest writings to his final incomplete drama, Pirandello was to explore the incoherence of human life in individual and social relationships. Both of the author's early Sicilian novels demonstrate the illusory nature of society's standards and human desires. While the heroine of *l'Esclusa* suffered the fate of being forced into the nonlife outside society, the characters of *Il Turno* experienced the full emptiness of struggle within social structure. Pirandello was now ready for a new novelistic experiment about the attempt to discard conventional social identity for an authentic freedom.

3

The Fugitive from Life

The Fugitive from Life: *Il Fu Mattia Pascal*

Pirandello's novel *Il Fut Mattia Pascal* (*The Late Mattia Pascal*) is generally regarded as the "point of arrival" where the author for the first time fully worked out the tragic dichotomy between an individual's longing for complete freedom and the forms of life that society imposes upon him. With that work the Sicilian writer first received national and even European acclaim. After the novel's serial publication in the *Nuova Antologia* during 1904, it appeared later in the Viennese *Fremdenblatt* in a translation by Ludmilla Friedmann. But when a French version by Henri Bigot was in the process of preparation for publication in the *Revue de Paris*, Matilde Serao intervened personally and had her novel *Dopo il Divorzio* (*After the Divorce*) substituted for Pirandello's. Despite the failure of recognition in France, the novel's success in Italy secured for Pirandello future publication by the major firm of Treves Brothers of Milan. During the early years of this century Verga's Sicilian novels and tales were still unappreciated, and D'Annunzio remained the greatest luminary among Italian writers. The success of Pirandello's third novel in attracting a fairly wide reading public resulted in large part from the author's effort to move beyond the Veristic preoccupation with the problems of life in a closed provincial world. His third novel represented precisely the desire to escape enslavement within society through the construction of a wholly original personality.

It is disgust with a wretched existence in a small Ligurian town that impels the novel's protagonist, Mattia Pascal, to create a new identity for himself. Accustomed since childhood to a carefree style of living, Pascal found himself in early manhood utterly destitute because of his own indifference, his widowed mother's naiveté, and the treachery of the administrator of the family estate. Whereas Pascal's handsome brother, Berto, managed to marry advantageously, Mattia so compromised himself that he had to wed a poor girl with a demon of a mother. Through a friend's charity Pascal was appointed town librarian with a monthly salary that barely sufficed to meet his family's needs. One day, shortly after the deaths of both his mother and his daughter, Mattia Pascal decided to go on holiday and get away from his nagging wife and mother-in-law with the money his brother had sent for their mother's funeral. At Montecarlo he almost broke the bank playing roulette. At last he was in a position to demand respect at home with his winnings. Mattia Pascal could hope to vanquish his mother-in-law and to regain his wife's early affection for him.

At that point of the novel fate interrupts the protagonist's plans to rebuild his former life. On his way home Mattia reads a newspaper account of his death by drowning in the mill-flume of what used to be his family's farm. His wife and mother-in-law identified the body as his, and the authorities declared that he had committed suicide because of financial problems. After his initial shock Mattia Pascal recognizes that fate has given him a marvelous opportunity to break with the past and become a new man. He can flee the worries of everyday life and overcome the restrictions that society establishes for those who have to conform to its customs. As a fugitive from the mediocrity of ordinary life he takes the fictitious name Adriano Meis. In the glorious exuberance of his liberated identity, Meis spends an enchanted year traveling about northern Italy and even along the Rhine Valley. But after awhile that fugitive existence begins to weigh upon Adriano with all its sterile loneliness. His instinctive need for human contact at last compels him to move into a Roman rooming house. Adriano Meis soon experiences the complications of his renewed involvement with social life, for he falls in love with his landlord's daughter. How can a man without legal identity apply for a marriage license? After one of the lodgers robs him of a large sum of money, Adriano Meis admits to himself that he can no longer sustain his masquerade, for he has no recourse to the police and civil authorities to protect his nonexistent rights. The time has arrived for him to simulate suicide by leaving his hat and cane on the parapet of a bridge by the Tiber, along with a note to which he has written the name *Adriano Meis*. Now that he has died a second time, he undertakes his resurrection as Mattia Pascal. But during the two years when he was attempting to remain outside life, others continued to go on living. To his amazement, his "widow" has remarried and has a daughter by her wealthy husband. Content to demonstrate the illegal status of that second marriage and the child's illegitimate birth by his mere physical presence in town, Mattia Pascal makes no effort to cancel his death certificate. He returns to his old post at the library, where he passes his days writing the memoirs that constitute Pirandello's novel of the late Mattia Pascal.

Along with the novel's formal structure it is necessary to speak of an expressive structure for the stages in Mattia Pascal's attempt and subsequent failure to elude life in society. Basically the novel falls into three broad divisions. The opening section comprises the first seven chapters, which deal with Pascal's youth, mismarriage and financial plight. This first division recalls the life of provincial confinement and frustration that Pirandello examined in his previous two novels. Transition toward the metamorphosis from Mattia Pascal to Adriano Meis is provided by the sixth and seventh chapters. The sixth chapter transports the reader and the protagonist from the limitations of the Ligurian town Miragno to the excitement and seemingly unbounded possibilities of Montecarlo with its casino. In the seventh chapter the protagonist stands between two forms of life after he learns of his alleged suicide in the millflume; this chapter is pivotal since it is here that the disillusioned librarian makes the choice to discard his conventional identity and assume what he hopes will be a genuinely free life outside the structure of society. The eighth through the sixteenth chapters from the second division all dealing with the existence, or perhaps nonexistence, of Adriano Meis, since he is no more than a creature of the imagination (*costruzione fantastica*), who can make no claims for others to recognize and respect him. In fact almost the entire section treats the limitations of Adriano Meis's nonlife, because the emphasis on the negative aspects of his vital experiment has started toward the close of the eighth chapter. The return to the mask of Mattia Pascal takes place in the third section, composed of the seventeenth and eighteenth chapters, which move forward with an almost bewilderingly swift pace in contrast to the slowly narrated disenchantment of Adriano Meis. The cinematiclike change in tempo from slow motion to accelerated action stresses the inherently grotesque nature of the protagonist's experiment to escape from the world of others. The novelistic structure therefore expresses the various planes of experience for the protagonist, from the insouciance of his pampered youth to his final decision to live as a dead man.

Pirandello was particularly sensitive to criticism that the plot of *Il Fu Mattia Pascal* was altogether too farfetched for any serious reader to accept it as plausible. For the 1921 Mondadori edition he included an appendix on the contradictions between reality and imagination, where he attempted to demonstrate how infinitely absurd and unpredictable life was for even the most wildly imaginative writer. While creative artists were usually expected to remain within the bounds of verisimilitude, life itself did not have to be contained by any barriers in its erratic and illogical course. For Pirandello, so-called normal life was full of excruciating situations that persons barely managed to tolerate until circumstances thrust the mirror of truth before them. When the hurt that had been held inside a person grew too agonizing, then he would be compelled to rip off the marionette-mask of his absurd existences. Living in society made puppets of individuals, of themselves and of others. The grotesqueness of life consisted in the mechanical construction of fictitious realities that would eventually be exposed in all their absurdity. According to Pirandello, his novel was no more than the imaginative revelation of the painful falseness that masked life.

As convincing proof of his novel's plausibility, the Sicilian author cited a notice in the *Corriere della Sera* for March 20, 1920, about a man named Ambrogio Casati who had visited his own grave. While Casati was serving a prison term, his wife and her lover identified the body of a suicide victim as that of Ambrogio Casati. Seven months after Casati's death certificate was issued, the wife and lover were married. It was not until early 1920 that Casati learned of his death and subsequently placed a bouquet of flowers on his own grave. Real life then furnished Pirandello with evidence that his imagination had not carried him beyond the limits of credibility. In fact, unknown to the Sicilian author, another famous writer at the turn of the century had also composed a drama with a plot strikingly similar to that of *Il Fu Mattia Pascal;* the source for that play had been a real-life trial in St. Petersburg that involved a case of bigamy, in which a complacent husband had simulated suicide so that his wife could remarry. Tolstoy's drama *The Living Corpse* bears such a strong resemblance to Pirandello's third novel that many critics and scholars have assumed that Tolstoy based his play on the Russian translation of *Il Fu Mattia Pascal,* but the date for the composition of the Russian drama was 1900.[1] Real life, whether in Russia during the last decade of the nineteenth century or in Italy at the time of the First World War, provided examples of the absurd measures that individuals would take to escape the pressures of existing in a structured society. Both Tolstoy and Pirandello sought to portray the grotesque deformation of modern life. A third similar but admittedly fictitious case of identifying a corpse as that of one's spouse occurs in the first Italian grotesque drama, Chiarelli's *La Maschera e Il Volto* of 1916; in that play Count Paolo Grazia has been forced by foolish vanity to pretend that he has thrown his faithless wife into Lake Como, whereas in truth he has banished her to exile outside Italy. Shortly after his court acquittal the count must make a legal declaration identifying as the remains of his wife a corpse that was retrieved by some fishermen from the lake. All these authors—Chiarelli, Pirandello, and Tolstoy— point out that life in society is an increasingly complex series of bureaucratic and judicial procedures that the individual can never truly succeed in eluding. Their grotesque art is the accurate mirror of life's absurdity.

The technique of the first-person interior monologue

creates the impression of an autobiographical confession. Mattia Pascal is forever speaking to another, who might take the form of some casual acquaintance or of a curious passerby who happens to observe the librarian placing flowers on his grave. The narrator-protagonist feels constantly compelled to justify his past actions. Sometimes he will say to himself, "How do I know this?", and then he will proceed to give an explanation for his strange behavior. Mattia Pascal claims to be writing his memoirs with the assistance of the librarian Don Eligio Pellegrinotto, a person who is always trying to bring order out of chaos, whether in Miragno's decaying library or with the facts of Mattia's three lives. Since this Pirandellian novel is a book of confessions, it must be placed as a fictitious successor to a long Western tradition of confessional literature that goes back to St. Augustine and reaches a high point with Rousseau. Because of the way *Il Fu Mattia Pascal* represents a deliberate attempt to demolish the form of confessional literature, it anticipates Svevo's *La Coscienza di Zeno* of 1923. Svevo wished to show how all literary confessions were fundamentally dishonest, inasmuch as the conscience-stricken authors carefully selected the episodes in their past and ended by detaching them in an unnatural and distorted fashion from the continuous stream of vital experiences. The narrator of *La Coscienza di Zeno* forever lies to himself, his analyst, and the readers of his diary about the utterly selfish nature of his motives and the insincerity of his desire to renounce sensual pleasures. Although Mattia Pascal's confessions are not conscious or unconscious lies, the vision with which he surveys the incidents in his various lives is humoristic, since the narrator no sooner makes an assertion than he at once begins to dismantle it with his cold reflection. All life is seen as lacking in substance, and thus the protagonist chooses isolation. The novel opens with an admission of life's uncertainty: "The only thing I knew for sure was that my name was Mattia Pascal . . ."; and it comes to a desolate close six months later, after the narrator has finished the work of his memoirs by declaring: "I am the late Mattia Pascal." Novelistic first-person narration in *Il Fu Mattia Pascal* serves to advance the humoristic investigation behind life's provisional forms. It is indeed no surprise that Pirandello dedicated *Umorismo* to Mattia Pascal the librarian.

Mattia Pascal is both actor and spectator in the novel. During his two years as Adriano Meis he is especially restricted to observing the life of others. Pirandello takes advantage of the protagonist's physical restrictions to focus on important figures in the work. After an eye operation, Meis must remain for forty days in a darkened room. During that period he has various guests, as on one evening a séance is held in his room. All he can discern in the dim light are outlines, and he must rely more on nonvisual impressions, such as tone of voice, than on what he is able to see. By listening to the half-Spanish, half-Italian jargon of the girl, Pepita Pantogada, he correctly judges her to be a willful and contemptible creature. Later, when Meis beholds the girl in full light, her stunning beauty so distracts him that he briefly forgets her inferior moral qualities. The author has artfully related psychological reaction to Meis's physical restriction.

Another example of Pirandello's technique of the restricted point of view can be found in the eleventh chapter, "Di Sera, Guardando il Fiume" ("In the Evening, Looking at the River"), where Meis encounters his arch-enemy, Terenzio Papiano, for the first time. One night, when he is in his room reading, he hears voices outside on the balcony of the rooming house. At first all he can make out are the voices of a man and a woman. His curiosity (and that of the reader) is aroused when he discovers that the man's voice is not that of his landlord, the only male in the rooming house besides himself. The entire scene is relayed by what Meis can hear and see through the shutters over the window of his room, which looks out on the balcony and the Tiber. That rather brusque technique of first introducing a character with a *macchietta* type of portrait is abandoned here as the author avoids physical details to focus on the inner qualities of the strange man on the balcony and his relationship to the dwellers in the rooming house. Meis comes to realize the hold that the stranger exerts over the roomer Silvia Caporale, who submits to the man's cross-questioning and allows him to address her with the familiar pronoun. Meis is now able to learn that the man's anger and agitation have to do with the presence of the new roomer (Meis himself) in the building; the hostile attitude of the stranger threatens to destroy the precarious vital invention that the late Mattia Pascal has created for himself. In his excitement Adriano Meis pays attention to details like Signorina Caporale's putting her hand on the man's shoulder only to be rebuffed by him. All of the scene's intensity and anxiety is heightened when the intruder orders the Caporale woman to fetch the landlord's daughter Adriana from bed. The protagonist's long wait by his shutters for the appearance of Adriana Paleari on the balcony adds to the sense of dread that the stranger's arrival has caused him. The dialogue scene when Adriana does finally come is extremely short: the intruder peremptorily orders Signorina Caporale to bed and starts to interrogate the girl. After the man seizes the girl by the arm, Meis is no longer able to restrain himself and slams the shutters. Adriana calls him to the balcony. To his further astonishment, he sees a young man with a rather idiotic expression on his face coiled on a trunk in the hallway; he surmises that the youth must be Papiano's brother. Out on the balcony the stranger ceases his angry inquiry and assumes a deceitfully smiling countenance when he is introduced as the husband of Adriana Paleari's recently deceased sister. All of Papiano's basic character traits have been presented already through the protagonists's physically limited area of vision: his irritability, his disregard for the feelings of others, his ability to simulate friendliness when necessary. The mood of the scene is that of a sinister intrusion. Although the true stranger in the Paleari household is Adriano Meis, the regular dwellers like Signorina Caporale and the landlord's daughter seem to welcome him, while they fear Papiano. This technique of constructing a character portrait through suspense-filled degrees of a limited point of vision and by setting a pervasive mood partake of the same impressionistic method that Joseph Conrad employed in his novels and tales.[2]

For many of the readers who followed the installments of Pirandello's third novel in the *Nuova Antologia*, the work must have seemed like a romantic story of evasion from the responsibilities of everyday life. Mattia Pascal's disguise as Adriano Meis does indeed constitute a story of the challenges and difficulties that an individual must face and overcome after he has chosen to be a walking invention of pure imagination. The novel can thus be appreciated as merely a series of hurdles that the protagonist surmounts; the reader's interest is sustained by the vicarious thrill of seeing how each new complication is solved. As such, *Il Fu Mattia Pascal* would be no more than an example of escapist literature, elevated perhaps to a metaphysical dimension by the author's humoristic concern to expose the fictional basis of social existence. There is, however, a profoundly human dimension to the novel, since it is an exhaustive study of the impossibility of an individual's forging a life that is wholly his own, independent of the sentiments of others and the institutions of modern society. Through carefully limited focus and the forever-questioning technique of interior monologue, the author probes the worlds of Mattia Pascal and Adriano Meis and determines the tormenting reasons why the protagonist must die twice, only to accept the nonlife of withdrawal to a dilapidated library. The novel thus relates to the investigation in Pirandello's tales and later plays of the contemporary alienation from inauthentic society.

The World of Mattia Pascal

Since one of the protagonist's eyes persists in squinting, his entire view of the world is conditioned by defective vision. The description he gives of himself is something of a *macchietta*, emphasizing how a red curly beard has crowded his face to the disadvantage of his tiny nose. Like the anti-heroes in Svevo's novels, Mattia Pascal displays ineptitude in meeting practical problems. As a child he never paid attention to the lessons of his tutor, Del Cinque, who abandoned the effort to educate the Pascal brothers and had even borne the insulting nickname "Pinzone," taken from his pointed beard. While their saintly, widowed mother retreated to three rooms in the family's townhouse, the Pascal boys had thoughtlessly invaded the deserted rooms and roamed through them as if in so many immense chambers of experience. In his childhood Mattia did not appreciate the apparently lifeless mansion, but after he was cheated of his patrimony, he never tired of recalling the antiques, faded tapestries, and upholstery with their musty odor, as well as the deathlike stillness of the furniture. During his fugitive years as Adriano Meis, moving from one hotel to another, the image of the family mansion with its familiar objects kept on returning to his mind, like the picture of a lost paradise where he could find identity. But in truth Mattia Pascal did not realize how precious his home was until after it was irreparably lost. An American author, who has considered the importance of place for her own fictional characters, affirms that sensitivity to place indicates a depth of personality:

> There may come to be new places in our lives that are second spiritual homes—closer to us in some ways, perhaps, than our original homes. But the home tie is the blood tie. And had it meant nothing to us, any other place thereafter would have meant less, and we would carry no compass inside ourselves to find home ever, anywhere at all. We would not even guess

what we had missed. (Eudora Welty, "Place in Fiction," in *Critical Approaches to Fiction*, ed. Shiv. K. Kumar and Keith McKean [New York, 1968], p. 262)

Pascal, as Adriano Meis, was to search in vain for a second spiritual home. But the character portrait that Pascal makes of himself in his first life is anything but flattering: a fatuous youth, utterly spineless, self-indulgent, and not particularly sensitive to others' longings or to the special setting that would remain his one true spiritual home.

Life in Miragno comes to the reader as perceived by Mattia's twisted vision. It resembles the same stagnant environment as in *l'Esclusa* and *Il Turno,* and it has the identical effect of deforming those who are condemned to remain there. The dramatic situation in Miragno is reduced to one of survival—but not survival against the forces of Nature as in Verga's agrarian society; rather, survival against the duplicity that corrodes the very quality of life. For Pirandello, in contrast to a writer like Hemingway for whom place is never hostile, the setting as well as its inhabitants is frequently malevolent. Those who fail to cope with the environment are condemned to perish in it, as does Mattia's mother, who loses her vast estate to her trusted administrator. Only one member of the Pascal family understands how to create a successful social role in that provincial world where mendacity and self-interest prevail: Mattia's brother Berto, who uses his good looks and fine manners to live on the dowry his wife brought him, even though his victory involves cutting off every warm sentiment toward his mother and brother. On the periphery of the Pascal family stands paternal-Aunt Scolastica, the man-hating old maid who tried to awaken the widow Pascal to her administrator's disloyalty; yet the aunt was not motivated by genuine affection but merely by determination to defeat a thief. Of all the characters, Aunt Scolastica shows the greatest awareness of social role as the normative pattern of behavior; propriety, inflexibility, demanding that everyone should fit into a rigid scheme of correctness. While Berto seeks the appearance and privileges of status, Scolastica asserts the obligations of position. The rest of the inhabitants of Miragno exist as creatures of habit and unexamined belief, constituting an inelastic society. In Mattia's distorted sight, the memory and sometimes the spectacle of place might soothe the pain of living, but the human environment always causes suffering.

Battista Malagna, the estate administrator, emerges triumphant in that shallow world by seeking only his own advantage. His is a dynamic ethic that appropriates everything in its grasp to itself. Malagna is an individual for whom *bontà* (kindness, or goodness understood as doing something to benefit another person) would be an alien term without significance. As throughout the novel, this figure is seen through the eyes of Mattia Pascal, who has every reason to depict him as the mole who undermined the very ground upon which the Pascal fortune was founded. Whenever he speaks of Malagna, the narrator employs descriptive terms to suggest a kind of oozing, amorphous creature that spreads over everything that comes near to it:

> All of him slid down; his eyebrows and eyes slid down here and there on his long, broad face; his nose slipped down on his stupid moustache and goatee; his shoulders sagged away from the back of his neck; his enormous, loose paunch hung almost all the way down to the ground. Since his paunch fell so heavily over his short legs, the custom tailor was forced to cut his trousers with so much slack at the waist that from a distance it seemed that Malagna was wearing a very long skirt or that his paunch stretched all the way to the ground. (P. 256)

To Mattia Pascal this hateful caricature of a man should at least correspond to his own story-book image of a consummate thief. In addition to the exterior portrait, Pirandello presents something of the inner life of Malagna in his relationship with his first wife, Signora Guendolina, whose social class is higher than his. Malagna's autonomy comes to an end through his tyrannical wife, who constantly reminds him of his inferiority, and he rather resembles an Italian Georges Dandin in his endeavor to win acceptability by imitating the ways of the gentlemanly class of Signora Guendolina. He is not even permitted to eat and drink as he pleases, for his wife suffers from a stomach ailment caused by truffle croquettes and wine. Both husband and wife end by abstaining from wine in public while drinking it in secret. Pirandello's novel points out how even a victor in life's shabby affairs such as Battista Malagna is checked in his relations with others and compelled by his interpersonal limitations to play a charade.

The baseness of life in Miragno is perhaps best exemplified by an episode in the fourth chapter where the protagonist relates the one successful act of revenge he has committed against the thief. Malagna grieved that he did not have an heir to receive the fortune he had stolen from the Pascal family, and shortly after Guendolina's death he married a peasant girl, Oliva Salvoni, who had once cared for Mattia and expressed indignation at the administrator's acts of thievery but was prepared to wed for financial security. As the years passed, however, no heir was born; and Malagna started to abuse his wife. The old man also began to frequent the home of a distant relative of his, the widow Marianna Dondi-Pescatore, who had a rather attractive daughter, Romilda. Malagna hoped to prove his virility with Romilda, and the widow Pescatore was willing to prostitute her daughter to her own venal interest. The name *Pescatore* means "the fisher," and indeed the widow uses Romilda as bait. Mattia would never have become involved with Romilda if it had not been for the admiration that his friend Mino expressed for her. The entire relationship of Mattia-Mino-Romilda is a classic case of mediated desire. Mino has no true personality of his own: with Berto he played a Dandy; with Mattia he performed as an idiotic adventurer. Living as a submissive shadow of one or the other of the Pascal brothers, Mino seemed, with his adulation, a ridiculous figure. Yet it was a comment of his about Romilda that ensnared Mattia in a course that led to his marriage. Mattia decided to visit the Pescatore home, where he at once observed the contrast between the tattered older pieces of furniture and the gaudy additions that must have come as gifts from Malagna. After Pascal reported his favorable impression of Romilda to Mino, his friend's interest incited in him a passionate desire to have her. Romilda herself in the novel gains her only identity from her suitors or her overbearing mother; she is an evanescent figure with sorrowful green eyes and a luminous complexion. By contrast, her bony, withered mother possesses a fierce personality and spiteful temper in her own right. It was the old woman who cast the net that trapped Mattia. She left her daughter alone with the silly young man one afternoon when they were out picnicking, and Mattia succumbed to Romilda's appeal for his protection. Soon the news came out that the widow's daughter was expecting a child by Malagna, who was only too eager to have an heir. Realizing that he had been made a dupe, Mattia took his revenge by visiting Oliva and providing her with an heir. Once Malagna was sure of having a child, he publicly denied any intimacy with Romilda. Unfortunately for Mattia, the vengeance scheme backfired on him and he had to marry Romilda. This story of cuckoldry goes back to Italy's novella tradition of the *beffa,* a joke played on elderly husbands by young wives and virile lovers. Along with the Boccaccian tradition, a similar situation can be noted in Machiavelli's play *La Mandragola* (*The Mandrake*), where a young lover makes it possible for an impotent lawyer to have a child by his beautiful wife. Pirandello himself used the basic plot situation of this episode in his later Sicilian play *Liolà* of 1916. The fact that the events occur in Miragno illustrates the meanness, stupidity, and hypocrisy at the core of the provincial world. One person appropriates the values of another so that everyone ends impoverished. Those who weave schemes often turn out to be victims. The joys of intelligent contrivance and sensual delight, which characterize the source of the episode in Boccaccio and Machiavelli, disappear in Pirandello's novel, with its bitter revelation of the deceit behind social relations.

All the futility and ignorance of Miragno finds its concrete symbol in the Boccamazza Library, where Mattia had to work for two lira a day to supplement the widow Pescatore's meager pension. None of the citizens make use of the library, which slowly crumbles with its accumulated years of dust. Pascal soon discovers that a major part of his responsibilities is to chase the rats—the only creatures that devoured the volumes in the building. The books sit covered with mildew, gradually disintegrating. The library's dilapidated condition and the townspeople's indifference to the deterioration of its volumes reflect the failure of civilization in Miragno's society. Sometimes the dampness that invades the building causes rather strange matings of volumes, as when the binding of a saint's life becomes attached to a treatise on the art of seduction—saintliness and lasciviousness are both extreme forms of vital commitment, such as could never be attained in Miragno's mediocre climate. Housed in a deconsecrated church, the Boccamazza Library is a shrine to absurdity.

Anyone who works in the library eventually surrenders to its deadly immobility. Although Pascal was hired to succeed the aged librarian Romitelli, the elderly man could not comprehend the reality of his retirement and continued to arrive at the library every day at precisely the same hour that he had done for years. Romitelli illustrates the two levels of comic and humoristic. Hobbling along on two canes that made it look as though he had four legs, the old man was deaf and nearly blind; but he persevered

in his "work," which consisted of reading historical diction-
aries and attempting to remember their contents. Libraries
are places where persons should read, and in the absence
of interested townspeople Romitelli assumed the task of
reading as a moral and intellectual obligation. The meaninglessness of the old man's methodical, clockwork routine
makes of him both a ridiculous and a pathetic figure. After
Romitelli died, Mattia was forced in his absolute isolation
to turn to the books to distract himself from thoughts of his
domestic problems. Compared to Romitelli and Pascal, the
autodidact in *La Nausée* who tries to master all the knowledge in the Bouville library according to alphabetical order
appears a positively constructive figure. Because the Miragno library was threatening to transform him into another
Romitelli, Pascal was partly motivated to flee the town in
order to escape the building's atmosphere of decay. In
truth, the essential bleakness of Pirandello's third novel
results from the fact that Mattia Pascal does resume his
work at the library, helping Don Eligio catalogue the texts
that no one wants to read. It is in the library that Pascal
composes his memoirs, which he intends to leave to the
Boccamazza Foundation with the provision that they are
not to be opened until fifty years after his third and definitive
death. The message, then, of his three lives is to be preserved in a building that stores useless information.

Even before Mattia Pascal fled Miragno and took the
alias of Adriano Meis, there were unmistakable signs of
that inner conversion which often characterizes confessional
literature. The entire first part of the novel is a deliberate
depreciation of temporal life, wherein the protagonist has
suffered the fall from an existence of ease to one of poverty
and degradation. Through viewing the silent, uncomplain-
ing agony of his mother as she huddles in a corner of the
Pescatore home, Mattia ceases to be the self-centered ignor-
amus that he has been; he is growing aware for the first
time in his life of the torment that persons can hold within

themselves. One day an explosion takes place in the widow's home when Aunt Scolastica arrives to take Mother Pascal away from that hateful place. Before she leaves, the aunt succeeds in plastering Widow Pescatore's face with a roll of wet bread dough. The Pescatore woman turns her anger on her son-in-law and pelts him with pieces of dough until she collapses on the floor from the fury of her emotions. At that moment Pascal has his first genuine flash of illumination:

> I can say that since then I have been able to laugh at all my misfortunes and at every torment of mine. I saw myself, at that moment, as an actor in the most foolish tragedy that one could ever imagine: my mother running away with that mad aunt of mine; my wife in the next room in her [pregnant] condition . . . ; Marianna Pescatore there on the floor; and I who could not provide bread for the next day's meal—I stood there with my beard covered by dough, my face scratched and dripping with what was either blood or tears caused by my convulsive laughter. I went to the mirror to find out the truth. There were tears, but I was also scratched all over my face. Oh, how pleased I was with my eye at that moment! In its desperation the eye was more determined than ever to look wherever it wanted to on its own account. (Pp. 274–75)

Two major Pirandellian themes are presented in this episode: life as an imitation of the stage and the mirror confrontation. Although Mattia employs the word *tragedia*, he devaluates its starkness with the superlative form of the adjective *buffa* to stress the comic absurdity of his domestic situation. His experience is to see himself living (*vedersi vivere*), which actually results in a momentary detachment of the conscious self from the stream of life's turbulent events. Not only does the mirror reveal his abject condition, but it also attests to the constantly distorted vision caused by Mattia's cockeye, which asserts its independence even at times of the most intense anguish. Mattia Pascal has been permitted to see the ridiculousness of his roles as husband and son. The earlier Pascal was in effect blind to everything around him.

This glimpse of the truth marks the first step in the protagonist's conversion.

As often in Pirandello's works, it is a death watch that precipitates events that might otherwise be slow in developing. The firstborn of Mattia's twin daughters died before he could feel a strong affection for her, but the second child survived for almost a year—long enough for her father to make the girl the sole purpose of his life. Within a period of nine days Mattia Pascal suffered the torture of double death watches, as he kept running back and forth from his home to Aunt Scolastica's in alternate vigils by the bedside of his daughter and mother. The mother's death severed a fond link with the past, while the girl's passing shattered any hope for the future. Both died on the same day, almost at the same hour. As part of his confession Mattia Pascal admits that his immediate reaction to the double deaths was simply to fall asleep. The exhausting torment of the two vigils prevented him from experiencing the grief which, when it came after he had rested, almost drove him to insanity with its fierceness. With no past or future, Mattia Pascal had only the disconsolate emptiness of the present. Not possessing a reassuring belief in an afterlife in which his mother and child could know the happiness that was denied them in human society, Pascal stood on the brink of suicide. Yet, instead of committing that fatal act, the protagonist took advantage of a series of chance happenings to kill not himself but the fictitious reality he had been compelled to endure in Miragno.

The Shadow of a Man

In creating the metamorphosis from Mattia Pascal to Adriano Meis, the author anticipated other writers, like André Gide who rebelled against the psychological determinism and consistency of character portrayal in the novels of Bourget. In place of logic and consequentiality, Pirandello and Gide sought to recapture life's unpredictability with its infinite surprises. Like Michel in Gide's *Immoralist,* Adriano Meis learns that to free oneself is relatively easy but that to be free is difficult. Just as the immoralist had his beard shaved off so that his altered appearance would reveal the authentic personality that manifested itself after a close contact with death, the protagonist in Pirandello's novel decides to have his beard trimmed. But in the humoristic context of the Italian novel, the anti-hero's reaction to his changed appearance is not one of joy in the palingenesis of his spirit, for the new image of himself in the barber's hand mirror makes Meis recoil in horror before what looks like a monster. During most of the time of his disguise, Adriano Meis has to endure the tell-tale cockeye of Mattia Pascal until surgery corrects the defect and completes the work of exterior transformation. He also has to dispose of his wedding ring, but although he throws the ring away, the habit of fondling his finger eventually causes others to suspect that he might have been married once. The creation of a new personality is only superficially achieved through tonsorial, sartorial, and surgical alterations, for the one true transformation must come from within the self.

No sooner has the protagonist discarded the mask of the provincial dunce than he is forced to make a new one for himself. Since it is impossible to live in society without an identity, he selects at random the name Adriano Meis. In addition to the name he must fabricate a past for himself, with parents, grandparents, a birthplace, education. In what Pirandello must have intended as one of the absurd coincidences of fiction with life, Adriano later meets in Rome a man who claims to be his cousin Francesco Meis and who even corroborates various details about their common family history; the protagonist therefore becomes the prisoner of his own fictions, never attaining the freedom that was the original goal of his new life of evasion. To construct his second personality Adriano decides to reeducate himself by concentrating his attention on the inanimate world, which will free him from the tribulations of man's activities. Having already died once to society, Meis resembles the man with a flower in his mouth, in the way that death liberates both of them from the routine concern with life's petty affairs; by adhering to matter, they wish to achieve release through the disappearance of the conventional ego.[3] Adriano Meis of course enjoys an advantage over the character of the later novella in that he is not sentenced to perish from a terminal disease. The fugitive of Pirandello's novel can stand outside human relationships and smile at the foolishness of others who spoil the beauty of living with their spitefulness. Along with a new name comes a renewed desire to appreciate life.

Yet the mere fact that Meis is alive and living in human society renders impossible the simplicity and directness of the existence that he imagines for himself. Although he has won a sizable fortune at the roulette tables, the sum must be carefully pensioned out to last the rest of his lifetime, since he cannot deposit it in a bank to earn interest or invest at the Bourse without presenting proper identification. Having gained that pension from the challenge of living, Meis still has no hope of finding employment, again because of lack of identifying documents. At Venice a gondolier refuses to believe he is Italian and accuses him of being Austrian—the most hated national identity that an Italian could ever assume. On a chilly evening in Milan Meis almost purchases a puppy from a match vendor on the street, but he has to deny himself even the company of a pet, since he would have to apply for a dog license and pay a tax. For the same reason he cannot buy a home, marry, or protect himself from thieves. One night in a dimly lit Roman street he rescues a woman from four assailants, and that act of heroic involvement almost results in his having to go and give a complete report of the incident at police headquarters. To become involved means to compromise his independence. Meis cannot even know the self-annihilating euphoria of the drunkards who pass him on the streets laughing and shouting, for his sorrows are not to be dissipated by wine. Pirandello's novel has been called the "triumph of the civil state" because of Meis's failure to live without a legal identity.[4] His success in sustaining the disguise for a period of two years was possible only in the politically relaxed conditions in the early years of the twentieth century, when persons could travel in Europe and stay in hotels without displaying a passport. Since the First World War no one would be able to play Adriano Meis's masquerade, because positive identification has been required for even an overnight stay at a touristic pensione in the most remote village.[5] But although the prewar governments did not overly intrude into the private affairs of citizens, it was still impossible to exist without the need or the risk of having recourse to the services of the state. In his third novel Pirandello does not regard the state as such a hostile force, unlike Verga who saw the central government as an exploitative power; rather, the state with its bureaucracy is seen in *Il Fu Mattia Pascal* as an unavoidable necessity.

Along with the protagonist's inability to survive without the aid of the state's legal apparatus, the novel stresses his failure to stay outside the lives of others. He is too sociable a person to be content with snatches of conversation from hotel employees and restaurant workers. Adriano Meis's sense of spiritual dislocation in hotels, where everyone remains a stranger, is reechoed in the novella "Nell 'Albergo è morto un tale" ("Somebody died at the Hotel," ca. 1915), which speaks of transient travelers as persons who "are absent not only from their towns and homes but also from themselves." According to Pirandello the traveler who stops at a hotel suffers the loss of familiar surroundings, being cut off from the accustomed reality of his life. Meis must always feel within himself the vacuum created by the break with his past that the bewildering and lonely life of a hotel sojourner can never fill. He becomes such a stranger to life and human society that one day in a hotel corridor he is reduced to conversing with a canary that he sees in a birdcage hanging from a window casing. Meis thus comes to understand the limitations of his self-chosen isolation.

Desire to reestablish a meaningful communion with others leads Adriano to take up residence in the Paleari household. The unpretentious style of furniture, the obvious need to supplement income by renting rooms, the disorder of the Paleari home introduce the protagonist again to the domestic problems of the Italian middle class. His host, Anselmo Paleari, formerly a supervisor in a government office but retired early, has no mind for banal, financial problems. He occupies himself with theosophy. The first time Paleari answered Meis's knock at the door, he shocked his future tenant by appearing in his underdrawers and with his head swathed in a turban of soap suds. With his obsession for occult philosophy, the landlord's thoughts are just as vacuous as the soap bubbles. He sees in Meis a possible convert to mystical knowledge. But the only person at the boarding house who effects a genuine conversion in the solitary stranger is Paleari's daughter, Adriana. Although she never persuades Meis to share her deeply religious sentiments, the girl succeeds in awaking his most refined feelings. Once he offends her by using a holy water font in his room as an ashtray, but, without complaining, the delicate creature merely replaces the font with a real ashtray. Adriana Paleari represents the greatest threat to Meis's claim to freedom. Love, for any man, demands at least a partial surrender of his freedom; for him it would mean exposure and the end of his charade. But Meis with his quickened sensitivity responds to the girl's need for his sheltering affection. The dead man loves in spite of himself, no longer able to maintain the new, smiling mask of cordial indifference that he hoped would safeguard him from the emotions of others. But it is as a corpse that he kisses Adriana one night in his room, which is darkened because of his eye operation. In the painful light of daytime Meis realizes the harm he has caused by yielding to the temptation to kiss the girl. Because of his strictly extra-legal status he can only bring havoc into Adriana's life. He can neither marry her nor compel her brother-in-law, Papiano, to return the dowry of Adriana's late sister. The irony of Meis's situation consists in the fact that only because of the gradual reeducation of his fugitive life has he come to value Adriana's fragile loveliness, which would never have left an impression on the frivolous Mattia Pascal; but precisely because he is a legal nonentity, whatever action he takes will result only in his hurting that gentle creature.

In contrast to Adriana Paleari's gracefulness, Signora Silvia Caporale, the only other woman at the boarding house, is a grotesquely deformed figure. Caporale is still another of Pirandello's beggars for a little kindly attention, a morally shipwrecked individual who cannot even purchase tender regard from the venal Papiano. This piano teacher and café entertainer, who relies heavily on wine to assuage her sorrows, could be classed with the misfits in Rosso di San Secondo's drama *Marionette, che passione!*, inasmuch as Signora Caporale behaves like a *sciagurata* incapable of withstanding life's cruelties. Like other Pirandellian female characters of advanced middle age, she lives in her memory of a youthful love for a fellow student at the music conservatory who died at the age of eighteen before he could realize his genius as a composer. Adriano Meis views the wretched woman as a less than human creature with a carnival mask face and eyes resembling those with lead weights in a mechanical doll. As a musician who once had the ability to compose songs and improvise brilliantly at the keyboard, Silvia Caporale has known the dream of a sublime romantic creativity, but she has surrendered her humanity to become a ridiculous and hideous puppet.

As the one person who succeeds in manipulating the

other residents of the Paleari boardinghouse, Terenzio
Papiano acts like a sinister puppet master. His might largely
derives from a moral elasticity that permits him to denounce
evil in others while practicing it in his own interest. Although he professes to be an Italian patriot and a fervent
admirer of Garibaldi, Papiano works as secretary to an arch-
reactionary aristocrat who plots the restoration of the Bourbon regime. With his penetrating gray eyes he has seen
through the patterns of society's hypocritical games and
learned all the rules to become a consummate impostor. It
is Papiano's self-satisfied attitude that makes Meis regard
him as a marionette who feels no need to question the conventional game of mutual deception on which society is
founded. In his double role as puppet master and marionette
of self-convenience, Papiano gains ascendancy over the
members of the household. Paleari's mind is too high in the
stars to perceive Papiano's treacherous schemes for control.
Although Adriana attempts to resist her brother-in-law, she
is too isolated to check him. Not only has Signora Caporale
allowed him to defraud her of her life's savings, but she
has also consented to fool Paleari by pretending to communicate with her dead lover, Max, in séances. Papiano has
the keen vision to recognize the loneliness of one person,
the weakness of another, the intellectual distraction of a
third—all of whom fall victim to him as he pulls the strings
of their passions.

Even Adriano Meis, who thought he could remain on
the periphery of life as a disinterested spectator to its absurd puppet show, joins the list of Papiano's victims. After
Papiano viciously uses his epileptic brother to rob Meis,
Adriano finds himself in the humiliating position of apolo-
gizing to the thief and embarrassing Paleari's daughter, who
insists on turning her brother-in-law over to the police. Both
Meis and Papiano are impostors: the first a man of such
absolute sincerity that he has tried to withdraw from society;
the second, living in full enjoyment of his social role, in

which he may practice fraud on others as long as he counter-feits the signs of his rank in the middle class. Pirandello has thus brought the drama of his novel to the confrontation between the impostor within society and the impostor out-side society. The solitary rebel remains defenseless. After his attempt at flight from the falseness of Miragno, Adriano Meis discovers that, as long as he lives, he will never be able to elude the masquerade of conventional forms. All that he has done is prevent himself from participating on equal terms with others. In his despair Meis lets Papiano take him to a reception at the palace of the Marquis Giglio D'Auletta. There he witnesses in miniature society's petty intrigues. The marquis anticipates a character type who will be fully portrayed in Pirandello's fourth novel, *I Vecchi e i Giovani:* the aristocrat who lives only to reconstruct a glorious moment in the past. Usually the marquis's palace attracts members of the clerical party, who unite with the old-guard aristocrats to oppose the central government. Meis also knows that the marquis's son-in-law, Don Antonio Pantogada, is the one person in Rome to have met him in his former existence as Mattia Pascal, when they were both gambling at Montecarlo. Wishing to take advantage of Pantogada's absence from the city, Adriano plans to flirt with the Spanish diplomat's daughter Pepita, in the hope of breaking off his attachment to the Paleari girl.[6] The pro-tagonist has reached the nadir of his grand experiment with freedom, for in his compromising situation he has to hurt and sacrifice the person he loves by feigning an amorous interest in a vain creature deserving only of his scorn.

As a result of his flirtation with the Spanish girl, Adriano receives a challenge to a duel from her lover, the painter Bernaldez. Once again Pirandello returns to the ritual of a duel, but in this novel the ceremony receives an especially humoristic treatment. How can a corpse fight a duel? Neither Paleari nor Papiano will agree to become so involved with the elusive Signor Meis as to serve as his second. Several

military officers in a café laugh at Meis's efforts to enlist
their assistance without following the proper procedures of
chivalric practice. Only a person with a conventional social
identity is entitled to take part in the gentlemanly affair
of honor. The duel cannot occur in *Il Fu Mattia Pascal*
precisely because Adriano Meis is no one at all. The protagonist imagines two symbolic representations of his nonexistence : a puppet and a shadow. Adriano Meis possesses
as much being as a puppet with a papier-mâché heart and
a straw brain since he has no right to feel or reason as any
normal human. At one time he had considered himself
superior to living marionettes like the Caporale woman and
Papiano, but in the end he recognizes himself as infinitely
inferior to them. He is merely the shadow of a man. In
truth, the man who walks about the streets calling himself
Meis has less consistency than the shadow he casts across
the ground. In the final two paragraphs of *Umorismo* Pirandello will comment that humorists pay more attention to a
man's shadow than to his body, and he cites Chamisso's
novella *Peter Schlemihl,* the man who sold his shadow to
the devil. By his earlier refusal to return home and disprove
his death-by-suicide, the protagonist of *Il Fu Mattia Pascal*
chose the "shadow of a life" over the grievous reality of
existence in the narrow world of a provincial town.[7] After
coming to behold the inauthenticity of the great world in a
cosmopolitan center like Rome, Meis must acknowledge to
himself his profound error in believing that he could start
anew and build a life of substance. All he has accomplished
is the creation of a shadowy existence whose nothingness
Pirandello the humorist reveals as the imperfect substitute
for the mask of life in society.

In the stunning collapse of his illusory dream of escaping
ordinary fictions through living a supreme lie, Adriano Meis
comprehends at last that he has sentenced himself to perpetual exile : "I saw myself excluded forever from life, without any chance of ever re-entering it" ("I and My Shadow,"

p. 398). For *excluded* the author uses the word *escluso,* the masculine form that corresponds to the title of his first novel about the outcast Marta Ayala. Whether through erroneous choice or the prejudice of the majority, those two Pirandellian protagonists, Marta Ayala and Mattia Pascal, suffer a similar banishment. Because of the extraordinary nature of his exile, Mattia Pascal must resort to the extreme solution that many of the characters in Pirandello's novelle take as the way out of intolerable circumstances: death, the withdrawal "in silence" after admitting defeat. A fictitious life like that of Adriano Meis requires a fictitious death— the drowning of the puppet and shadow. His false suicide off the Margherita Bridge by the Mellini River boulevard recalls an earlier novella of 1901, "E Due!", where within a few hours two self-tormented characters hurl themselves from the same Mellini parapet while also leaving behind their hats; those two suicidal figures act in fatal earnestness without a thought of simulating their deaths in order to begin new lives under fictitious identities. Just as Mattia Pascal once hoped to liberate himself from the slavery of his marriage in Miragno, Adriano Meis must break the chains of his self-chosen bondage as the shadow of a man.

The Quest for Meaning

By writing down the memoirs of his two lives, the protagonist, who works from the vantage point of his third existence, attempts to discover the meaning behind the experiments and the resulting failures of the masks that he wore in society. Are any significant patterns to be discerned within his prisoner and fugitive existences? The novel would then reveal a sense of logic in the events of his lives that could not be seen at the time those events occurred. As usual with confessional literature, there is the danger that the narrator might impose a meaning on past happenings that would not correspond to their true significance at the moment they actually took place. In Pirandello's novel the spirit of inquiry and constant debate prevent the protagonist from arriving at facile conclusions. It is not the task of Mattia Pascal to compose a reassuring book about the reasons for his acts; the memoirs are not to be considered an apology but rather the exploration of the two masquerades that the protagonist felt compelled to perform before a false world. The account of his past actions and his reflections would then provide a meaningful statement about an individual's failure to lead an independent and authentic life of his own.

Early in the novel, during one of his many polemical discussions with Don Eligio, the protagonist asserts the temporal relativity of truth. Mattia declares that truth is not absolute and unchanging but is modified according to attitudes prevailing at a specific time in history. As in Pirandello's essay of 1893 on today's art and conscience, there arises an essential contrast between man's present-day insignificance and his central importance in the universe before Copernicus. Mattia goes so far as to affirm that at one time the earth actually stood still while the sun revolved around it, until that dreadful day when Copernicus published his new system and thereby cast mankind from a cosmic throne that the boldest conquests of modern science have not succeeded in restoring. The protagonist is truly not so ignorant as to deny the new realities of Copernican astronomy, but he would like to possess the serenity and the feeling of self-importance that he encounters in ignorant peasants who unquestioningly hold on to the Ptolemaic system. For Mattia man's recognition of his own worth is at the most illusory if it is not founded on a cosmology that places human affairs at the center of the world.

Truth for Pirandello is always related to physical illumination. The truth that the convalescent Adriano Meis glimpses in his darkened room for forty days varies from the reality of the sunlit day that follows the admission of his love for the Paleari girl. The fugitive's mystical landlord explains to him the nature of truth, which is the awareness of existing that every person carries within himself like a glowing lantern. In the darkness of man's earthly exile, that lantern of illusion sheds a feeble light to make possible a direction in life. The commonly held beliefs in Beauty, Virtue, or Honor, which appear as eternal and inalterable essences during certain periods of history, are according to Anselmo Paleari beacons of different-colored glass whose flame is nourished by the collective sentiment of an era. The epoch in which the landlord and his reticent tenant live happens to be one when the great gust of doubt has extinguished the beacons' flames. Adriano Meis, who until his operation devoted little time in pondering on human destiny, would perhaps accept Paleari's definition of truths as the collective agreements of a particular historical moment; but this Pirandellian protagonist is unprepared to reach his landlord's conclusion that death itself is only an illusory phenomenon that prevents mankind from participating in an eternal universal life. Later, in *Umorismo*, Pirandello will repeat Paleari's mystical words with their faith that man might end his exclusion from the world. In his third novel, however, his protagonist does not aspire to mystical elevation; his problems emerge from his relationship with a society that excludes one who tries to stand apart. Like his landlord, Meis feels that theirs is a dark age torn in different directions by the lack of a collective sentiment. Pirandello's novel *Il Fu Mattia Pascal* represents in part an artistic realization of the picture of bewilderment and alienation that the young author sketched in his essay *Arte e Coscienza d'Oggi*. Mystical transcendence will not be possible until the very late writings.

During a few moments, especially at the ebullient time of his first flight, Adriano Meis does experience intimations of a higher life beyond the barriers of routine social relationships, but he never fully appreciates the possibility of a genuine spiritual liberation. One evening at dusk, when he was traveling through Turin, he came closest to going beyond the false self of the Other as he watched the play of the dying daylight on the waters of the Po: ". . . the air was marvelously transparent; everything in the shadows seemed enameled in that transparence; and I, while I stood there looking on, I felt so intoxicated with my freedom that I feared I might go mad" (pp. 316–17). In the evanescent flux of sensations that moved across the stream of flickering impressions on the river's surface, Adriano Meis almost ceased to be a fictitious identity. At one moment it seemed that he might succeed in piercing that armor plate with which the "ego" shields the true "I," through identification with the image of the Other. There is no complete break-through in Pirandello's third novel, and it is not until his final novel, *Uno, Nessuno e Centomilla*, that the repressed "I" displaces the Other on the mirror of identification. The protagonist of *Il Fu Mattia Pascal* is no Fausto Bandini fleeing commonplace troubles for the oblivion of a divine insanity. In later works like the novel *Si Gira* of 1915, Piran-dello speaks of a "beyond" of the self to which his characters aspire. In his unique position of a man trying to live outside society, Adriano Meis could perhaps have entered that beyond through the golden stream of twilight, but he chose to withdraw from that form of ascent and to return to the sane confinement of the body politic.[8]

Unable to soar beyond his conventional being, the pro-tagonist gradually recognizes the narrow bounds of his social prison. One of the first persons to expound clearly on the limitations of the self was the eloquent Cavaliere Tito Lenzi, whom Adriano met from time to time in a Milanese restaurant and whose witty conversation he enjoyed until it turned to personal inquiry about Meis's background. Lenzi understood that the individual existed for others and derived his only contentment from them, as he tried to demonstrate to Meis:

Our conscience? But, my dear sir, our conscience just doesn't work right! . . . It might perhaps suffice if it were a self-contained castle and not a public square; in other words if we could succeed in thinking of ourselves as isolated beings; and if our conscience were not by its very nature open to others. In the conscience . . . there exists an essential relationship—essential, be sure of that—between me who am thinking and the other beings of whom I am thinking. · . . When the feelings, inclinations, tastes of those others of whom I'm thinking or you're thinking are not reflected in me or you, we cannot be satisfied or tranquil or happy. (P. 323)

Lenzi's discussion recalls the statement in *l'Esclusa* by Gregorio Alvignani that conscience is the others in us. The individual cannot succeed in having a thought that is wholly his own; and of course the acts that follow those thoughts occur merely in response to the desires and interests of others. Adriano Meis's longing to be absolute and self-sufficient, and his program of creating the most noncommittal existence possible for a person living in a complex and mechanized society, are condemned to end in a fiasco. He reduces himself to an aimless wanderer along the streets of a labyrinthine city, quaking before the roar of the machines that run the world and supplant the very persons who invented them. The inwardly independent self that the protagonist would like to affirm is no more than the sterility of the shadow of a life from which he has resolved to retreat.

By standing apart in the shadows of society, Adriano does gain insights into the way men surrender their humanity to acquire a mechanical ease that fails to quiet their inner restlessness. That mechanical ease exacts a price by transforming men into inane puppets. Meis arrives at his perception of the puppet of facility one day, after Anselmo Paleari announces to him that a new version of Sophocles' *Electra* is to be performed that evening by automatic marionettes. The landlord poses a problem for his lodger, to imagine that at the climax of the drama, when the marionette representing Orestes is about to take revenge on his mother and Aegisthus, there should suddenly be a tear in the paper sky of the puppet theater. At that moment, according to Paleari, ancient tragedy, with its clearly determined motivation, would become modern tragedy, with its situation of impotency; Orestes would lose the inner force to assert his will and would appear as Hamlet, the modern hero paralyzed by superior forces. Whereas Paleari speaks with regret of the fall in stature of the tragic hero, Meis realizes the comfort and sense of complacency that men can derive by accepting the marionette role: "Lucky marionettes . . . over whose wooden heads the paper sky is kept intact! No bothersome uncertainties, no inhibitions, no melancholy, no pity: nothing! And they can sit back and enjoy their drama, loving and esteeming each other without ever fretting themselves or getting confused because that sky is like a ceiling which is proportioned to their stature and actions" (pp. 356-57). That puppet condition does not suit just a few dwellers at a modest Roman boarding house, for it includes the anonymous masses of the modern electrified metropolises. Unlike the Futurists, who wanted man to become an automaton, Pirandello viewed the marionette transformation not as a victory but as a loss. The protagonist of his third novel comes to see how much intensity of emotion and depth of thought are sacrificed for the wooden beatitude of puppets.

What is the guiding principle in a world where the individual must take others as the mediators of his thoughts and actions and where the temptations of mechanization will reduce him to automatic responses? Despite all the reflections that the protagonists made before committing decisive acts, it was chance that rendered possible his experiment with a second life. Pirandello returns again in this novel to the theme of fortuitous events, the right combination of circumstances that determine the course of a life for an individual and his family. Although a person may think himself master of his destiny, it is chance that manipulates him. In the novel Pirandello wishes to show how gambling symbolizes the supremacy of chance in the world. The original fortune of the Pascal family came from the kindness of fate when the protagonist's father won a large sum of money and a cargo of sulfur from the captain of an English tramp steamer visiting Marseilles. Gambling enters again in the Montecarlo episode, where the casino appears as the temple of Fortune and the half-crazed gamblers seem ardent devotees of the capricious goddess. Mattia Pascal has no magic system for controlling the truly independent moves of the little ivory ball about the numbers of the roulette wheel; it is fate alone that crowns his betting with success. Even though Pirandello lacks the brilliance of Dostoevski in portraying games of chance as man's encounter with the forces of the unknown, the Italian author still succeeds in stressing that fate is the uniquely autonomous power in the universe. For individuals to triumph in a world governed by chance happenings, it takes a spirit of accommodation to whatever stroke of good or ill fortune that fate accords. Pirandello cannot follow the opinion of a medieval Christian writer like Dante, who viewed fortune as an angelic minister impartially working to redistribute the goods of this earth. He also rejects the typical Renaissance image of fortune as the enemy who destroys man's dream of perfection. The reign of chance for the twentieth-century author merely demonstrates the absurdity of man's existence.[9]

Mattia Pascal took advantage of fortunate events to prolong a holiday from mediocre realities. The impossibility for that holiday to endure a lifetime is emphasized by Don Eligio toward the novel's close as the methodical librarian sagely remarks about Mattia's memoirs: "[they tell us at least] that outside the law and outside of those peculiarities, happy or sad, by which we are what we are, it is not possible to live" (p. 440). Yet Mattia to the end persists in evading the law by not having his death certificate revoked. Flight still remains the most meaningful avenue of experience for him and for other protagonists. The very title of a tale of

1923, "Fuga" ("Flight"), reiterates the longing of the Piran-dellian hero to break from the asphyxiating routine of a miserable existence; in that tale fifty-two-year-old Signor Bareggi refuses to return home to his attentive but simple-minded wife and their two daughters. Bareggi takes com-mand of a milkman's wagon and heads out for the freedom of the countryside away from the foggy oppression of Rome and his apartment on via Nomentana. The novella closes on a note of mystery after the horse and wagon come back to the milkman's home, but nothing more is said of Signor Bareggi. There is perhaps only one case of a Pirandellian character who succeeds in living outside conventional society. Old Guarnotta of "La Cattura" ("Captivity," 1918) has grown weary of the responsibilities of managing his vast landholdings; for fifteen years he has been dressed in mourning for his only son by his first wife. To his astonish-ment three neighbors "liberate" him from his living death of an empty existence by kidnapping him, in hope of a large ransom. After the captors learn from Guarnotta that his second wife would rather see him dead than part with money, they debate whether or not to kill him, for fear of being turned over to the authorities. At last they decide to make the old man a prisoner for life in a mountain cave, where they will provide him with food, clothing, and blan-kets. It is during his captivity that Guarnotta becomes a free and living man again. Earlier, he had been a prisoner of the memory of his son and of his loveless role as a land-holder. Living outside the temporal and spatial confines of normal society, which believes the old man is dead, Guar-notta establishes a genuine relationship of mutual affection and respect with his captors and their children. Out of the necessity of becoming a captive the old man has to abandon privileged recollection to live once again.[10]

In his disguise as Adriano Meis, the protagonist of Piran-dello's third novel stays within the limits of everyday society and consequently obeys the need to manufacture a new form and mask. Mattia Pascal comes to know only a poor counterfeit of freedom. His memoirs constitute the failure of language to forge a vital significance and arrive at the liberation of an unalienated, self-renewing existence expressed through the linguistic resources of human intelligence, memory and desire. Through recounting the history of his various lives the late Mattia Pascal conveys the message that to dwell within society signifies to live a constantly self-creating lie.

4

From History to Humor

The Bitter Heritage: *I Vecchi e i Giovani*

Luigi Pirandello's fourth novel, *I Vecchi e i Giovanni*, represents the author's confrontation with the mythical structures of history.[1] In that work the Sicilian writer subjected to humoristic analysis the myth of the Italian Risorgimento, which had inspired his parents' generation and his own early youth, for disillusionment with the new Italy produced by the movement for independence and unification is the novel's dominating theme. Pirandello himself recognized the painful task that he assumed in trying to assess the failure of the Risorgimental myth; in a letter of 1912 he pointed out the novel's personal significance for him: "I now expect to finish *I Vecchi e i Giovani* . . . the novel of Sicily after 1870, a most bitter and populous novel, wherein is enclosed the drama of my generation."[2] The period depicted in the work is 1892 to 1894, the time of a scandal in the Banca Romana and the insurrection of the Sicilian Fasci. Although the title might seem to suggest an antagonism between two generations, Pirandello interested himself in exposing the tragic personal patrimony that the youth of Italy received from the discredited heroes of the Risorgimento. He studied an era when the sincere enthusiasm and the spirit of sacrifice that had made Italian unification possible vanished in an atmosphere of compromise and corruption: the "bankruptcy of patriotism." Without an unsullied myth of the Risorgimento to inspire them to practical action, the Italian youth in this Pirandellian novel cease to be effective agents of historical change.

Although the novel first appeared as a serial in the *Rassegna Contemporanea* during 1909, the author carefully revised the work for publication in two volumes by Treves in 1913. Pirandello returned once more to the novel for a definitive publication by Mondadori in 1931. The attention that the writer lavished on the novel clearly indicates the importance that he attributed to that work. Pirandello was born seven years after the unification of Italy and three years before the annexation of Rome as the nation's capital. The novel's time span thus corresponds to the author's early manhood. His parents and even his maternal grandparents had actively taken part in the struggle for independence and unification. Pirandello's maternal grandfather, Giovanni Ricci Gramitto, had to take his family with him into exile on Malta for his participation in an attempt to establish a separatist government for Sicily in 1848. During Garibaldi's military campaign of 1860, Rocco Ricci Gramitto, Pirandello's maternal uncle, joined the army of the Thousand and remained with the Red Shirts for their later battles to annex Rome. On his return to Girgenti in 1862, Rocco introduced his sister Caterina to his comrade-in-arms Stefano Pirandello, and a year later Caterina and Stefano united their patriotic aspirations in matrimony. Luigi Pirandello, therefore, in *I Vecchi e i Giovani*, was writing the most personal of novels about the profound disappointment that his family and their generation experienced after the painful years of sacrifice to realize their dream of national glory.[3]

The intense sadness and sense of frustration that characterize this fourth novel can also be noted in several of Pirandello's tales that are concerned with the misery and disenchantment of the post-Garibaldian era. In the novella "Lontano" ("Faraway," 1901) the author portrayed the futility of sacrifice: while Don Paranza was away risking his life to fight for Sicilian liberation from Bourbon tyranny, his former colleagues were making a fortune in commercial ventures; at the age of seventy-eight the patriotic veteran lives on a tiny pension, occasional work as an interpreter, but mostly from fishing. Although Don Paranza sometimes goes to bed hungry because the fish are not biting, he still has his medals from the battles of '48 and '60 to comfort him. The right to wear war medals and to call oneself an authentic Garibaldian veteran is the subject of the tale "Le Medaglie" of 1904, where the former patriots are shown to be a petty exclusive club, meeting in a shanty building whose rent they neglect to pay; as far as the general populace is concerned, an impostor dressed in a red shirt with medals pinned to it will suffice as a decorative dummy for civic celebrations. United Italy's moral bankruptcy comes under examination in "Il Guardaroba dell 'Eloquenza" ("The Wardrobe of Eloquence," 1908) in the story of Bencivenni, a halfstarved veteran who considers the out-of-wedlock pregnancy of his step-daughter as an event paralleling the disgrace of his nation. Bencivenni rescues his step-daughter by committing suicide and leaving a note where he falsely takes the blame for embezzling funds from a philological society; the old man's suicide is his means of quitting a thieving Italy. Spiritual displacement in the new Rome of the unified nation overcomes the main character of the novella, "Musica Vecchia" ("Old Music," 1910), when he returns home to the city in 1909 after an exile of sixty years caused by complicity in the affairs of the Roman Republic of 1846 to 1849. Poor Icilio Saporini compromised himself by setting a patriotic hymn to music. After his long exile in America he finds Rome unrecognizable; to his utter grief Icilio discovers that the *bel canto* music of his youth has given way to Wagnerian sonorities.[4] Whereas in those preceding four tales Pirandello gives an exterior fictional account of the fruitless heroism of the Risorgimento, in the second of his "Colloqui coi Personaggi" ("Interviews with My Characters," 1915) he enters into a direct conversation with his mother's ghost on their family's participation in the wars of liberation. Pirandello regretted that he was born in an intermediate generation between the Risorgimento and the First World War. The interview with his deceased mother appeared in print at the time the author's son was beginning his military service on the Austrian front. In all those novelle, as well as in *I Vecchi e i Giovani*, Pirandello sought to examine the crisis of a patriotic conscience in a debased society.

This novel was written during the years 1906 to 1908, the same period when Pirandello composed the treatise *Umorismo* on man's need for illusions. In that treatise the author stated that since life did not have any true goal of its own, it was necessary for men to save themselves from the void by giving importance to some goal. As a humorist the author felt that he had to reveal the emptiness of those illusions. His novel *I Vecchi e i Giovani* represents an attempt on Pirandello's part to behold historical process with a humoristic vision. The bitter heritage that the Risorgimento left Italian youth in the final three decades of the nineteenth century appears as the result of the self-deluding aspirations of an entire generation to found a kingdom of justice and greatness. To create his novel Pirandello faced an enormous aesthetic problem. The work has the form of a historical narrative in the third person, according to

multiple-selective omniscience, where the story arises directly from the characters' minds.[5] Historical writing tends toward synthesis, but Pirandellian humor works through
analysis, always uncovering the contrary of any positive
statement. As a consequence of the ceaseless humoristic inquiry, the author's effort at presenting an epic picture of a
society at a crucial moment in its history would seem at
first to be doomed to failure. Instead of the panoramic portrayal of struggling humanity that is to be found in Verga's
works, Pirandello focuses attention on bizarre character-
types, many of whom appear at the start of a chapter with
minute descriptions of physical features and mannerisms
only to be submerged in the confusing whirl of the novel's
events without ever contributing to the advancement of the
narrative. Not following Hegelian or Marxist world views,
Pirandello did not create characters who would appear as
participants in the dialectical affirmation of the laws of
historical progress. Although the characters may indeed be
interpreted as the major conveyers of significance in the
universe of the novel, they do not contribute to the advancement of history but are merely participants in a grand
marionette show where the master puppeteer remains absent. Throughout the apparently isolated cases of tortured
individuals, the novelist attempted to demonstrate how
history should be considered another of man's ideal constructions that no conscious or unconscious self-deception
could prevent from crumbling in time. The disintegration
of the ideal Italy built on the illusions and sacrifices of his
parents' generation provided Pirandello with a supreme
example of the basic unreality in life that he as a humorist
had to unmask.[6]

As a major novel of Sicilian history, *I Vecchi e i Giovani*
must be classed with two other works that investigate the
social and political upheaval which followed the collapse
of the Bourbon regime and the island's adherence to the
united Italian government: *I Vicerè* (*The Viceroys*, 1894)

by Federico De Roberto and *Il Gattopardo* (*The Leopard,* 1958) by Giuseppe Tomasi di Lampedusa. Although Pirandello's work does not display the same clear, formal structure of De Roberto's novel where each of the three parts closes with an important historical event, both of the books denounce the acts of treachery committed against the Sicilian people by ruthless political leaders. The chief difference in tone between *I vicerè* and *I Vecchi e i Giovani* arises from the contrast between De Roberto's cynicism before betrayal and Pirandello's anger over injustice. On superficial examination *I Vecchi e i Giovani* seems a highly complex novel, with its crowd of characters from the aristocracy, bourgeoisie, semi-professional groups, and peasantry, while Lampedusa's novel possesses a deceptive simplicity because of the concentration on the adjustment of one character, Don Fabrizio di Salina, and his family to the changes brought by the Garibaldian invasion. In truth, *Il Gattopardo* is one of the most powerfully symbolic books ever written, where almost every word suggests a transformation of men to animals or conveys the message of a fall from pagan divinity to commonplace mortality. Although Pirandello employs various recurring symbols throughout his novel, he is not interested in weaving the intricate symbolic tapestry that distinguishes Lampedusa's work. All three of these novels present a princely family that has to arrive at an accommodation with a new reality that favors the ascendancy of the crass middle-class entrepreneurs to political control in Sicily: the House of Uzeda in *I Vicerè,* the Laurentano family in *I Vecchi e i Giovani,* and the lordly Salina in *Il Gattopardo.* In each of the novels death plays a significant role, since they all deal with the death of a social system with its values and traditions. Pirandello's work, even more than that of the other two novelists, stresses the dying of a myth of national glory.[7]

In its exterior structure *I Vecchi e i Giovani* falls into two parts. The setting for Part One is Sicily, in the province

of Girgenti. To a slight extent the author had already suggested the region's stifling atmosphere in *Il Turno*, but here
the picture of the environment is sinister with the air of
decay that hangs over the squalid provincial capital Girgenti
with its mournful gloom of thirty churches. Ambitious
youths must either flee the suffocating climate or succumb
to its Oriental lethargy, joining the idlers who promenade
on the town's main street. The façades of buildings are
cracked; sometimes the interiors are plushly furnished, but
no one uses the rich furniture. Pirandello also recaptures
the odors of Girgenti: the dust that is rarely swept away, the
mold on rotting walls. Only the place names evoke the
grandeur of the past: "Via Atenea, Rupe Atenea, Empedocle
. . . names: flashing names that rendered all the more de-
pressing the wretchedness and ugliness of things and places.
The Akragas of the Greeks, the Agrigentum of the Romans
had ended in the Kerkent of the Moslems, and the mark
of the Arabs had remained indelibly set on the minds and
customs of the people. A taciturn languor, dark distrust and
jealousy" (p. 571). In contrast to the Arabic sloth of the old
city is Porto Empedocle, bustling with the sulfur industry:
"that little seaside village that had grown in so little time
. . . and now become an independent commune. . . . the
houses were piled up, without room, packed almost on top
of each other. The loads of sulfur were heaped along the
beach; and from morning to evening there was a continual
racket" (p. 469). Beyond the somnolence of Girgenti and the
strident animation of Porto Empedocle stands the desolate
malarial countryside where the peasants still live in feudal
subjection to city-dwelling landlords. The author reveals
how this entire district is caught in the stranglehold of the
reactionary clerical and Bourbon parties allied with the
unscrupulous entrepreneur Flaminio Salvo.

Rome, the embodiment of the new Italy, is the scene at
the start of Part Two. The climate of the restored national
capital is that of a demoralized society whose one-time

heroes have pursued venal careers in politics. In the concluding chapters the action shifts back to Sicily, where
government troops savagely suppress the insurrection of the
socialist *fasci* of combined labor unions. Sicily and Rome are
thus the two poles of the historical myth of modern Italy.
Pirandello stresses the bewilderment of Italian youth before
an age they cannot understand : the Revolution died without
bringing about a spiritual renascence; unification failed to
elevate the under-developed regions of the South; and
neither peasants nor industrial workers could realize the
reforms advocated by the socialists. What the characters in
the various classes lack is an awareness of cosmic and historical process. The myth of the Risorgimento, the bland
promises of the new parliamentary government, and the
utopian dreams of socialism—all these modes of interpreting
and shaping history are unable to impart a sense to events.
Between the bitter heritage of Sicily and the empty rhetoric
of the new Rome there opens the abyss of incomprehension
and explosive resentment.

Throughout the novel the various chapters tend to be
broken into smaller sections, each of which presents a
different arena of interest. This rather cinematic shifting of
focus of interest in no way results from Pirandello's inability
to sustain constancy of view and can only be attributed in
part to the novel's original publication in serial form. It was
the author's desire to fashion a series of highly dramatic
scenes where new characters would enter or depart as the
force of circumstances required it. Pirandello's method
works to provide an overall impression of the diverse figures,
young and old, who were victors and vanquished in Sicily's
tragicomedy of suffering. The author sought to recapture
the painful interaction of those ruling from 'above' and the
large slave class laboring from 'below' across that gulf of
incommunicability. Through personal dramas Pirandello as
humorist tried to reach some understanding of history.
Whether the scene is Sicily or Rome, a princely palace or a

slum dwelling; the author analyzed the motives of his characters to uncover the naked truth behind their acts: the guilt of the old and the shame of the young.

The Old

With the irony of historical process, the man who stands at the head of the older generation is not a former war hero or even a proud representative of the aristocracy. Through control of the sulfur industry the banker Flaminio Salvo has become the determining force in Girgenti. In a Hegelian interpretation Salvo would figure as a "maintaining individual" whose egotistic enterprises would set the standard for behavior in civil society. The financier could never rise to the level of a "world-historical individual" because his activities are not motivated by a transcendent ideal. By contrast, the title character in Verga's *Mastro Don Gesualdo* amasses a fortune in real estate and grain out of an intense longing to impart meaning to his life. To the moment of his death Verga's character clings to his land with the sensual devotion of a lover, while Salvo negates the value of all that he has struggled to accomplish. Salvo needs no "religion of *la roba*" to sustain him as he accumulates riches from a destructive lust for power over others. Despite his material success, Flaminio Salvo is defeated in spirit from the very start, whereas Mastro Don Gesualdo never surrenders and is merely conquered (*vinto*) by life itself. Miserly and sadistic, Salvo is a dried-up shell compared to Verga's passionate hero.[8] The words that become key terms in representing this burnt-out but vicious figure are *sazio* (sated), *stanco* (tired), and *nausea* as he beholds a lifetime of work constructed on the sufferings of others.

Like the characters in "Formalità," Salvo employs a formal language of deception of himself and others by which he regards himself as a victim working for everyone else in

Girgentian society, who imprison him in the role of com-
mander. He feels his life's work has acquired an autonomy
separate from him to serve *"gli altri"* who look to the financier as the supreme model for them to imitate. His interior
monologues reveal the self-duplicity of a man who relishes
assigning parts to others while pretending to appreciate
independence: ". . . The servility that I discover in everyone is making me lose [my pleasure in commanding]. Men!
I want men! I see about myself automata, puppets that I
have to place in this or that pose and which remain before
me in the pose I have given them as if to spite me. . . . Tomorrow I shall die. I have commanded! Yes, that's it: I
have designated roles for this person or that person, for so
many who have never been able to see anything in me other
than the role I act for them. No one has ever had the
slightest suspicion about that other life, the life of feelings
and ideas that is stirring within me" (p. 643). Pirandello unfortunately does not reveal that "other life" in Salvo. Only
once toward the close of Part One does the banker relax
the mask of despotic ruler, when he confides to his young
chief engineer, Aurelio Costa, that a person must always
seek his own desire regardless of the judgment of others or
even of oneself.

Everyone must be sacrificed to Salvo's selfish calculations.
In the hope of controlling the price of sulfur on the international market, he vindictively allows striking miners to
starve. The banker displays no remorse after the brutal
murder of his mistress, Nicoletta Capolino, along with Costa,
although the responsibility for their deaths is largely his own
since he thrust the two together and provoked the rebellion
of their love affair. Salvo feels that life has sufficiently
punished him through his family: his wife is a lunatic; a
son, the only person he ever loved, died in adolescence. His
daughter, Dianella, also comes to lose her sanity after the
death of her beloved, Costa. Flaminio always thinks away
his guilt by resorting to "a strange game of conscious fic-

tions" ("uno strano gioco di finzioni coscienti"), a refined self-deception that relieves his mind and safeguards his own sanity. In his domestic and commercial relationships Salvo persists in his role of tyrant, because he considers the freedom of others to be a denial of and threat to his supremacy. Whether with his daughter or his associates, he is always holding a cross-examination to ferret out the thoughts of others in the hope of determining whether their inner feelings correspond to their exterior submission to his will. But his violation of another person's conscience never succeeds in setting his doubts at rest. Salvo's vulnerability is most evident in his relationship with Costa. Fifteen years before the start of the narrative, Costa, who was only a boy, rescued the banker from a rather ridiculous death, that of drowning in a public bathing area when his feet became entangled in a string tied to two floating pumpkins. That absurd occurrence changed the course of Costa's life, for Salvo decided to show his gratitude by taking the boy into his home and financing his education. In time, the fullest consequence of that chance event was to be Costa's murder, which contributed to dissolving the resentment that Salvo held against his rescuer as a person to whom he had to feel indebted. It was always the feeling of weakness toward the youth that the banker gave out as the reason for rejecting him as a son-in-law, rather than social prejudice over Costa's being the child of a lowly laborer. Yet the very person that Salvo wished to become Dianella's husband was none other than young Prince Lando Laurentano. This financier proves himself another Georges Dandin or M. Jourdain attempting to force his way into aristocratic society. Following his humoristic method, Pirandello reveals in Salvo the discrepancy between what the banker claims his acts represent and the truly pretentious reality of his motives. The most significant feature of Salvo's—the one that distinguishes him from the Garibaldian veterans whom he despises and from the youth whom he manipulates—is that he does not require myths to sustain his enterprises. The banker has no need for privileged recollection as the tortuous phrasing of his thoughts with past conditional tenses and pluperfect subjunctive contrary-to-fact clauses serve only to project him into a possible future where no one would escape his manipulation. Salvo's desiccated being reflects a post-mythic age.[9]

In *l'Umorismo* Pirandello wrote that "because social relations are many times nothing but a calculation in which morality is sacrified, the task of humorism is that of discovering, through a laugh and without indignation, hypocrisy behind morality." Humoristic analysis of the fictions people use to mask hypocrisy with morality is evident in representing the efforts of Salvo's legal secretary, Ignazio Capolino, to maintain his position of apparent luxury and authority. First he married Salvo's least attractive sister to gain her dowry, but, as Pirandello remarks in *l'Umorismo*, death has a way of sneering at persons and their ambitions, because after five years the woman died childless and Capolino had to return the funds. Sight, with nouns and verbs of vision, is Capolino's chief faculty for turning his gaze from a humiliating reality, as when he later won Salvo's financial support by pretending not to see the banker's amorous involvement with the lawyer's second wife, Nicoletta. In the novel's supreme moral irony, Capolino, with Salvo's backing, defeats the candidates from the Garibaldian and socialist parties to become parliamentary deputy from the *clerical* party. This man, whose *persona* depends on prostituting his wife, wins a position of political leadership in that vitiated society. Inwardly the lawyer does rebel against the degrading compromises necessary to his success. Hoping to be secure in his roles as *avvocato* (lawyer) and *deputato* (representative), he has undermined his status as *marito* (husband) before the public's eyes. Both husband and wife strive never to arrive at that moment of mirror experience to see themselves living. Husband and wife play a continual game, a comedy of polite and gracious lies and a show of mutual devotion; the art of performance prevails :

> that was a dramatic moment, an intermezzo for the comedy that husband and wife had been acting every day for two years . . . for each other. . . . They both knew quite well that they would never succeed in fooling one another, and they did not even try to do so. It could not be said that they were acting for pure love of their art, for both of them secretly hated the need for those fictions. But if they wanted to live together, without creating a scandal before the eyes of other persons, without too much disgust for themselves, they understood that they could not act in any other way. And thus they were eager to dress up, or better still, to mask that hatred with kind and courteous lines; to treat the fictions as a sad and costly work of charity that was conducted as an obligation or competition to show their remarkably good manners. Husband and wife finally acquired not only an affectionate appreciation of each other's merits but even a sincere gratitude toward each other. And they almost loved one another. (P. 599)

Though nauseated by the knowledge of infidelity, Capolino and his wife avoid jealousy and revenge by carrying on their marital farce. Situations of paradox fascinated Pirandello, whose later plays were in part to constitute a theater of paradox where "normal" social conventions are reversed and made tolerable through the characters' tortuous logic. Through his humoristic awareness of the contrary, Capolino and Nicoletta are loathsome creatures who have violated the sacredness of their conjugal vows, but when viewed with the sentiment of the contrary, they are to be pitied as intelligent and sensitive individuals who in their moral weakness have sold themselves for material security. The fragility of their constructed life is made evident when Nicoletta elopes with Costa, only to be murdered later by an enraged crowd of striking sulfur laborers; Nicoletta so resents the happiness that Costa and Dianella Salvo might have enjoyed that she is prepared to destroy her marriage and risk her own life. Capolino, who because of a dueling injury has to wear special eyeglasses that make him look like a caricature of his former self, adjusts his vision to avoid the mirror of the truth about his wife's elopement; and he restructures his life by taking vengeance against Salvo when he persuades the banker's sister, Adelaide, to leave her husband, Prince Ippolito Laurentano, whom she married in only a church ceremony, and to flee to Rome with him so that they can marry in a civil contract. The lawyer's act of defiance against his slave-master Salvo does not represent an attempt at self-liberation, for he will go on fawning before his governmental superiors and begging the favor of his wealthy third wife and her Roman relatives. Capolino has merely changed his master.[10]

While Salvo and Capolino represent the new bourgeois dominators of Sicily, the island's aristocratic past is recalled by the members of the Laurentano family. Despite their common heritage, the Laurentanos display a staggering diversity in their political allegiance. Elderly Prince Ippolito has remained loyal to the Bourbon cause, while his sister, Caterina, is a Garibaldian patriot. The prince's son, Lando, is a socialist. Of the entire family only Don Cosmo, Ippolito's younger brother, is indifferent to politics. Each of the Laurentanos, even the recluse Don Cosmo, reaches out for what Dostoevski called in the *Notebooks to the Possessed* "the bonds to create," which might rescue them from the mediocrity, stupidity, and vulgarity of the mercantile class led by Salvo and Capolino. Every member of the aristocratic family assumes a different attitude toward human time. Austere and inflexible, the senior prince is perhaps the Pirandellian character most aware of time. At his estate of Colimbètra he has preserved a page from history by surrounding himself with a guard of twenty-five men dressed in Bourbon uniforms. His blind adherence to the pageantry of a dead past and his voluntary exile at his villa from the living world at Girgenti for over thirty years render him at the same time foolish and almost admirable. Despite the ridiculousness of his refusal to accept the reality of Italian unification, this aristocrat has the courage to live by his values, unlike the many shallow opportunists who have profited under the new regime. His is the most colossal example of privileged recollection in all of Pirandello's writings. With his moral inelasticity Prince Ippolito differs from Don Fabrizio di Salina in *Il Gattopardo*, for Lampedusa's character makes a public settlement with altered realities. But Fabrizio's apparent willingness to accept change stems from his passive nature, for he truly wishes to hold on to the values of the nobility and church. Prince Ippolito fights for his beliefs. In his desire to enjoy "the pleasure of history," the Prince of Laurentano clearly anticipates the time-preoccupied title character in the play *Enrico IV*. Just as the servants who form Enrico's "court" consider themselves no more than "six puppets hung on the wall," the members of the prince's guard are described as puppets in red breeches and blue jackets. Placido Sciaralla, their would-be "captain," has almost lost the ability to distinguish between his uniform and himself; the costume has become his mask. Like wound-up toys these soldiers practice military drills, winning for themselves the derision of the local populace, who call them so many little Don Quixotes out to attack windmills. Yet with all his Quixotic foolishness, Don Ippolito works from his domain with the bishop and the leaders of the clerical party to defeat the electoral campaign of the central government. For unlike the Prince of Salina, Ippolito does exercise a very real political role in the new state whose institutions he succeeds in coordinating with his role as a disdainful exile. The independant feudalism incarnated by Don Ippolito leaves its impression on bureaucratism statism. A living anachronism with his toy soldiers or *giocattoli*, the prince of Laurentano triumphs over present time by extending the past into the future.[11]

It is a crystallization of the life of the past, with no becoming, that Don Ippolito seeks to achieve by restoring the glories of Sicily's Grecian heritage within the confines of his estate. He shares with Lampedusa's Leopard prince a similar disposition to reverie, but whereas the lord of Salina employs astronomy as his spiritual anesthetic, the ruler of Colimbètra lulls away his cares with archaeology. While most of the Grecian statues that he has excavated from his own grounds are collected in the prince's private museum, the headless statue of Venus Urania stands provocatively outside his chapel to symbolize the aristocrat's contradictory nature: the sensual pagan as opposed to the pious Christian, the same opposed attitudes of Eros and Agape that preoccupy Don Fabrizio di Salina. Throughout the novel Pirandello frequently uses such symbols to illuminate a certain facet of a character's inner life, such as Capolino's new spectacles. As part of his archaelogical research, the prince is also preparing an erudite volume on the topography of Girgenti in Greek and Roman times. Like many scholars, Ippolito suffers the illusion that the "word" can somehow determine reality, as if signification could define the earth. The desire to re-create the past in all its concreteness rises from the need to elude the mediocre and disappointing present.[12]

This preoccupation with dimensions of time reflects a dread of dying. All of the prince's actions—political, archaeological, and marital—are motivated by his concern over death. In his political battles Don Ippolito fights the destruction of his own noble class. Archaeological investigations permit him to combat the ravages of time. It was a vain attempt to reassert his vitality and end the loneliness of his isolated position that caused him to enter into the illegal and ill-fated marriage with Adelaide Salvo. Whenever the prince looks at his withered hands, he feels the approach of death. Unlike Enrico IV, Don Ippolito does not resort to the insane game of hiding age by regarding a youthful mirror image of himself in a portrait. The prince's true salvation comes from his love for outer Nature. As throughout all of Pirandello's writings, Nature in a blade of grass, the roar of the sea, the moonlight shining through the leaves of olive trees just *is;* it does not have to signify anything, but persons possess the freedom to read into it whatever can console them for the collapse of life's artificial constructions. Although the prince of Laurentano cannot alter time and the world, he searches for the truth that unchangeable Nature might reveal to him. His vision of Nature possesses the harmony of an ancient pastoral, and the prince is a worthy descendant of Theocritus with the poetry that he relives in the Sicilian landscape. As in a painting of a pastoral scene by Poussin, the prince has already had his tomb constructed within a grove of oranges and pomegranates. Although his wife's desertion will cause him to close himself once again in a total retreat from present reality, his sensitive appreciation of natural beauty will help to soothe the anguish of his wait for the death he cannot escape.

In contrast to the magnificence of her brother's exile, Donna Caterina Auriti-Laurentano solemnly secludes herself from society by living in a dark slum-dwelling at Girgenti. She is the novel's victim of time and martyr to the myth of history. Married in her youth to the revolutionary Stefano Auriti, she chose in 1848 to join in his banishment to Turin. Too proud to accept financial aid from her loyalist brother, she endured hunger and poverty in the northern city. Only after her husband fell at the battle of Milazzo in 1860 did she return to Sicily, expecting to see justice and freedom established through unification with the mainland. All the privations that she was willing to suffer were for the glorious dream of a united Italy, and Caterina's martyrdom began only after she realized that her sacrifices had been for naught. She shares her disillusioned exile with her widowed daughter, Anna. Both of them dress in black, mourning not only for their dead husbands but also for a dead myth. Their home is as dreary as a prison, and they almost never leave it—they have enclosed themselves in a structure of dark despair, impotence, and resignation to futility. The heroic Donna Caterina has become a living corpse:

> The gloomy mortification of her pride, the fierceness of her character that at the cost of unbelievable sacrifice she had never betrayed even before fate's cruelest assaults had so changed the features of her face that it no longer showed any trace of her former beauty. Her nose became long and pointed, hanging over her withered mouth that had deep ridges here and there because of lost teeth; her cheeks were hollowed; her chin thrust out sharply. But the eyes, under the thick black brows, especially showed the ruin of her face: the eyelids drooped, one more than the other; and the eye that was more closed than the other, with its slow glance that was veiled with intense anguish, made that wasted face look like a waxen mask of horrible pain. Her hair meanwhile had remained black and lustrous, as if in mockery to make the destruction of her other features more noticeable. (Pp. 509–10)

In Pirandello's narrative and theatrical writings it is always the eyes that betray the inner travail of his characters. Donna Caterina's features have hardened into a mask of mutilated life. In referring to her the author frequently employs the adjective *cupo* ("gloomy") for the darkness that has closed about her soul. When Prince Ippolito sees his sister for the first time after a separation of forty-five years, he cannot recognize her. After Caterina looks at a miniature portrait of herself, which her brother has saved, she declares that the girl pictured there is dead.[13] The portrait is a mirror of the past. Neither Caterina nor Ippolito can triumph over time. Her sullen withdrawal from light and life is of course due to the failure of the liberal ideals of her youth. She saw in the Risorgimento the opportunity for Sicily to emerge from centuries of neglect, but the reality of misgovernment after 1860 forces her to acknowledge that conditions were better under the Bourbons. The author reserves his severest criticism of the government's exploitation of his native island for the angry outbursts of Donna Caterina; at times this character works more as a vehicle of Sicilian protest than as an artistically realized individual in the novel's drama of despair. Pirandello uses her speeches to express his own indignation at the new despotism that enslaved Sicily. Because of her contempt for the central government, Donna Caterina vehemently opposes the election of her son, Roberto, to parliament as a candidate for the liberal party. Her son's ultimate disgrace in the bank scandal drives her into a catatonic state and finally to the evasion offered by death. Her dying is merely a passing away into the total darkness to which she had surrendered when she lost the bright hopes of her youth.[14]

Absolute skepticism distinguishes Don Cosmo Laurentano, the recluse of decrepit Villa Valsanìa. Unlike his brother, who wishes to spend his exile in luxury and beauty, or their sister, who has deliberately stayed on in a slum neighborhood to show her disdain for life, Don Cosmo is indifferent to his surroundings. As long as the roof does not cave in on him, this eccentric figure with Spartan habits does not even notice the rain that drips through the rent ceiling. But the life that Cosmo has tried to avoid begins to crowd in on him when the prince's wedding takes place at Villa Valsanìa. The cracked walls are covered over with artificial decorations that never succeed in masking the villa's true condition, just as the feigned good humor of the wedding guests fails to conceal the grotesqueness of the poorly matched marriage. Cosmo's clothes also have a symbolic function. Living away from the fashions of the city, this near-hermit dresses in a casual, unpretentious manner. The clothes that he used to wear when he took a more active part in Girgentian affairs are preserved in a chest. Don Cosmo has also locked away an old cassock, which symbolizes the religious fervor of his youth when he studied at the seminary until the hypocrisy of his companions so sickened him that he let reason conquer blind faith. Twice in the course of the novel's events the chest is opened, as the present invades Cosmo's privacy. The first time his housekeeper persuades the old gentleman to put on an old frock coat to receive the wedding guests. Like the frock coat in the tale "La Marsina Stretta," the garment fits too tightly under the arms; it also smells of camphor. When elegant Prince Ippolito sees his brother in the coat, he tells Cosmo to remove that "monument" from the past. The second invasion of the present is absolute, when a group of socialist revolutionaries fleeing the government's troops arrive on a stormy night to ask for refuge at the villa. Don Cosmo entreats the fugitives to take off their drenched clothes and put on his old but dry garments. One of the revolutionaries dons the cassock, which fits him like a strait-jacket. The chest is completely emptied as the past is made to serve the needs of the present moment. Don Cosmo wishes to live neither in the present nor the past, but in a twilight hour of his own. Although other persons attempt to encroach on his retreat, he always succeeds in withdrawing to the solitude of his thoughts, which no one is ever able to invade.

Total renunciation of all ideals has given the recluse a sense of serenity that shields him from all hurt. Flamino Salvo, the most active combatant in the novel, admires Cosmo alone among all his acquaintances because of the old man's wisdom in detaching himself from life's involvements. For a while after his break with the seminary, Don Cosmo continued to devote himself to reading philosophers like Kant, Hegel, and Rosmini, but as the years passed, he came to view all metaphysical systems as sand castles that would quickly fall apart. His attitude resembles Pirandello's portrait of Montaigne in *Umorismo:* ". . . the skeptic that tolerates everything without believing in anything, for he has no enthusiasms or aspirations—a man who uses doubt to justify inertia as tolerance" (*Tutti i Saggi* [Milan, 1960],

p. 106). For Cosmo life must be observed but not experienced. His passivity recalls that of Don Fabrizio di Salina, since both characters regard action as futile, a burden that they should never assume. This skeptic is one of Pirandello's mouthpiece characters, for as a spectator and commentator on the tragicomedy produced by the frenetic activities of the other characters he serves as the novel's chorus and the voice of the author himself. It is Cosmo who delivers the novel's message to his nephew, Lando, while the other socialist fugitives are sleeping:

> One thing alone is sad . . . to have understood the game! I mean the game of the mocking demon that each one of us has inside him and that takes delight in representing outside ourselves as reality what a little while afterward he himself shows to be an illusion of ours, deriding us for the trouble we have taken on account of that illusion, and also deriding us for never being able to delude ourselves as has happened to me because outside of those illusions there is no other reality. . . . And thus, do not complain! Trouble yourselves and torture yourselves, without thinking that all of this will come to no conclusion. If it does not conclude, it is a sign that it must not conclude and that it is vain to expect a conclusion. It is necessary, that is, to follow after illusions; to let the nasty little demon play his game within us until he is tired of it all; and it is necessary to think that all this will pass . . . will pass. (P. 831)

Persons attempt to impose stops on time, to divide history into glorious moments, to pretend that there are conclusions. Pirandello will close his final novel with the chapter heading "Non Conclude," denying the human tendency to establish artificial periods. Cosmo's awareness of universal and historical process as a purposeless game (*senza scopo*, without a goal) is the novel's central theme, which renders all the more pathetic the sacrifices of the old to build the new Italy and the aspirations of the young to reform. For yesterday's reality is today's illusion. Having resigned from life and those illusions which sustain its myths, the old man makes himself a creature without reality. What he seeks to make for himself is the detached nonbeing of objects that witness human events without feeling. Unwilling to fight time like his brother or scorn its betrayal like his sister, Cosmo would prefer to dwell within a timeless moment; but he sadly recognizes that such an escape is only illusory. His dwelling and garments belong to the temporal world from which he has tried without success to exclude himself. In breaking away from the game of illusions, Don Cosmo has paid a price—loss of joy in life.[15]

At the opposite pole from Cosmo's disenchantment is the naive faith of the Garibaldian veteran Mauro Mortara, a character type adapted from Pirandello's poem *Pier Gudrò* of 1894. The stages in Gudrò's career are exactly the same as in Mauro's: youthful anticlerical pranks, exile on Malta, work as a stoker on a ship, big-game hunting in the Orient, combat in all the major battles of the Thousand. Like Mortara, Gudrò cherishes his medals. Both of these figures are suspicious of the proletariat movement. But in the fully humoristic dimensions of his nature, Mauro Mortara is a far more human figure than the pasteboard hero of the early poem.[16] Although Mortara's savage physical appearance and gigantic stature inspire terror and respect in the country-side, this peasant who is the true lord of Villa Valsanìa is revealed in a comment of the omniscient author as being both "ferocious and comic." Seen outside of the rustic setting of the territory around Girgenti, with the brace of pistols strapped to his waist, Mauro Mortara, appears a ridiculous wild man. The author associates various animals with the old warrior peasant to illustrate his character: Mortara is "faithful like a dog and courageous like a lion." To aid him in his vigilant guard on Don Cosmo's villa he has three fiierce mastiffs, with which the old man holds endless con-versations. Along with the leonine and canine facets of his nature, Mortara also possesses some of the majestic spirit of a leopard. Among his treasures of a lifetime of violent activity is a leopard that he killed and stuffed years before in Libya. But when anyone examines the stuffed leopard, he discovers that the relic of past courage has an eye missing and is covered with dust. Mauro Mortara is as much an anachronism as the stuffed leopard; both resemble forgotten musem items.

Old Mortara lives completely in a world of his own illusions and attempts to force everything and everyone else to conform to his distorted vision of Italian greatness. He has turned his eyes from all the injustice, oppression, and poverty in the unified country. Ever since unity was achieved, Mortara has held on to the blind conviction that the Italy he had fought to create has become the first nation of the world. As a concrete symbol of the veteran's blindness, there is a room at the villa where Mauro has erected a "Shrine of Liberty" to the memory of General Gerlando Laurentano, Ippolito's father, who committed suicide during exile on Malta. As always, the peasant has founded his devotion on an illusion: General Laurentano never worked for a united Italy; instead he suffered political banishment for advocating Sicilian autonomy from Bourbon rule. The course of events that culminates in Mortara's tragic enlightenment to the truth about Italy begins when Prince Ippolito sends the old man to Rome to fetch Lando home. The encounter between the old and the new Italy when Mouro confronts Lando leads nowhere, for although the young prince pities and even admires the veteran, there can be no communication between them. As throughout the novel, no one—even those of the same age group or political persuasion—penetrates the barriers that the characters establish to protect themselves from the sentiments of others. For the seventy-eight-year-old Mortara, the trip to Rome represents a pilgrimage to a holy city. He walks ecstatically along the streets of the capital until the day he witnesses the arrest of Roberto Auriti, whose father died in Mauro's arms on the battlefield of Milazzo. The old man's dream of Italian greatness—the most fragile of ideal mythic constructions—is forever shattered, and at last his eyes are open to the misery and corruption of the unified government. Symbolically, Mauro tears the military decorations off his shirt and tramples on them.

Pirandello portrays the human tendency to rationalize the truth in Mortara's desperate efforts to find an explanation for the demoralized spirit of his nation. The outbreak of the Socialist rebellion provides him with a scapegoat for the failure of Italy to realize the aspirations of the revolution. Those rebels have to be the enemy who are dishonoring their country. Mauro has substituted one illusion for an even more preposterous self-deception. In a final, reckless attempt to reaffirm his faith in Italy, the old man leaves the villa and joins the troops that are combating the riotous villagers. After a furious battle, among the bodies lying in a village square there is one that bears four medals on its bloodied breast—medals that are tragic emblems of former Garibaldian glory and fallen ideals. The governmental soldiers wonder, "Whom had they killed?" This is the concluding question of *I Vecchi e i Giovani,* for the murder of the old patriot is Pirandello's anguished protest against the destruction of the principles that inspired the Risorgimento.[17]

Among those who betrayed Mortara are Francesco D'Atri, prime minister of the central government; Robert Auriti, boy hero of Garibaldi's campaigns; and Corrado Selmi, parliamentary deputy from Sicily. None of these three was able to sustain the purity of his youth: "In conspiracies, in combat they had been in their element; in peace they were like fish out of water. . . . They felt they had to commit late in life and badly all the foolish acts that as youths they had not had time to do . . ." (pp. 652–53). To remind him of his senile acts of self-disintegration, D'Atri has a porcelain ape that sneers at him from atop a bracket. To himself the prime minister no longer seems like the man whom others once considered the greatest hero after Garibaldi. In his

mirror D'Atri glimpses fragments of other possible selves for
him, but the grotesque image that has triumphed in the
looking glass is that of a silly old man who has dyed his
hair canary yellow to mask his age. This last act recalls the
passage in *Umorismo* where Pirandello speaks of an elderly
woman who is both comically hideous and pathetic because
of the make-up, dyed hair, and youthful fashion of the
apparel with which she tries to keep from losing her young
husband. For at the age of sixty-seven this dignified statesman had committed the folly of his life by marrying a
woman young enough to be his granddaughter. After she
gave birth to a child by Selmi, D'Atri publicly accepted the
baby as his own, ignoring the equivocal smiles of his colleagues and parliamentary rivals. He did not have the good
fortune to die a hero on the battlefield, but outlived his
fame and degraded himself by his December-May marriage
As a diminished man D'Atri attracts contempt and pity.
Although he has never misused his office for personal gain,
the prime minister attempts to suppress documents that
could incriminate parliamentary deputies and cause the fall
of his cabinet. In his political as in his domestic affairs,
D'Atri seeks to conceal the truth.[18]

Pirandello modeled the character Roberto Auriti on his
uncle Rocco Ricci Gramitto, who after 1870 settled in Rome
to a life of self-indulgence.[19] Similarly, Auriti is shown
living in the capital where he has established a strange
menagerie of a home with a singing teacher as his mistress
and her vagabond brother and complacent ex-tenor husband
as constant companions. He, who had been the youngest of
the Thousand, surrendered to an enervating torpor. Born
in the critical year of 1848, in middle-age Auriti feels caught
between the young and old. Despite his boyhood heroism,
he never displayed the aggressiveness that was required in
Rome's competitive atmosphere to seize the spoils that the
many patriots, for mere amusement and reward, won for
themselves. Like most of the authentic veterans of the

Risorgimento, Auriti has ceased to be a man; they are living memories and walking legends. Time for them is the invincible adversary that has won a war of attrition with the weapons of age and infirmities. It is solely because of the legend of his childhood glories that the central government chose Auriti as the parliamentary candidate from Girgenti; otherwise no one would have ever selected the weak-willed lawyer to run for public office. He is no more than a war-hero puppet that the government, secret police, masons, and mafia wish to manipulate so as to remain in power. In order to succeed against the reactionaries and socialists, Roberto would have to advance a coherent program of economic and political reform. Since he is unequal to the task, Auriti has to fall back on his record, reminding persons that he was captured at Aspromonte with Garibaldi. The eternal smile that he keeps on his lips never truly masks the fact that Auriti has lost faith in the ideals of his youth. His is only a formal patriotism that rings false and rhetorical to the populace. Naturally, Roberto loses the election, running a poor third. It is Italy, not a particular individual candidate, that goes down in defeat before a Sicilian electorate that can no longer tolerate hostile legislation and unfair administration. After his arrest in a bank scandal for signing I.O.U.'s to cover the debts of his friend Selmi, Roberto Auriti loses his only reality—the reputation acquired through his boyhood exploits. The one-time hero becomes a zero, since his life, in typically Pirandellian terms, is to be "hooked" and condemned because of a single accusation of guilt.[20]

Whereas Mauro Mortara never claimed the pension that was his by right, Corrado Selmi thought the world owed him an elegant livelihood as proper compensation for his heroism. Selmi achieved success thanks to his dynamic way of assaulting problems without worrying about the morrow. Machiavelli's comment in the twenty-fifth chapter of *The Prince* on the favor Fortune bestows on the bold perfectly describes Selmi's career. In the darkest hours of the revolutionary struggle it was always he who found the means to surmount obstacles. After devoting eleven years to the battle for unification, he entered parliament, and in gratitude to his constituency he effected legislation to have his home district freed of malaria. Yet, although Selmi recognized how the central government was defrauding Sicily, he did nothing to alert parliament to the crisis it was creating. For despite all his exterior charm and daring, Corrado Selmi is a deeply flawed individual who eventually loses control over circumstances.

Selmi's guiding philosophy rests on a fear of standing still and becoming imprisoned in mere form. He feels that to think too much will kill reality and that to live is to flow unconsciously and spontaneously. This deputy declares that life for him is a feather continually blown along by the wind of adventure. Selmi tries to avoid striking an attitude or pose that might result in a fatal pause in the stream of life. He calls himself a "traveler without baggage" who never assumes burdensome responsibilities. Of all his actions Selmi regrets only one: his affair with D'Atri's wife. His ultimate fate resembles that of the character Mateo Sinagra of the novella "Da Sè," who collapses after fortune turns on him. Once an investigatory committee has denounced him before the Chamber of Deputies for receiving secret bank loans, Selmi decides to take his life, for he realizes that his flight from responsibility has reached its end. He will be frozen in the form of disgrace, as he can already see in the newspaper headlines that report his fall from favor. His name printed atop the newspaper page reminds him of a gravestone, his own. Like the usual Pirandellian suicide, Corrado Selmi calmly takes a carriage ride out to the summit of the Janiculum so that he can enjoy for the last time the peaceful view of the city. His final act before poisoning himself is to write a letter exonerating Auriti of blame. By this last defense of his friend, Selmi hopes to redeem himself. Of all the characters in the novel, Selmi most cherishes life. Yet, when the disastrous consequences of his blind activism catch up with him, he must renounce his intense love of life.

Among the members of the older generations, the most wretched and truly outcast are two Girgentian revolutionary organizers whom everyone contemptuously calls "Propaganda and Co.": Luca Lizio, the inarticulate theorist, and his mouthpiece orator, Nocio Pigna. In physical appearance they represent respectively the tall, lanky, thin man and his squat, rather hunchbacked partner of comedy teams, for the author heaps scorn upon them as third-rate performers in a drama of demagoguery. The studious Lizio, who can barely utter two syllables, has found in the loquacious Pigna the barrel-organ of propaganda for which he is able to play grinder with the tunes of Marxist commonplaces like "Social Revolution" and "Brotherhood of Man." They work through the deliberate perversion of language with slogans and abstract dogma that they themselves do not fully comprehend. When the two establish a union hall for Girgenti's *fascio*, they decorate it with timeworn, imitation-damask hangings that once served in church for festal occasions but now bear party mottoes. Lizio and Pigna are priests of a new religion that the anti-Socialist, anticlerical Pirandello regarded as being as empty and formal as the traditional Christian religion. The propagandists cannot succeed in their goal of re-educating the people to prepare for a radical revolution partly because of the abstractness of their program, which the ignorant populace fails to fathom, but also because of the low esteem in which they are held by society. Everyone refuses to distinguish the individual man from the program of reform that he advocates. Although Lizio and Pigna are supposed to be fighting for the working class, they themselves do not work, they sponge off the labor of two of Pigna's seven daughters, who take in sewing. Lizio manages to survive on people's sympathy because of the suicide deaths of his father and brother, but society constantly hounds Pigna and sees to it that he cannot find work. Pigna once worked as a sacristan, and his skill at oratory comes from the close attention he paid to his priest's sermons. But when his eldest daughter became romantically involved with a canon, the ensuing scandal caused him to be driven from his post. For a while he had a job as a clerk in a lottery office until persons accused him—unjustly—of pocketing some of the bets. Made unemployable, Pigna stands "espulso dalla società" ("expelled by society") and rendered superfluous even in his own home. Since he does not wish to stay outside the society that has rejected him, Pigna plans to overthrow it and become indispensable to the new order. Pigna's case is not isolated in Pirandello's writing, for similar tormented characters appear in tales like "Dono della Vergine Maria" ("The Gift of the Virgin Mary," 1899) and "La Patente" ("The License," 1911) as well as in the dramatic version of "La Patente," but only in the novel does the outcast vent his anger as a revolutionary.[21]

From the might of a Flaminio Salvo, ruler of the establishment, down to the misery of the revolutionaries, the author presents a gallery of humoristic portraits of individuals in pursuit of illusory goals. Only two characters—Salvo and Don Cosmo—perceive the pointlessness of activity, and the first of these lacks the strength of will required for renunciation. All the figures share the guilt, in varying degrees for their participation or nonparticipation, for the crimes of betrayal against their Sicilian homeland. Yet, although the author scrupulously exposes the insincerity motivating his characters' actions, he depicts all the inner torture and sense of spiritual void that transformed a generation of heroes into inane, worried puppets.

The Young

With few exceptions, Pirandello's treatment of the young lacks the convincing human depth that characterizes the older generation in the novel. Rarely are the novel's youthful figures represented fully in their painful awakening to life, in contrast with the anguished adolescents in novelle like "La Veste Lunga" and "In Silenzio." The general impression created by the work's portrayal of the younger characters is one of incompleteness, as if the drama of the young has still to be realized. There are certain characters, like the De Vincentis brothers, Ninì and Vincente, who were obviously never intended to emerge as major figures; Ninì, for instance, is clearly meant to be such a vacuous, cream-puff character that Dianella Salvo in her insanity can substitute him for Aurelio Costa. But Costa himself never comes to life: others speak of the exceptional qualities of this young engineer, but the author fails to bring those qualities into prominence as an operative force in the novel. Costa's brutal murder together with Nicoletta marks the end of any hope for the youth of Italy within this novel's structure. Coming from the lower classes, Aurelio Costa with his education should have been able to assume a firm position in the professional world, marry a woman of the bourgeoisie like Nicoletta, and negotiate labor reforms as a mediator between the capitalist Salvo and the sulfur workers. It may well be that Pirandello expressly left the engineer in the novel's penumbra since, like the rest of Italian youth, his potential would remain truncated.

Pigna's daughter Celsina is still another youthful character whose development is not altogether realized artistically. The reader usually learns about her from what others say rather than from direct dramatic presentation: how she won first honors in a technical institute for men, how her stubbornness in following her own way closed the conventional career of teaching to her as a means of leaving poverty behind. Through her own initiative Celsina arrives in Rome, supposedly to attend a socialist meeting but with the hope of discovering a way to get her talents recognized. By chance the husband of Auriti's mistress hears Celsina's melodious voice and predicts that she could be a successful operatic singer. After all this preparation the author abandons Celsina completely. leaving her in a twilight scene practicing a song by the banks of the Tiber. Although her last word seems to express optimism: *Volerò* (I shall fly), in defiance of her lover's prophecy that she will be ruined, the term recalls the title of Pirandello's tale "Volare," on the plight of a girl in the metropolis turning to prostitution to escape drudgery. In Celsina's situation are the germinal elements of a new feminist drama, a woman from "below" trying to use her abilities to elevate herself socially and to succeed in her own person. But here, in the case of Celsina, the novel does not show the fully realized coordinate relationship in presenting the young and old that its title appears to proclaim.

Only with Dianella Salvo does the author display the same tender concern he shows for lost girls in tales like "Il Ventaglino" and "La Balia." Hated by her father, who regrets that she did not die in her brother's place, Dianella is in truth even less fortunate than the daughter in the tale "Felicità," because the insanity of the banker's wife has deprived the girl of a mother's love. Ever since her childhood Salvo's daughter has cherished the dream of one day marrying Costa, who has never once become aware of her feelings for him. The only character who offers love to the girl is Ninì De Vincentis, whose personality is so bland that no one could return his affection. Dianella comes to establish a sentimental rapport with Mauro Mortara, for the old savage and the frail girl share a common adoration of nature. The silence of the immense solitude around Villa Valsanìa soothes the disquiet in Dianella's soul. She feels that she resembles a rivulet whose natural course has been blocked— by her father's disdain and her mother's madness. Mortara alone knows how to open the great source of tenderness in the girl. Just as the old man is able to converse with the trees, Dianella feels she can flee her aloneness to partake of a higher, universal life that the rustle of leaves and the hum of insects bring to her. Those moments of pantheistic rapture briefly lift her out of the pathological melancholy of the luxurious prison-home where her father exercises his tyranny upon the girl.[22]

Although direct contact with Nature makes possible intervals of relief, the tension that Dianella tries to ease in the tranquillity of the countryside grows unbearable whenever discordant reality closes in upon her retreat. Unfortunately, Salvo's daughter never arrives at a moment of full identification with Nature, either by fusing with it for a sublime instant of ecstasy, participating in its concrete physical substance, or by permitting it to contain her in its completeness. The girl reveals all the sadness of the reflective isolation of consciousness when she has to confront the spiritual nothingness of her father's world. Dianella feels crushed under the banker's riches. The fragile forms of consciousness are forever shattered in insane fury at the news of Costa's death. That delicate equilibrium, maintained in the girl's mind only by the hope of love, breaks down from the pressure of unalterable events. The submissive girl at last rebels against her father, repeatedly calling him "Wolf!" as the predatory beast that has slaughtered the engineer, and she asks for the protection of Mortara as the hunter who will destroy the voracious wolf. What has been denied Dianella in the world of supposedly sane relationships, she will obtain for herself in her state of lunacy, for the demented girl imagines that she is holding Costa in her arms and receiving his caresses. In actuality, the De Vincentis boy is attempting to nurse her back to sanity. Madness is only a case of thought, a certain deviant but still coherent manner of knowing reality. For others like her father, Dianella will be a pathological figure who might be cured. But in Pirandello the word *pazzia* is not necessarily the equivalent of *malattia,* as was evidenced in "Quand'ero matto." Dianella Salvo's madness serves as the logical mental construct of the life of loving affection that she has always desired and will never forsake.

While the Salvo girl has to lead a life of deprivation

amidst the material possibilities of the banker's fortune, Prince Lando has so many choices of a mode of living that he feels the unity of his psyche to be threatened. In no way can he be classed with the rebel-victims among the anti-heroes of the modern novel. Although the prince is ready to scream out "No" to the world, he is in no manner one of its victims. His rebellious spirit in part wells out of a Nietzschean superabundance of vital energy, which propels him onto a course of blind activism. Outwardly the prince continues to frequent the gatherings of the smart set in Rome at race tracks and chic restaurants, although the charmed existence of fashionable society bores him. This exterior conformity to the empty rituals of his social class arises from a reluctance to appear different from others as well as from a desire to display an outward stability. Lando belongs to the decadent era of Rome's pleasure-seekers, and Pirandello does not hesitate to lay bare the fundamental vulgarity of the reduction of life to a superficially refined quest for sensual stimulation. The inane chatter of friends at exclusive clubs distracts the prince from violent thoughts. Lando even feels alienated from his slim, handsome body, which seems to hold him prisoner in the negligible identity of a gentleman of noble birth and a member of the Roman establishment. To discover his ultimate identity, to construct a genuine personality and at the same time to move forward on the current of life—here are the contradictory problems that plague the young prince as he regards his reflection in a mirror.

With the character of Prince Lando Laurentano, the author studies the mentality of a rebel, and in so doing he anticipates the dramas of men in revolt against society or destiny in the works of Camus, Sartre, and Malraux. The act of rebellion entails an assertion of the self; its consequences, in Pirandellian terms, involve the destruction of the death-dealing social forms that channel life into rigid habits and customs. Lando's adherence to the Socialist Party is, as his closest friend, Lino Apes, observes, only nominal in nature, since the prince does not truly wish to work for the peaceful restructuring and reform of society. On his own estates in Sicily he has already created an example of enlightened agrarian reform, with fair distribution of farm land, the founding of rural schools, and the publication of a weekly newspaper to diffuse information. Yet, the success of his personal initiative leaves the prince still dissatisfied, propelling him toward the violent revolt that seems the sole escape from the sterile atmosphere and mediocrity of the world in which he must live. When the bibliophile prince contemplates his well-stocked library, he concludes that the vital flux has been trapped in the crystallized form of books: ". . . artificial compositions, fixed life; caught in unchanging forms, logical constructions, mental architecture, inductions, deductions—away! away! away! To move oneself, to live, not to think! . . (pp. 681–82)." The nonthought of anarchical rebellion comes across in the vehement rejection of the logical order and linguistic uniformity in the constructed universe of books. Longing for an opportunity to take energetic, impulsive action, the prince hopes that a great flood will burst forth to sweep away all the vestiges of society's arbitrary life forms.

News of the Sicilian uprising elates Lando, although he knows that the revolt will end in failure. Like other rebels in twentieth-century literature, he prefers the inevitability of failure to the patient preparation for a systematic attack against the establishment. But unlike the heroes of Malraux's novels, Lando acts only for the thrill of revolt rather than for any higher principle that would redeem the absurdity of entering into a rebellion that must fail. Pirandello's character possesses the lucidity of mind to see that the noblest of principles led the heroes of the Risorgimento to reconstruct an Italy modeled on the rhetorical tradition of ancient Rome and the vain, materialistic progress of the more advanced European nations. The prince's essential nihilism corresponds to the assault on the source of life that Nicola Petix attempted for the destruction of man. Yet, spiritual redemption does come to Lando after he actually returns to Sicily and witnesses scene after scene of the animal horror of warfare. The prince even makes a visit to a graveyard, where he entreats the cemetery attendant to open the lids of coffins so that he can examine the expressions of astonishment on the faces of the victims who did not expect to die. Pirandello explicitly draws a parallel between this graveyard scene and the one in *Hamlet* when Apes comments that he has to play the role of Horatio to Lando's Prince Hamlet. For the brooding prince of Sicily renews the struggle of his Danish counterpart against a paralysis of the spirit, refusing to become a puppet immobilized by the rent in his paper sky. Alone among the Socialist fugitives, Lando accepts guilt for the massacre of innocent persons. On the eve of his exile the young prince learns from his Uncle Cosmo the illusory nature of his attempt to destroy fixed social forms and ceremonies. With the awakening of a moral conscience in Lando comes a renascence of humanity: the one hope for the young.[23]

Because of his social rank and wealth, Prince Lando had several avenues of vital direction open to him. Donna Caterina's grandson Antonio Del Re—Pirandello's self-portrait as a youth—never succeeds in breaking away from the gloomy shadows of home in Girgenti's slums. He is another of Pirandello's myopic anti-heroes whose efforts at imitating the dynamism of life are doomed to defeat by their limited vision. Del Re yearns for the comfort of Celsina Pigna's love, but she knows that he wants to make her into a doll for his own solace. The girl in fact hands him an old rag doll to provide him with a surrogate for her affection. Not possessing Lando's luxurious distractions, Antonio is the most desperate and potentially violent youth in the novel. He plans to commit some outrageous crime that will prove him capable of resolute action. His inability to find a constructive outlet for aggressive tendencies derives from a crisis of late adolescence, for Antonio is only eighteen at the novel's beginning. He childishly demands a perfection in life that is nonexistent, especially during an era of political corruption and communal distintegration. After he moves to Rome to pursue studies in science, the backwardness of the faculty and the rowdyism of the students at the University of Rome inspire him with such intense aversion that he withdraws from classes. Although Antonio lacks Lando's ability to effect destruction on a large social scale, this youth wishes to use his scientific knowledge to invent a bomb that he would drop from the gallery of the capitol upon the Chamber of Deputies. That one act would avenge Sicily for the injustice of the central government, and by its sensationalism Del Re could emerge from his anguished isolation and dominate reality for a self-annihilating moment. But instead of transforming his arid intellectual revolt into an active negation, Antonio behaves like a ridiculous puppet when he attacks Corrado Selmi with a dagger, blaming the politician for Auriti's arrest. In the novel's cruelest irony and most extreme absurdity, Selmi is already dying from poison. This assault is the violent confrontation between the disenfranchised Italian youth and their moribund senior leaders. Del Re's act is of course doomed to meaninglessness. The youth must return home to Sicily like a naughty child, rather than like a man who has achieved freedom through a supreme crime.[24]

There hangs over the young a continual temptation to madness. When constricting political, social and economic realities threaten to demolish the fragile dream-buildings of illusions, the young who have not had the chance to act positively in the real world will either turn inward to live a fantasy of desire or will lash out furiously against the forces of constriction. Both the lunatic and the rebel seek uncompromisingly to rebuild the world according to their ideals. Dianella, Lando, and Antonio were born in a country where hope had died. Refusing to relinquish their ideals, the young will affirm their desire for perfection through revolt or flight into insanity.[25]

From History to Humor

All the characters of this novel, young and old, with the exception of the recluse Don Cosmo, struggle against spiritual paralysis. Each one experiences some form of exile, political or sentimental. The novel opens and closes on a day that follows a storm, and in the interval between those two tempests Pirandello represents the death of the political myth that inspired Italians from the time of the collapse of the Napoleonic empire to that of the unification of their country. As the author observes the victors who immediately began to decline in the monotony of banal life after they had passed from the turbulence of battle to the calm of an attained ideal, his attitude recalls that of Cervantes as analyzed in *Umorismo,* who had a need to create a *Don Quixote* instead of an epic poem. Pirandello expressly states in *Umorismo* that there are no heroes: "The humorist does not recognize heroes; or rather, he permits others to represent them. As far as he is concerned, he knows what legends are and how they are created, what history is and how it is shaped: they are all compositions which are more or less ideal. And the more they make claims toward reality, the more ideal they are. Compositions that he [the humorist] delights in tearing apart . . ." (p. 158). Instead of writing to glorify the Risorgimento, Pirandello the humorist writes to repeat how the reality of one generation must be viewed by the youth of a succeeding generation as vain illusion. Although the humorist takes delight in dismantling myths, he recognizes the depth of devotion aroused by those myths. Through sentiment of the contrary, he pities all those whom the pointless action of historical process has led to full delusion with hope.

5

Novels of the New Rome

The Writing Machine: *Suo Marito*

In his fifth novel, *Suo Marito* (1911), and his sixth novel, *Si Gira* (1915), Pirandello anticipated both Alberto Moravia and Jean Paul Sartre by writing novels of alienation in the twentieth century. Moravia's *Gli Indifferenti* of 1929 and Sartre's *La Nausée* of 1938 analyze the bewilderment of protagonists who can no longer relate either to other persons or even to material objects. While Moravia's anti-hero Michele sees himself as an indifferent puppet moving automatically along the rain-swept streets of Rome, Sartre's Roquentin abandons work as an archaeologist and later as a historian because life holds no meaning or intrinsic order for him. Pirandello's *Suo Marito* and *Si Gira* study the collision of cosmopolitan tastes and provincial values within sensitive, creative individuals attempting to find their way in the new Rome, which by the final decade of the nineteenth century had again emerged as the true center of Italian political, intellectual, and artistic life. The Sicilian author does not present the positive struggle between a complex urban society and an individual ambitious for recognition and success as Balzac does with his representations of Paris as an arena of triumph or defeat for provincials like Eugène de Rastignac. What Pirandello analyzes is a lonely and frequently unsuccessful battle for self-recognition. He shows how the move to the Roman metropolis with its sophisticated literary coteries, salons, and musical circles exercised a devastating impact on impressionable provincial artists whose work prior to arriving in Rome had arisen spontaneously, even naively, from the traditions and customs of their native regions. The mechanistic rhythm of the new environment exerts a dehumanizing effect on those individuals, threatening to transform them into machines.

No sooner had *Suo Marito* appeared in print than the author yielded to pressure to have the work withdrawn from circulation, for it was embarrassingly obvious that Pirandello had derived his story of a young authoress coming to Rome with a senator's sponsorship from the career of Grazia Deledda. The unflattering portrait of the authoress's husband, a notary archivist who resigns his post to manage his wife's affairs, bore such great similarity to Deledda's enterprising husband that that Sardinian writer justifiably felt offended by Pirandello's work. It was only twenty years later that Pirandello returned to his novel and began to prepare a revised version, changing the title from *Suo Marito* (Her Husband) to the ironical *Giustino Roncella nato Boggiòlo* (*Giustino Roncella, né Boggiòlo*) with its play on the exchange of roles between spouses. Because of the demands of his work as a dramatist, Pirandello was unable to carry the work of revision beyond the second paragraph of the fifth chapter, exactly in the mid-point of the novel's eight chapters. Finally, in 1941, the revised sections, followed by the original concluding chapters, were published by Mondadori in the omnibus collection of Pirandello's novels.[1]

Although most critics dismiss this novel as a failure, emphasizing the author's attempt at revision, his occasional intrusions into the narrative, and the use of third-person technique, Pirandello still shows considerable ease in handling the novelistic material. Unlike the meandering method of *I Vecchi e i Giovani,* this work displays the author's ability to create a singleness of effect in the story of a marriage's collapse under the strain of adjustment to a new way of life. Each chapter's subject is clearly announced by a title like "The Banquet," "The Lord of the Island," or "Fly Away"; and the novelist never strays away from the center of interest in the various scenes in the chapters. Throughout the work Pirandello makes the reader both see and hear the characters. In the banquet scene of chapter 1, where the heroine, Silvia Roncella, is initiated into Rome's most distinguished literary circle, the author works like a cameraman, moving skillfully from one clique to another, recording the blasé facial expressions and the malicious comments of the guests. Whenever he encounters a strikingly grotesque figure like the club-footed dwarf poet Cosimo Zago, the cameraman-author pauses for a close-up that reveals the infinite sadness concealed under a pose of superior detachment. It is only when the author tries to contrast the artificiality of the banquet at a chic restaurant overlooking ancient ruins with the eternal natural rhythm of life in the distant countryside that direct comment begins to distort the scenic representation and reduce it to the level of a caricature of pettiness.

Part of Pirandello's success in recapturing scenes with either large groups of characters or comic encounters between two persons lies in his use of language, in this novel, as extremely narcissistic and intransitive. No matter what the number of speakers, there is little or no dialectic. One comic example occurs at the opening of the third chapter where Silvia's elderly Uncle Ippolito receives an American journalist who asks for an exclusive interview. Since the eccentric old man speaks no English and the reporter understands little Italian, the two try to communicate by stressing syllables: *ni-po-te* or *par-to-ri-re* as language loses significance. The two men end by merely smiling at each other. Language throughout the novel is represented as a commercial commodity, which publishers like the reporter's newspaper purchase at so much per word. Persons fail to reach each other with words, a situation rendered all the more pathetic since Silvia is a writer. Through such linguistic devices as in the scene between the uncle and the reporter, Pirandello makes the reader aware of a perilous sense of loss, which pervades the whole work and gives it stylistic unity.[2]

Social discourse in the new Rome, which provides the setting for the first seven chapters (except for chapter 5), is that of persons without deep roots who could just as easily be living in Paris, London, Berlin, or St. Petersburg. The members of the Roman smart set cannot articulate a sentence without slipping in French phrases. High priestess of this world is Dora Barmis, consulting editor in the novel for the fashion magazine *Le Grazie,* who jestingly proposes that she will compile a text of "cultured" conversation with a list of impressive names of the day like Nietzsche or Wagner, which people with no deep interest in philosophy or music can "drop" into the idle chatter of salons. Giustino Boggiòlo actually wants Barmis to train his wife in the culture that will secure her acceptance in the leading literary circles. At the novel's start, in the banquet scene, Silvia remains a silent figure while her husband monopolizes the conversation. Only through writing does she at first succeed in asserting herself over the social discourse that either her uncle or her husband imposes upon her. The uncle believes that she should speak as a proper provincial homemaker, and Giustino thinks of the image that Silvia should present as a major new author. Silvia never becomes the superficial conversationalist according to Barmis's style, because she resists being appropriated by a discourse not of her own creation.

An expert on current trends in interior decoration, Barmis assumes the task of advising Boggiòlo on the furnishing of Villa Silvia, where he plans to install his wife so that she will play a role in the capital's cultural life with her own brilliant gatherings of celebrities. For Silvia Roncella that villa stands as the concrete image of a false, insipid form of life where she, with the values of her native Taranto in the deep south of Italy, can take no part except as an impostor among a crowd of counterfeiters. The very details of the villa's interior decoration symbolize the alienation at the heart of the novel: estrangement, transfer of self, surrender of autonomy. At Barmis's direction the husband has arranged for separate chambers for himself and his wife. Alienation here deals with the aggression that one person visits upon another's being to appropriate that other self. The three stages of the novel's development are appropriation (as when Boggiòlo took his wife's bows at the banquet), sacrifice (when the husband resigned his government post to manage Silvia's career), and at the end the reassertion of self, with the marriage irreparably shattered. Villa Silvia symbolizes Giustino's attempt to enslave his wife: having no longer any income of his own, he has taken care to furnish a quiet study where she can labor, writing dramas that will pay for their expenses. That studio, for Silvia, becomes a prison workhouse where she must serve as a writing machine grinding out commercial manuscripts. The villa, with its façade of urban sophistication, represents the viciousness and shallowness of the new Rome, where Silvia falls victim to her husband's transgression.

Pirandello's virulent satire of the Roman salons reflects his profound disappointment with the artistically and intellectually bankrupt society of the national capital. Instead of scholars the author found pedants; instead of dedicated artists, dilettantes. His novella "Il Sonno del Vecchio" ("The Old Man takes a Nap," ca. 1905) describes a disastrous afternoon for an aspiring young playwright whose attempt to read a drama to the guests of a salon fails miserably because of distracting conversation from a famous journalist and the loud snores of an elderly statesman. The direct relationship of the tale to the novel is evidenced by the fact that the journalist Casimiro Luna is a character in both works; in the tale Luna appears as a walking caricature whose whole life is a continuous fiction. But whereas in the novella Pirandello succeeds in keeping an aesthetic rein on his contempt for the fatuous literary coteries, in the novel his attack grows so fierce that the social grasshoppers of the salon world seem no more than ludicrous figures who spend most of their time squabbling with each other. Even a carefully delineated figure like Dora Barmis, with her bizarre apparel and affectation of a Bohemian poverty, appears an outwardly constructed character with no authentic inner life of her own. Perhaps of all the Roman characters only one, who is sketched in a few lines, comes to life as a pathetic *macchietta:* the evanescent elderly woman Ely Facelli, who rents rooms to Boggiòlo and his wife on their arrival in the capital. This figure is one of Pirandello's humoristically depicted characters in her efforts to disguise the ravages of her advanced age with a blond wig and thick layers of face powder; she forever dreams of finding a publisher for her gigantic lucubration on the true history of the Longobards in Italy. Only in the portrait of the equivocally smiling old woman does sarcasm give way to a poetically vital sympathy. In this novel the salon is the microcosm of the new Roman society that has no ties to the capital's ancient and ecclesiastical traditions. These salons appear to offer the promise of a vigorous national culture, but instead they represent the vacuity of the recently unified country.

In the fifth and eighth chapters the novel's setting

changes to the northern region of Piedmont, the homeland from which Boggiòlo was exiled when the government sent him to work in Taranto and to which he must return after the definitive break-up of his marriage. Silvia's feelings toward her husband's home in the mountain valley village of Cargiore are a mixture of resentment and fascination. After the birth of her son, Vittorino, the authoress has to spend several months in the village convalescing while her husband enjoys the triumph of promoting her drama *The New Island* in its premiere performances throughout Italy. At the same time that Boggiòlo is excluding her from the life that she has deserved because of her literary productions, Silvia's mother-in-law and the wet nurse relieve her of caring for the baby. She has been cut off from her two works of creation: her drama and her son. Also during her exile at Cargiore, Silvia's Uncle Ippolito dies and is buried in the village cemetery. The old man's death serves to sever the authoress's ties to her former life in Taranto. In her absolute isolation from her past and present Silvia sees herself as an *"esclusa"* (p. 940), exiled to the unreal lunar landscape of Piedmont. Despite her loneliness the authoress awakens to an arcane sense of life in the mysteriously moonlit valley with its snow-capped peaks, icy rivulets, and faraway echoes of peasants' songs, Through the creative renascence of her spirit Silvia is able to write poems for the first time, about her impressions of Piedmont, although her husband will later reject the verses as lacking in commercial value. Even after her return to Rome, to labor in the villa's prison study, the authoress emerges from a period of artistic sterility by writing a novella on the eccentric local characters of Cargiore, like her mother-in-law's aged, would-be lover, Martino Prever, and the village curate, Don Buti, who tries to demonstrate God's might with his telescope. That tale of life in Cargiore could very well be Pirandello's novella "Gioventù" ("Youth") of 1901, where there is another Martino Prever, who committed suicide when his beloved had to wed against her will. In the novel it was Martino's brother who took his life out of amorous despair. As in the writings of the Piedmontese author Cesare Pavese (1908–1950), the moon works a nocturnal magic in both Pirandello's tale and novel, evoking a sense of peace and disquiet at the same moment. Pirandello's handling of the Piedmontese setting in *Suo Marito* especially recalls Fogazzaro's re-creation of the Valsolda region, even to use of the French-like dialect of the area to impart a local flavor to the dialogue. To the heroine of the novel, Piedmont is a land of death, where she loses her uncle and, by the end of the work, her son. Although the valley setting might seem at first to offer an idyllic contrast and alternative to the atmosphere of contention in Rome, it is a realm where dreams die. With the burial of her child Silvia knows that her marriage is part of her past.[3]

Pirandello's study of the protagonist, Giustino Boggiòlo, possesses so much humoristic ambiguity that the character can be viewed as an insensitive exploiter of his wife's talents or as a self-sacrificing martyr to her literary ambitions.[4] He admits that he married Silvia not for love, but from loneliness after being separated from his mother because of his transfer to Taranto; his situation is similar to that of a schoolteacher in the novella "Notte" ("Night," 1912) with an identical need to reach out for the consolation of feminine companionship in a distant and strange region. What Boggiòlo fails to appreciate is that his wife's respect for and faithfulness to him are founded in the Tarantine conception of the husband as the man who works to provide for his family. It is in fact the shock at learning of Boggiòlo's resignation from his position in the state archives that causes Uncle Ippolito's fatal stroke. Upon his marriage to the Roncella girl, Giustino agreed to pay no attention to her literary activities as long as she carried out her domestic duties. But when one day a check for a thousand marks arrived from Germany to secure translation rights for one of Silvia's stories, Boggiòlo's whole attitude changed, for he was forced to recognize the enormous profit that could be realized from literature. He then took the responsibility of acting as his wife's secretary, literary agent, and general manager. Little by little he began to crowd Silvia out of her own career— always with the rather legitimate explanation that he was protecting her financial interests from publishers who might take advantage of her inexperience in commercial negotiations. By the time of their arrival in Rome, Giustino Boggiòlo feels assured that his wife's success is due not so much to the intrinsic merit of her writing but to his own efforts to promote her works.

It is in Rome that Giustino deliberately starts to thrust his wife into the background as he demands public recognition for his entrepreneurship. At the banquet in Silvia's honor the husband rises to accept the toast that Senator Borghi offers in praise of the talented young authoress. Like a typical press agent, Boggiòlo is prepared to make a pest of himself in order to have his wife's writings advertised in the newspapers. Unlike many Pirandellian characters, Giustino Boggiòlo does see his mirror image in other persons— with the decisive exception of his wife, before whom he remains blind to the end. As long as he advances Silvia's literary reputation and increases the sales potential of her works, he stays indifferent to others' laughter. Whether persons print calling cards with his name listed as "Giustino Roncella, né Boggiòlo" or refer to him as "the monkey atop the elephant," he accepts his ridiculous role and derives every possible material benefit from it. Boggiòlo constantly deceives himself as to the true nature of his motives. In one respect he acts as a husband who cannot do enough to further his wife's career, even going so far as to master English, French, and German in order to handle contracts in foreign countries. But in another light Giustino must be viewed as a man who secretly desires to supersede his wife in the profession that she has entered because of her innate gifts and discipline. Boggiòlo's appropriation of his wife's

being goes as far as his actually counterfeiting Silvia's signature and handwriting to prepare souvenir albums that he
fills with choice maxims from her writings along with some
of his original contributions. What he can never counterfeit,
of course, is his wife's ability as an author. Basically, the
husband feels his male ego threatened by his spouse's success and tremendous earning power, and he attempts to
remove that menace to his self-esteem by directing Silvia's
activities, treating her like a push-button automaton from
which he can extract a drama or a novel to hawk in the
literary market. In the novel's humoristic ambiguity there
arises the question as to who is dependent upon whom to
derive substance as a person. The reciprocal master/slave
relationship is obscured by the problem of determining who
is creator and who is the created one. Is Silvia indebted to
her husband for his sacrifices to advance her socially and
commercially, or must Giustino be considered a debtor for
the importance he has achieved as the manager of his wife's
literary career? Between the two there arises an ever-increasing resentment over the sacrifices and debts incurred during
the move to Roman society. Mutual dependence deprives
the marital couple of individual integrity.

As usual in Pirandello's writings, neither husband nor
wife can communicate with the other. Boggiòlo never speaks
of his need to affirm his self-sufficiency before the world
that is ready to applaud Silvia's creations. The wife equally
fails to let him know how his crass commercialism degrades
her. Like most major Pirandellian characters, Silvia begins a
stranger to herself, dimly aware of other possible selves within
her being. Her writings first served as an outlet for the disturbing other self, and an attentive reader of Silvia's books—like
Dora Barmis—could easily see that the gentle, conservative
Tarantine homemaker truly possessed a spirit with the savage
thrust of a dagger. Giustino's worst strategic error in regard to
his wife consists in opening the doors of their home in order to
have a salon. Not only does his act betray Silvia's southern

Italian image of the husband as an almost insanely jealous guardian of his wife, prepared to keep out intruders with double locks and bars on the windows, but it also exposes the authoress to ardent male admirers, who appeal to the unexplored part of her nature that she fears to acknowledge. In order to contrive a sense of stability for her being, Silvia Roncella needs the solid bonds of province, tradition, and family. Degree by degree in the novel those bonds are broken. Boggiòlo himself comes to recognize that the presence of their baby might restore an equilibrium to Silvia's dangerously mobile personality. But the husband has so surrendered to the mechanics of his managerial role that. instead of going immediately to Cargiore for the child, he thinks only of traveling to Paris for the premiere of *The New Island* and of finding a companion who could inspire Silvia to complete a new play. As the typical man of action who has become a mere machine, Giustino Boggiòlo destroys his marriage.

For the ideal companion in his wife's literary labors, the husband selects the senior figure of the Roman world of letters, a man who, because of his age and prestige as maestro, would seem most likely to offer Silvia the fatherly understanding she requires to regain a feeling of inner security. But the writer that Boggiòlo leaves with his wife is a humorist, who by the very nature of his creative thought can never believe in fixed personalities and lasting sentimental bonds. Pirandello was later to admit that in the figure of the writer Maurizio Gueli he intended a self-portraiture, a study of a man held in thralldom to an insane woman, for the relationship between Gueli and his madly distrustful mistress, Livia Frezzi, is directly modeled on the Sicilian author's marriage to Antonietta Portulano. Gueli has been compelled to recognize the existence of another personality within himself that his mistress's jealous mind has created: instead of the austere, self-denying *persona* that he presents to the world, there is Frezzi's image of a man who lives only to indulge himself. Just as in real life Pirandello's wife refused to read any of his works, Livia Frezzi rejects Gueli's writings as a vain offering of himself to others. Within the fiction of the novel, Gueli is shown as having abandoned writing for the past ten years in an effort to prove to his mistress the strength of his devotion to her. Like Marta Ayala, the Frezzi woman innocently suffered ostracism from society after her husband cast her out of their home on the unfounded suspicion of an affair with Gueli. Excluded from the company of others, Livia grants such a total possession of herself to the writer that he almost accepts the sacrifice she demands of him in compensation for her fate. To show the falseness of the pleasure-seeking image that she holds of him, Gueli turns down invitations and tries in every possible way to avoid the society of others. But a mere glance at someone on the street suffices to enrage Livia as evidence of his treachery. In his battle to negate that other self, Maurizio Gueli has also become an *"escluso dalla vita."* The once intense vigor of his creative energies has been tamed and checked like the current of the Tiber against its banks outside the writer's townhouse.

The spontaneous force of Silvia's talent appears like a new source of life for Gueli, who hopes to find spiritual salvation in a return to writing. The relationship between Gueli and the Frezzi woman constitutes an enclave within the novel: a representation of the tyranny which self-sacrificing persons exercise over each other. This enclave functions as a secondary sequence in the novel to parallel the master/slave relationship of Boggiòlo and his wife. Livia Frezzi employs her nearly insane demands to gain power over Gueli. Pirandello's innovative perception here is to see madness as a means to acquiring power over another's actions. Sociolinguists have observed the struggle for control in this manner: "One person may be said to have power over another in the degree that he is able to control the behavior of the other. Power is a relationship between at least two persons and is not reciprocal in the sense that both cannot have power in the same area of behavior." [5] Through his love for Silvia the older author wishes to escape the aggression from his mistress and banish the image of a sensualist which Frezzi has imposed upon him. For years Gueli has had to live with two truths: the truth of his integrity as he has always viewed himself, and the odious but thoroughly consistent truth of what he has become for his mistress. In the eyes of Silvia (here the verb *vedere* is of paramount importance) he desires to behold a reflection of the noble truth. Gueli's weakness comes from his failing to reject Frezzi's sacrifices.

Thwarted in her roles as wife and mother, Silvia has literature only as a reason to live; and Maurizio Gueli represents literature to her, not as enforced machine labor but as a sublime act of creation. Their decision to flee together to Ostia arises from a mutual desire to elude aggression and regain the freedom of artistic creativity. Silvia's attraction to the senior writer, at first thinking of him as a possible collaborator in literary projects, is in Pirandello's words a descent down "the easy ladder" of self-deception. For the cold embrace that the two exchange at Ostia, they have to pay a price of public scandal after the Frezzi woman appears and shoots Gueli. That incident determines the final playing of personal roles. Maurizio Gueli, with an arm amputated, will return to his mistress in an almost contrite admission of the truth of her vision. Because scandal always falls more heavily upon women than men, Silvia Roncella finds herself an outcast like Marta Ayala; but unlike the heroine of Pirandello's first novel, the authoress possesses the literary talent to rise above social opprobrium and firmly establish her renown as a playwright without her husband's management. The timid, unassuming provincial has taken on the personality of a strong-willed artist fully capable of promoting her own cause.

Along with the theme of multiple personalities and diverse truths, this novel also elaborates another typically Pirandellian motif: the parallel between daily life and the stage. It must not be forgotten that when Pirandello published *Suo Marito,* he had not yet launched into a career as dramatist. Silvia's two plays in the novel, *Se non così* and *L'Isola Nuova,* were to become in Pirandello's theatrical productions respectively *La Ragione degli Altri* of 1915 and *La Nuova Colonia* of 1928. The author always sought to stress those moments and situations when everyday life takes on the nature of theater with its contrast between illusory realities and truthful fictions. In an episode of the novel's final chapter the parallel of life and stage takes place when Boggiòlo—by then a disillusioned man who has turned over all earnings and property to his wife—is secretly watching a rehearsal in a Turinese theater by the dramatic company that first produced *L'Isola Nuova.* During the original rehearsals of his wife's play, Giustino felt himself to be a moving force in the magical world of the theater, arguing with the director and actors to make them translate into stage effect the beauty and savage vigor of Silvia's text. Now, with the break-up of his marriage, he knows that he can enter the theater only as a beggar. As Boggiòlo sits weeping in the shadows of a box, the company's leading actress, who allowed him to attend the rehearsal unseen by the other actors, grows aware of the strange simultaneity of the two dramas taking place in the theater: the one on the stage, which somehow rings false compared to the other, the true drama of despair occurring within the box. The actress can barely resist the temptation to ask her colleagues to halt their play-acting and to come to watch the spectacle of lost humanity in the auditorium. Ten years after the publication of *Suo Marito,* Pirandello was to revolutionize the modern theater with a play where real life explodes upon the artificiality of the stage: *Sei Personaggi in Cerca d'autore.*

Once again in a Pirandellian work a death watch resolves

a situation of anxious waiting. Whereas in *L'Esclusa* the funereal vigil reunites an estranged couple, in this novel Vittorino's dying seals the separation between husband and wife. Ironically, the child was born on the evening of the premiere of *L'Isola Nuova* and dies on the night of the Turinese opening of *Se non così*. Vittorino belongs to the same class of unloved children as in the author's novelle. Silvia wanted to give the boy her love, but her husband and her mother-in-law took the child away from her. Boggiòlo himself never paid the boy any attention, except to regard him as the only remaining bond with his wife. After Silvia is summoned from the Turinese premiere to be with her dying son, Giustino makes his last attempt to resume his managerial role by taking advantage of the event and dictating a press release about the death with special orders to suspend performances of the play. But the atmosphere of this death watch is one of finality, heavy with the sickening fragrance of the flowers that crowd the child's room.[6] Pirandello resorts to maudlin sentimentality in the scene where Silvia weeps over Vittorino's toys. The bereaved writer gives the dead child a kiss of farewell, and after his burial she returns with a journalist to her new life in the literary world, leaving behind the husband who once thought he was the true author of her success. Giustino was only "her husband," and her leaving him condemns him to nonexistence as he is reduced to being a signifier without a signified. Boggiòlo's ultimate failure consisted in not seeing his wife as another Self who by the novel's close is able to put behind provincial traditions to take her place in the new Rome.

The Moving Machine: Si Gira!

Although in *Suo Marito* the situations of everyday life seem infinitely more dramatic than the staged scenes of the theater, in *Si Gira* life resembles a cheap and sensational movie where everyone plays a stupid and insipid role. The world presented in Pirandello's sixth novel is that of the Roman movie studio Kosmograph in the era of the silent film. Pirandello's attitude toward the nascent motion-picture industry alternated between fascination and repulsion. Not long after the original publication of *Si Gira,* the writer participated in founding the film company Tespi. Several years later, with the advent of "talkies," he produced the essay "Se il film parlante abolirà il teatro" (1929) on the threat to the future of the legitimate theater posed by the enormous success of sound pictures; Pirandello concluded that films would move from representing drama to expressing a new language of pure music and vision. In *Si Gira* the movie world is shown as one of silly young actresses giggling as they race along in flashy limousines provided by the studio: the god they worship is speed, the new dimension of beauty introduced by the automobile and hailed by the Futurists as lovelier than the ancient Winged Victory of Samothrace. Everyone pays homage to the movie industry. Famous writers bring sketches for scripts that will assure artistic greatness for the productions of the movie camera, but directors politely turn away authors explaining that their story ideas are too bold for a medium in its infancy. For high salaries serious actors have permitted the camera to exile them from the living theater audience and to reduce them to phantomlike images that flash across a screen. In the hollows of space and time as reproduced in vapid scenarios, those flickering screen images appear as the signifiers of a creative death. Whatever life the devouring camera reveals on the tapeworm coils of the film strips acquires the monstrous irreality of moving statues in a waxwork museum. Placed in focus on a movie set, the actors wait like victims for the black spider of the camera to draw away their vitality for the mechanical play of illusions in this new entertainment industry. The camera thus becomes another of the instruments of alienation, according to Pirandello.[7]

As the silent, dutiful servant of this life-recording and life-killing machine, cameraman Serafino Gubbio becomes the novel's reflecting conscience as he writes down his impressions in the work's seven diarylike journals. Pirandello wished to emphasize Gubbio's importance when he changed the novel's title from *Si Gira,* as it first appeared in the June to August 1915 issues of the *Nuova Antologia,* to *Quaderni di Serafino Gubbio Operatore* (*Journals of Serafino Gubbio, Cameraman*) ten years later for the work's publication in book form. Gubbio's notebooks resemble the first-person narrative technique of an inner crisis that André Gide employs in journal novels like *The Immoralist* and *Strait is the Gate.* Gubbio's crisis comes from his unwillingness to accept the role of automaton turning the camera's handle. To everyone at the studio Gubbio has no personal identity other than their nickname for him, "*Si Gira*" ("Shoot!"), since he is the silent hand that operates the camera. As he stands bent over his machine, the cameraman seems fused with his instrument. There are two eyes in operation: the insentient camera eye, which merely reproduces, and the human eye, which interprets. The thinking, feeling mind possesses more than camera vision. To the actors the cameraman is only a *thing* whose presence is a mechanical necessity. While Serafino Gubbio aspires to be no more than a professionally impassive spectator, he remains a profoundly sentient being who never fully succeeds in repressing his emotions. The seeing human mind looks beneath surface realities. The style of Gubbio's journals directly reflects his anxious desire to overcome the intensity of his all too human feelings and at last arrive at a state of mechanistic impassivity. Like his camera, the protagonist is also recording situations, which he represents in fragmentary passages which form the novel's film clips. Since for Gubbio the function of a camera is to extract and later reproduce the living meaning of a given situation, he similarly sets down his reflections in a succinct manner, which almost makes of the novel a collection of essays on Pirandellianism, as in the following passage:

We shall have a false conception of individual unity. All unity exists in the mutual relations of the various elements; which means that if one changes even to a slight degree the relations, the unity must also be changed. This explains how a person who is by reason loved by me can by reason be hated by another. I who love and that other who hates are two : not only that, but the one whom I love and whom that other hates are not one and the same . . . they are also two. And we ourselves can never know what reality is given to us by others; who we are to this person and that. (P. 1095)

Gubbio's reflections render *Si Gira* a precursor of the essay-novel (*romanzo-saggio*) that Moravia was much later to create with *La Noia*. The prose in this work possesses a taut quality that contrasts with the exhilarating, adventurous style of *Il Fu Mattia Pascal*, although both novels are written in the style of the interior monologue, for these journals of Serafino Gubbio do not constitute a confession of past error but a picture of present inner conflict.

What tortures Serafino is an awareness of that same "beyond" ("*oltre*") of the self and life that Mattia Pascal had glimpsed in the early days of his masquerade as Adriano Meis but could never reach. Every time Gubbio views the day's film shooting, he has to witness the presence of that beyond as it is revealed in the facial expressions and the gestures of the actors on the projection-room screen. He feels within himself the pressure of a superfluity that he believes is the plague of all mankind since it divorces humans from immediate contact with nature and prevents them from finding contentment solely in the satisfaction of their animal needs. That superfluity compels men to search in the course of their lives for a sense of certainty that is only illusory, and the consequent failure to find that certitude causes men to judge life as meaningless. It is the same discovery that material objects are superfluous (*de trop*) that convinces Roquentin in *La Nausée* of the world's absurdity. Gubbio finds man's condition to be one of superfluous disconnectedness, like the pieces of film strip left

on the floor of a film-editing room, and even the structure
that a director can impose with his guiding consciousness
onto the remaining film seems arbitrary and artificial. Further, in the life of man without God, there is no director.[8]

In his attempt to be an impassive spectator, Gubbio
studies the eyes of others, hoping to discover that certainty
which no one in truth possesses. Above all, the cameraman
desires to penetrate the barriers between himself and
others, for even though contact with outer nature may no
longer be possible, he yearns to establish a viable relationship with other fellow-suffering humans. Herein lies the
basic contradiction in his being, the source of his dialectical
tension: the recognition of the necessity in an industrial
civilization to remain an insensitive outsider (Camus's
stranger) as opposed to a terrifying wish to break from one's
isolation to reach the other. The interior monologue lends
itself to Gubbio's desperate appeal for others to notice him
and to participate in his feelings, since it can use direct
address to attract attention, as in this question: "Have you
ever laughed at the fable of the fox and the grapes? I never
have. Because no wisdom has ever appeared wiser to me
than this which teaches us to be cured of every desire by
despising it." (p. 1197). Often the cameraman pauses in his
notes as he tries to convey an exact impression of his
emotions at a particular moment in time, explaining for instance that what might arouse disgust in him now was, in
the past, only the object of his curiosity. The "*I*" of this
novel is constantly endeavoring to communicate with the
"*you*" of others.

Because the novel follows the process of one given mind,
the resulting singleness of impression tends to make of the
work a compilation of scattered but thoroughly investigated
moments of individual experience. In his camera technique
Serafino Gubbio employs the method of the close-up to
enlarge the content of every moment, without allowing any
detail to be missed. The text then becomes a graphic repre-

sentation of the protagonists's inner disintegration as he fails to establish contact with others and has to surrender to the metallic embrace of a machine.[9] There is a continual ebb and flow of aspirations and disillusionments. No sooner does Gubbio assert that he has accepted alienation than he shortly afterwards rebels against his servitude to machines: "But no, I am no longer *a thing,* and this silence of mine is no longer an *inanimate silence.* I wanted to make others aware of this silence, but now I am suffering it so fiercely!" (p. 1157, original italics). In such a passage the language is palpably disintegrating. That silence is absolutely necessary to Gubbio's practice of his profession, for if a quiver of genuine emotion should ever throb in his hand, he could no longer be a cameraman. As he surveys his past, the protagonist points out the decisive moments that determined his involvement with the machine age. During his poverty-stricken youth in Naples he wanted to pursue the study of the humanities, placing emphasis on classical literature; but after a distant relative left him a small legacy, Gubbio yielded to his parents' desire for him to take up technical studies in Liège so that he could acquire an in-depth knowledge of the workings of machines. Although his technical diploma brought him no immediate material rewards, a chance meeting with an old acquaintance secured for him the position as cameraman for Kosmograph Studios. Again in a Pirandellian work it is a fortuitous event that produces the entire chain of consequences across a man's life. This novel's apparently fragmentary form attests to the impossibility of shaping events in time and ordering them coherently. The retrospective accounts of the various journals show Gubbio to be not so much an ordering consciousness as a creature living in anguished reflection on the painful situations in which he has had to participate.

Even more than in *Il Fu Mattia Pascal,* Pirandello has succeeded with this novel in breaking away from the school of psychological determinists like Bourget and Capuana. The mentality of Serafino Gubbio is a picture of inconsistency. In its initial passage this novel appears as a vitriolic polemic against machines and the civilization that abuse man's inventiveness:

> Man who in the beginning was a poet used to deify his own sentiments and worshipped them; now having tossed away his own sentiments as encumbrances that are not only useless but also harmful, he has become wise and industrious. He has begun to build of iron and steel his new divinities, and he has become their servant and slave.
>
> Long live the Machine that mechanizes life!
>
> Do you, gentlemen, still have some soul, some heart and some mind? Give, give them up to the voracious machines that are waiting for them! (P. 1050)

This attack on mechanical civilization is of the same spirit as the anti-industrial sentiments that were expressed in Pirandello's 1893 essay on contemporary art and conscience. The metaphors and similes of *spider, tapeworms,* and *waxworks* are the protagonist's weapons in taking revenge on the machine age. All about him Gubbio hears such an incessant din of industrial noise that he wonders if mankind might be driven to a mad act of cosmic destruction so that the world could begin anew. Like the title character in Svevo's *La Coscienza di Zeno,* Pirandello's anti-hero recognizes the pathology of modern times and thinks that a general holocaust might shock man back to an accord with his own feelings.[10] Pirandello's novel was of course published at the moment of Italy's entry into the First World War. Whereas the Futurists hoped the war would wipe away the vestiges of pre-industrial society, the supremely anti-Futurist Serafino Gubbio longs for a return to an age of poetry and sentiment. Yet, within the same sections of the journals as those in which he launches his attack on machines, Gubbio comes close to admitting to a sense of pride in his professionalism. He even confesses to a fear that he might lose his position if industrial progress discovers some means for the camera to operate itself. The cameraman has won a place for himself in the mechanical process that he would not readily relinquish. Ironically, as Gubbio works his machine by cranking the handle, he resembles that dynamic superman of continual operation that the Futurists wished to substitute for the obsolete romantic man of strong emotions. His is a drama without any possible solution as he stands caught between two modes of life: the sentimental and the mechanical.

By writing his journals Serafino tries to regain that human superfluity which must be suppressed within the mechanical, routine framework of his daily labor at the studio. In no way can it be said that the narrator of the journals maintains a noncommittal "I am a camera" attitude during the various tableaux that he presents in each section of the novel. Despite his avowed intention to remain neutral, Gubbio reacts with the deepest possible compassion toward the bewildered individuals whose pathetic and ridiculous fates he happens to observe. Although a single still photograph can do no more than fix forever an individual at a particular moment of his life, and although that same person has to grow old while his image on the fading photograph remains young, the moving-picture machine is able to re-capture the past through the technique of the flashback. The novel's cameraman evokes several intense moments of his life, showing himself to be an impassioned witness, rather than a coolly detached recorder of events. In the journals of Serafino Gubbio the motion picture becomes a mirror of man's anguish.

Perhaps the loveliest tableau of the novel occurs in the opening section of the second journal, when the protagonist relives the sweet memories of the *Casa dei Nonni* in the countryside near Sorrento, where in his youth he worked as a tutor for the grandson of the Mirelli family. Those pages could easily be compared with the most lyrical of Proust's *A la recherche du temps perdu*. The tableau begins in the descriptive past tense as the narrator recalls the grand-parents' home with its charming old-fashioned furnishings that always seemed to welcome him. As in the Proustian affective-memory process, certain fragrances and aromas cause the line between past and present to vanish, such as the scent of jasmines in the garden, and cinnamon-flavored coffee. Along with the redolence of the past there are the visual elements of colored tiles, faded wallpaper, light filtering green through the sun-blind. At a certain point the tense changes to the vivid present as the scene comes fully back to life. Suddenly the name *Giorgio* rings like a bell in the narrator's memory as he reexperiences the "limpid" calm of the peaceful home. Olfactory, visual, and auditory elements work together in the surge of the past back to the present. In the intimacy of that house the narrator found a refuge from the pressures of the mechanical civilization that threatened to enslave him. But even that sheltering retreat was not safe from violation. After the loss of his only son, Grandfather Carlo removed the nameplate from the garden gate, hoping to fool Death out of entering again. As usual in Pirandello's writing, the attempt to cheat Death was futile, for soon afterward his daughter-in-law died. The idyll of the country home came to a close after the grandson Giorgio left to pursue a career as a painter in the international colony on Capri. When the youth returned, he brought with him an agent of destruction more fatal than Death itself: his fiancée, the Russian adventuress Varia Nestoroff, who eventually caused Giorgio's suicide after she wrecked the engagement of his sister, Duccella, to Baron Nuti. The fully tragic consequences of that contact between cosmopolitan sophisticates and unaffected outsiders come clear to the narrator some years later when he revisits the villa. The pastoral sweetness of the second journal is juxtaposed against a squalid present moment in the sixth notebook: a new tenant has occupied the house; the flowers are without scent. Grandmother Rosa and Duccella are living in a wretched

apartment, trying to forget their miseries in religious superstition. The darling elderly lady and her enchantingly attractive granddaughter have become ugly and misshapen caricatures of their earlier innocent selves. This second tableau
serves for more than a demonstration of time's destructive
might. The reader is made to share the actual experience of
Serafino's consternation and disillusionment as the narrator
relates his horrified shock at the grotesque change in those
two beloved women from his past: ". . . I was outside of
everything, absent from myself and from life; and I no
longer knew where I was nor why I was there. I had images
within me, not my own but of things, of persons; images,
appearances, countenances, memories of persons and things
that had never existed in reality outside of myself. . . . I had
believed that I could also see and touch them, but no,
there was nothing! I had not found them again because
they had never been: shadows, dreams . . ." (pp. 1187–88).
Indeed the effect of the second tableau in the brutal present
has been to annihilate the beauty of the narrator's gentle
memory and to render it unreal.[11]

Even on the first night after his arrival in Rome to seek
employment, Gubbio had encountered life's unreality, but at
that period he was not prepared to differentiate between
reality and its substanceless shadow. At that time a homeless
traveler, he took as his guide through the Roman streets,
which were deserted except for nocturnal phantoms, a
humorist philosopher, Simone Pau, whose facial features recalled an ancient comic mask. The passages in the first journal where the two wander along the city's narrow streets on
a chilly November night are more than an imitation of
D'Annunzio's descriptive cameo style in a novel of Rome
like *Il Piacere,* for they depict the journey of lost souls in the
pitiless modern metropolis. Serafino at first thought his friend
was playing a joke on him when their walk ended at the
"Ospizio di Mendicità," a casual shelter for derelicts who, in
the institutional white nightshirts they had to don, looked

like members of a monastic order. To the narrator's surprise
Simone Pau informed him that he had made a home at the
shelter, where he received a room of his own and meals as
compensation for giving lessons to the orphans who lived
there. Pau, like Dr. Mangoni of the tale "Niente," sought
freedom by possessing nothing, denying himself the most
ordinary comforts; he did not even use his room but slept in
the common dormitory. During the daytime he frequented
cafés and libraries, gathering material for bizarre articles
that he published in philosophical reviews. Pau's ascetic
resignation from life did not give him the authentic freedom
of a truly uncommitted individual because he involved himself in the lives of the shelter's vagrants, who for various
reasons had ceased to play society's game. To show a breathing symbol of human fate condemned by mechanical progress, the philosopher pointed out to Gubbio a vagrant with
an enormous red nose who kept holding tightly to a violin.
That derelict violinist had once inherited a printing firm in
Perugia, but he abandoned the family profession to dedicate
himself to his violin and wine. The vagrant's fate might
seem to give some indication of the direction life would have
taken for Signor Orsani in the novella "Formalità" if he had
not entered his father's bank instead of following a musical
career. Despite his attempts to flee the tyranny of machines,
the violinist again and again had to take odd jobs like feed-
ing lead cakes to a monotype press in order to have the funds
to redeem his precious instrument from the pawn shop. The
moment of explosion occurred when a motion-picture company hired the vagrant to accompany a player piano with
his violin. That demand to subjugate his artistic temperament to the automatic rhythm of a machine so infuriated
the man that he went berserk and had to be incarcerated
for two weeks. Upon his release from jail the vagrant ceased
to play his violin. The narrator admits that at the time of
his stay at the shelter he was aware only of his participation
in a grotesque adventure and that he never expected to

suffer a degradation similar to that of the violinist. Yet it was in the shelter that he renewed an acquaintance that led to employment as a cameraman. The wretched violinist enters Gubbio's life again, in the third journal, when Pau brings the vagrant to the Kosmograph Studio, encouraging him to play for a tigress that the film company has purchased to make the picture *The Lady and the Tiger*. The sight of the superb animal in her cage, a fellow victim of the industrial age, awakens the violinist from his inarticulate withdrawal into a nearly catatonic state; he too has been living for years within the bars of an invisible cage. He breaks his silence, and gives expression to the anguished recognition of the nothingness that has plunged him to the depths of society by playing the violin for the last time in his life. Shortly afterward the vagrant dies and therein gains his liberation, the only kind of freedom available in a world where all humanistic values have given way to soul-devouring machines. The violinist is a figure emblematic of the outcome of moral vagrancy, whose significance Gubbio comprehends only by slow degrees as he ponders on his encounter with the residents of the casual shelter and their hopeless retreat from an empty social existence. The art of Pirandello's narrative technique is to make the reader participate in the process of gradual discovery and enlightenment in the protagonist's consciousness.[12]

Sometimes the pieces of the sentimental puzzle fit together almost of their own accord. Two apparently unconnected events that are reported in the second notebook serve to introduce the story of Varia Nestoroff, the huntress of men. On the same day that Gubbio killed a snipe during a hunting expedition in the Roman countryside, he also read a newspaper report of the tragic death of an engineer friend of his who was torn to shreds by a wild beast in Africa. The association of those two incidents of savage slaughter illuminates the predatory nature of the Russian *femme fatale* who, after Giorgio Mirelli's suicide, became one of the stars at Kosmograph. In real life as well as on the screen she plays the part of a siren who ruthlessly brings about the destruction of the men who adore her. The cruel game that Nestoroff excels in performing is one of reverse sexual mediation: she scorns those who desire her while she inflames the passions of individuals like Giorgio Mirelli who would worship only the divine effulgence of her beauty. Always eager to affirm her independence of others but in reality proving her reliance on their opinions, Nestoroff has formed a liaison with Carlo Ferro, the most bestial member of the acting cast at the studio, just because everyone else despises him. In an effort to understand the death-dealing behavior of the actress, Gubbio traces her dubious past in St. Petersburg and Berlin, where survival for Nestoroff meant abuse from her unscrupulous husband and the men who helped to advance her career on the stage. This Russian beauty appreciates in males only brute force; incapable of tenderness toward men, she desires either to debase or to be debased.

As an actress Varia Nestoroff experiences a crisis of identity, which is to be a major situation in Pirandello's dramas. The roles that the studio assigns her are grotesque, as befits colossal spectaculars, but she takes them so seriously that her screen performances seem extravagant and ridiculously intense. She repeatedly seeks in vain to recognize herself in the inappropriately vehement figure who spoils film after film by over-acting the inane parts. It is the presence of the "beyond" of her personality that takes possession of the actress and manifests itself in her exaggerated screen images. Nestoroff dwells in the Lacanian "mirror-stage," where she remains imprisoned in the images of identification that she has taken from other persons to constitute her ego. The major mirror for the actress is the motion picture, with the film images that it provides for her. If Nestoroff has given of her whole being to every role, why does she fail to find herself in the mirror of the motion

picture? In a similar manner she fails to discover her ultimate identity in the images that her various lovers hold of
her. Six portraits of her by Mirelli hang in Nestoroff's apartment to remind her forever of the dreams of feminine loveliness that the young Neapolitan artist found realized in the
Russian emigrée and that he tried to make eternal in the
glowing colors of his canvases. As if in defiance of Mirelli's
sublime vision, she has dyed her hair an unnatural coppery
tone and deprived herself of the beautiful coloring that gave
her countenance an expression of purity. The different
images on the paintings and films are forms that imprison
facets of Nestoroff's contradictory personality; they compel
her to see herself living and they prevent any spontaneity.
Pirandello saw in the situation of an actress, who must be
continually confronted with her public images while always
longing to be "herself," the most distressing illustration of
the contemporary search for personal identity. At the time
Si Gira was published, the author had had relatively little
theatrical experience. Seventeen years later, in 1932, he
produced a play, *Trovarsi* (*To Find Oneself*), in which the
actress Donata Genzi sacrifices the chance for a private life
to preserve the identity of her professional career. In this
novel Nestoroff struggles between the turbulent "beyond"
of her personality and the Others within her ego-image.
Varia's reaction is to rebel against all limiting forms with a
murderous fury that spares no one, including herself.[13]

Gubbio himself admits to forming fixed images of other
persons, refusing to believe that they can be different from
the way he first pictured them in his mind. For him Baron
Aldo Nuti will always be the fop, the vain gentleman only
too aware of the advantages that rank and wealth have
brought him. Within the narrative's formal scheme Nuti
turns out to be a victim who can never break away from the
cameraman's unflattering vision of him. He is above all the
wind-up toy that the Nestoroff woman found amusing for a
while but soon tired of and tossed aside. A puppet with a

broken mainspring, Nuti resorts to fictitious defenses to deny his betrayal of Mirelli and his desertion of Duccella—asserting that he was merely attempting to provide evidence of the actress's treacherous nature by pretending he wanted to take her from the painter. Although Pirandello often wished to demonstrate the relative quality of truth, Nuti's "truth" in the novel appears as only a mechanical invention to restore the character's vanity, which the actress shattered when she used him to break off her engagement with Mirelli. The baron is only a puppet awaiting a manipulator.

Nuti and the Russian actress both represent that period in the history of Italian film around 1914 when the industry, then at the height of popular success and production, began to change emphasis from historical costume epics to the bourgeois drama of conflicting passions. In pictures, whose plots reveal an obsession with self-destruction, the dominant figure was the siren who not only led others to perdition but ruined herself. Nestoroff is a typical *diva* from that period of professional hysterics who humiliated other actors and directors, while Nuti comes from the class of aristocrats who actually did buy their way into productions in order to gain parts playing decadent representatives of their own social class. On-screen romances mirrored real-life affairs between actresses and aristocrats. Kosmograph resembles studios like Cines in Rome, where stress on the star system resulted in artistic decline and financial disaster. Pirandello's novel is a remarkably accurate portrait of Italian film diva-ism, its grotesque acting style with exaggerated movements of hips and arms, and its cult of dreadful fate. Here it is the diva Nestoroff who succeeds in manipulating Nuti, persuading him to demand the dangerous role of the hunter who shoots the tigress—a part originally for her lover, Ferro. Within the staged falseness, tawdriness, and frivolity of the film studio, authentic emotions explode with violence when that insignificant puppet-baron of human vanity attempts to rebel and makes his final desperate effort to redeem his image of ineptitude and fatuousness by firing at Nestoroff and thereby allowing the tigress to destroy him. The scene of the double death clearly indicates the artistic transition on Pirandello's part from narrative to theater, with the perception unique to the Sicilian author of the collision between stage and real life. The triangular story of Mirelli-Nestoroff-Nuti was to furnish the background for the second play in Pirandello's trilogy of the theater-in-the-theater: *Ciascuno a Suo Modo* (*Each in His Own Way*) of 1924. In the figure of Nuti one can note the germinal situation of a character trying to establish his autonomy outside the work of art where he has to play a contemptible part.

That inability to escape one's role plagues still another character in the novel: Dr. Cavalena, who in his submission to his jealous wife stands as a comic parallel to Maurizio Gueli and Livia Frezzi. Whereas in *Suo Marito* the omniscient author identified with the sufferings of the Roman writer, in *Si Gira* he presents Cavalena as a clown who masks his baldness with a foolishly curly wig. Cavalena can never forget that he is first of all a physician, duty-bound by his profession to treat the sick. To please his wife he has also excluded himself from life: resigning his commission as Surgeon Lieutenant in the Militia, abandoning general practice, withdrawing from journalism as a free-lance writer, giving up teaching positions in the technical schools. Like Gueli he attempts periodically to rebel against his wife and immerse himself in life, only to find he is hopelessly behind the times because of his earlier retreat from the arena of intellectual events. But all of his sacrifices are due to his sacred obligation as a physician to remain with his mentally ill wife, who in his professional opinion suffers from paranoia. As stated elsewhere in the novel, a man may not enter into his profession, but the profession enters into him and makes him its prisoner. Gubbio knows Dr. Cavalena by the nickname everyone at the studio calls the physician, "Suicide," from the scenarios he attempts without success to sell to Kosmograph, which invariably include a case of suicide. Once again in a Pirandellian work, a nickname serves as a label or mask to emphasize one facet of a man's personality: here, Cavalena's suicidal impulse. The narrator's sympathies go entirely to Cavalena's daughter, Luisetta (modeled on Pirandello's daughter, Lietta), the true victim of the domestic tragicomedy.[14] Having always lived in the shadow of her mother's insanity, Luisetta is accustomed to accepting the unreal as the norm for life and she readily lends herself to a phantom love with Nuti after the baron enters the Cavalena home as a lodger and falls ill from cerebral fever. In the baron's hallucinations he believes Luisetta is Duccella, and the girl pathetically accepts the affection that comes to her from those delusions. This situation is the reverse of that between Dianella Salvo and Ninì De Vincentis. The entire Cavalena household lives a humoristic situation where father and daughter pay the penalty for Signora Cavalena's irrational fictions. Gubbio recognizes in the Cavalena family the gulf between life's happy possibilities and its actual wretchedness. Instead of on economic security and domestic peace, the cameraman has to focus on the bitterness and spiritual desolation created by an unbalanced mind.

Throughout the novel, as Gubbio succeeds in penetrating and photographing the dark areas of human despair, three key impressions emerge out of the deliberate discontinuity of the journals: the grotesqueness of modern life, its shadowy insubstantiality, and the awesome silence that falls between persons and prevents them from communicating with each other. The reader repeatedly encounters the words *grottesco, ombra* and *silenzio* in situation after situation as the narrator explores the cruel deformation and constant inanition of human existence in an era of mechanical progress. Simone Pau in the casual shelter, Varia Nestoroff with her screen image, Nuti with his injured pride, Signora Cavalena and her jealous suspicions—these figure among the grotesque images that Gubbio records visually in the flashbacks, montages, and close-ups of his film journals. The farcical claims to freedom, moral truth, and integrity of those diso.iented and ludicrous characters underscore the absurdity of the chaotic and alienated world of the industrial age. Even when the narrator is most critical toward his characters and their exaggerated passions, he never completely fails to view them with the compassionate attitude of the humorist who, while carefully noting psychological distortions and masks of deception, retains a sentimental attachment to those tormented creatures.

The world of this novel appears a vast shadow play of elusive figures who pass in and out of Gubbio's life like the images of a feverish dream. As it is used in the journals, the word *ombra* can be translated "phantom," "ghost," or "shadow." Rome at night seems a ghostly city inhabited by phantom spirits who prowl along the Tiber for want of a comfortable home where they might find rest. In sequence after sequence of the novel, the shadows of the past haunt the narrator as they return to him on the stream of memories. Gubbio would wish to find in life a solidity of experiences, feelings, and thoughts; instead, the effect of moving time is to deprive him of every illusion of a tangible reality, leaving him only shadows. The tempestuous love affairs that Signora Cavalena imagines for her husband and the caresses that her daughter accepts from a delirious youth possess as much concreteness as the tragic love that Giorgio Mirelli extended to the Russian actress—phantom loves in an inauthentic world where madness has at least the same meaning as any other intense emotion. Indeed, Gubbio works for an industry that makes commerce of shadows; as a cameraman he has to divest the flesh-and-blood actors of their corporeal reality and make of them mere screen images. On his first bewildering night as Nuti's fellow lodger at the Cavalena's home, Gubbio beholds the image of his fear in the enlarged shadow that the sleepless cameraman casts on the opposite wall of a passage as he gropes to find his way in the strange house. By some mysterious power the shadow leads him to the door of Luisetta's room: the forever loving but always un-loved Gubbio longs in vain for the girl to reciprocate his feelings. As in *Il Fu Mattia Pascal,* Pirandello the humorist has written a novel of shadows: of the dark masks that eventually reveal the anguished truth of the nothingness behind life.

There hangs over the narrator of the journals a sentence condemning him to silence. The novel begins as an angry outcry against the contemporary supremacy of the Machine that kills life and art. In his effort to escape the racket of machines, Serafino Gubbio searches for the silence of sunlit homes, the quiet of empty city streets late at night, the tran-quillity of a countryside undisturbed by the roar of auto-mobiles. But the silence that the protagonist finally attains is a silence of things (*silenzio di cosa*): an inanimate state where he is reduced to being a mute presence. Throughout the novel Serafino's colleagues at the studio speak to him only when necessary, usually to give orders that the camera-man can execute without reply. He is at last delivered from the necessity to participate in the noisy business of life on the day of the double deaths. Standing in the cage in order to film the scene where Nuti is to fire at the tigress, Gubbio continues to turn the handle of his camera as the beast rips the baron to pieces and then heads toward him—to be felled in time by a shot from outside the cage. His rescuers have to pry Gubbio's hand from the camera since he persists in turning the handle. The shock of witnessing and filming Nuti's death deprives Gubbio of his voice. With his final, permanent silence he has become the perfect automaton, achieving the condition of nonhumanity that tempts most major Pirandellian characters in their evasion from the agony of living. Although the royalties from the tiger sequence will make him wealthy, Serafino Gubbio will go on—alone, mute, and impassive—shooting scenes in *silent* films. He will be able to contemplate with a mechanical serenity the unending parade of life's phantoms. In a world run by machines, the cost of survival is to become a machine.

In both *Suo Marito* and *Si Gira,* Pirandello investigated the collapse of the ethical foundations of Italian society before the First World War. At the very moment when all of European civilization seemed to be threatened by the mechanized onslaught of the war, the author became part of the theatrical renascence of his country. Ten years later, however, in 1925, he was to produce his final novel on the death of human personality.

6

The Destruction of the Marionette

The Prisoner of Time: *Uno, Nessuno e Centomila*

For both its subject matter and technique *Uno, Nessuno e Centomila (One, None and a Hundred Thousand)* presented such an enormous challenge to Pirandello that he spent over thirteen years writing the novel. He first mentioned the work in the same letter of 1912 in which he announced plans for completing the revised version of *I Vecchi e I Giovani*, stating that the new novel would be the most bitter and profoundly humoristic of his narrative writings since it dealt with the dissolution of life itself. The literary problem that the author faced consisted of creating a novelistic form that would be expressive of the formlessness in the disconnected thoughts and sundered selves of a personality that has exploded. After 1915 Pirandello had to put his narrative work

aside, except for the writing of occasional novelle, to dedicate himself to the theater. As late as the Summer of 1922
he still hoped to finish the novel within a few months, but
the ever-increasing demands of his career as playwright prevented him from realizing his desire for another three years.
By the time *Uno, Nessuno e Centomila* at last appeared as a
weekly serial in *La Fiera Letteraria* for 1925–26, the author
had already established his international fame as a dramatist with two of his most important plays, *Sei Personaggi*
and *Enrico IV*. His final novel should be regarded as another
example of the process of humoristic decomposition that he
was to apply to drama in the trilogy of the theater-in-the-
theater and that he had earlier applied to history in *I Vecchi
e I Giovani*. In his last novel the author explored the chaotic
inner world of man in order to render the devastating effect
of an individual's discovery that his personality belonged to
others and that to himself he had to be no one at all.

The novel's outer structure is remarkably symmetrical
for a Pirandellian work, being deliberately and deceptively
"constructed," like a mathematical demonstration, in eight
stages or books to illustrate the multiplicity of the human
personality. Throughout the novel the reader listens to the
voice of the dissolving consciousness of Vitangelo Moscarda.
Each book marks a definite step in Moscarda's disintegration
and subsequent fusion with the cosmos. In Book I a chance
comment by Moscarda's wife causes him to discover the
"stranger" in himself, that physical image and personality
which others attribute to him in contrast to the totally different picture that he holds of himself. By the end of the first
book Vitangelo determines to establish his exact identity for
others and then to undo that alien identification. After reflecting in the second book on man's artificial need to fabricate a meaning for life and thereby to break from nature,
Moscarda recognizes how his wife, Dida, has replaced him
with a marionette husband named Gengé, whom she regards
as a pleasant imbecile. Book III starts out with a declaration

of his intention to destroy, through a systematic program of madness, those one hundred thousand Moscardas that others might create; to his profound dismay Vitangelo has to admit that his public image is that of a usurer, simply because his father as a banker used to charge excessively high interest rates. Books IV and V are the novel's precise center, and in them the most important "events" of this humoristically reflective work take place as Moscarda demolishes his image as usurer, innocuous husband, and indifferent businessman by committing acts that appear absolutely inconsistent with the way others view him. But the attempt to prove that one can be something other than the public believes him is taken as evidence of insanity. Having thus liberated himself from an imprisoning form, Moscarda considers in the sixth book other possible roles he might assume, like physician, lawyer, professor, or parliamentary deputy. Naturally, he will not in truth endeavor to enter any of those professions, since they too represent constricting forms. Herein lies the major difference between Vitangelo Moscarda and Mattia Pascal: whereas the protagonist of Pirandello's third novel immediately begins to construct a new form for himself after fortune gives him the opportunity to flee a grievous existence, for Moscarda there is no turning back in any disguised form to the society that he has rejected. In the last two books Moscarda completes the mission of rational and social suicide. First, he almost dies physically from a gunshot wound inflicted on him by a young woman who fears the seductive logic of his anarchical thoughts. Finally, he reaches an agreement with the ecclesiastical authorities, who use their influence to prevent the courts from declaring him insane and having him committed to an institution. With the funds that he has taken from the by then defunct bank, he builds a hospice, where he is the first to seek shelter. Voluntarily reduced to an anonymous existence, he spends his days in the rapturous contemplation of nature, of which he feels an integral part.

The movement of the novel's structure is from Moscarda's initial imprisonment in social time to his liberation in the timelessness of eternal nature.

Because of the novel's prevailing humoristic ambiguity, it would be quite possible to judge it as either the story of increasing self-awareness or as a study of the development of madness.[1] To stay within the thoughts of Vitangelo Moscarda involves condemning society, since it unjustly labels a person as a usurer or a madman without ever trying to know him as he sees himself. The reader can, however, regard the eight books as a documentary record of a man who is insanely disintegrating, wrecking his marriage, and destroying the business that his father painstakingly built for his indolent and resentful son. Moscarda's final pantheistic serenity could be seen as the triumph of a demented spitefulness toward the relatives and friends who always tried to protect Vitangelo's financial interests.[2] Because of those levels of contradictory readings, Pirandello's novel recalls Maupassant's tale *Le Horla,* which in its definitive version appears as the first-person journal of a narrator who may either be under the thralldom of a foreign will or be succumbing to insane hallucinations. Both the French tale and the Italian novel are stories about writing stories: the text serves as a mirror, the signifying reflections of events signified in the disintegration of the protagonist. Through the linguistic mirror of this diary there occurs such a bewildering series of doubled images between the text's writing *I* and the written *I* that the critical reader could justifiably agree with the opinion of the humoristic author that one can never behold the crystalline image of absolute truth. As in "Quand'ero matto" there is a psychotic "overinclusion" of the pronoun *io,* demonstrating the protagonist's uncertainty of the *Me-Self* upon steadily losing autonomy. It could be said of Moscarda that *"He* is an *I* looking for a *Me"* in the gallery of mirrored reflections.[3]

One feature of this equivocal novel is, however, clear:

there is never a moment of stasis as the reader is carried along on the tortuous stream of the narrator's thoughts. Pirandello does more than let the reader merely observe the chaos of an exploding psyche; he immerses the reader in the narrator's shocked consciousness, with his wounded sense of individual dignity and ferocious need to assert his personal independence from the marionette identities that others grant him. At the novel's center lies a basic conflict between the individual's longing to retain his precious oneness and the multiple demands of society for him to play several roles at the same time. Moscarda would like to live without the mediation of others, without that unavoidable link with the rest of humanity which binds every social being in a chain of compromising relationships. But the work's last chapter carries the title *Non conclude,* for there is no true conclusion or resolution to the novel: Moscarda's evasion may be no more than an insane flight or the saintly victory of renunciation of a base materialism.[4]

In its initial situation, when Moscarda is made to see the strangers in himself, the novel recalls the story "Stefano Giogli, uno e due" of 1909. The title character of that novella soon learns after his wedding that his bride has fashioned for herself another Stefano Giogli, who does not at all resemble her husband as he believes himself to be. The "real" Stefano eventually grows jealous of that hateful metaphor of himself which his wife cherishes, but he never succeeds in making her recognize the objective existence of other persons outside herself. In her mistaken desire to please the tastes of her purely imaginary husband, the wife even changes the style of her coiffure, although the true Stefano insists that he prefers her original hairdo. Vitangelo Moscarda, or more correctly Gengé, as his wife calls him, has a similar argument with Dida over her hair style. Stefano Giogli Number One, however, never arrives at the theory of life and society that drives Moscarda to mad rebellion. The narrator of the novel realizes that there is not only a

Moscarda Number Two but at least a hundred thousand or more Moscardas, as many as there are persons who have formed images of him. A technical point of importance between the tale and the novel is that the story of Giogli is related in the third person by the omniscient author, while the novel is narrated by the increasingly alienated protagonist, who disclaims any superior knowledge.

This dispersion of the self into innumerable identities is also a theme in one of Pirandello's earliest plays: the one-act drama *Cecè*, first published in 1913. In that playlet the elegant gigolo Cecè, who makes his living by circulating in the smart sets of every leading Italian city, admits to an acquaintance with the problem of having always to divide his being into different identities according to the varying circumstances in which he finds himself: ". . . Isn't it torture to think that you live scattered in a hundred thousand persons? in a hundred thousand persons who know you and whom you do not know? Who know everything about you and whose names you don't even know? At whom you must smile . . . you will concede that we are indeed not always the same! According to our disposition, the moment in question, the relationship, we are now one way, now another: cheerful with one person, sad with another; serious with this one; joking with that one. . . ." What is a nuisance for the bored sophisticate Cecè in his life among the "beautiful people" and a continual source of irritation for Stefano Giogli in his domestic life becomes a cause of metaphysical anguish for Vitangelo Moscarda that he must overcome even at the cost of destroying his financially carefree, luxurious existence.

For Cecè, Giogli, and Moscarda, multiple personality results from the relationship between the self and others. A polymorphic condition arises as the seemingly single, unified personality decomposes from the daily multiplication of new images formed by others upon coming into contact with the individual. The process of multiplication first occurs outside the individual, who may live for years without ever becoming aware that his apparent oneness is illusory. Moscarda was twenty-eight when his wife remarked one day as he stood by the mirror that his nose sagged to the right. That discovery of a physical defect, which he had never noticed but which others saw, compelled Moscarda to realize how everyone else pictured him far differently from how he imagined himself. As Pirandello observes in *Umorismo,* man must wear an "exterior mask"—his physical countenance—that frequently differs from the "interior mask." To Moscarda's astonishment he finds himself a stranger with a crooked nose, circumflex eyebrows, ill-shaped ears, and a slightly bent right leg. From the realization of the different physical image that others have formed of him, Vitangelo comes to understand the unflattering picture of his moral character that the townspeople of Richieri project on him. In time he arrives at nearly the same conclusion as Gregorio Alvignani, that conscience or consciousness is the others in him. Moscarda must bear the hundred thousand selves while remaining nobody to himself alone. That pluralistic fragmentation of personality caused by outside pressure differs from the interior doubling of the self that Pirandello relates in his "Dialoghi tra il Gran Me e il piccolo me" of 1895 and 1897, where the two sides of the author's own personality debate over a life of solitude and study as opposed to the comforts of marriage; the nonconformist Great Ego is prepared to make every possible sacrifice to pursue a literary career, while the bourgeois Little Ego prefers good food and abundant hours of rest. The inner cleavage and debate of the early dialogues anticipate the schizoid dividedness of self in Prince Lando rather than the spiritual dispossession by others that Moscarda suffers; in all the cases, however, the end result is similar, with the multiplication and contention of alien selves within the self.

Whether as the outcome of exterior forces or inner conflict, the human personality in Pirandello's works explodes into thousands of anguished selves.[5]

In the relationship between Moscarda and his father lies the narrator's ultimate identity. As in Svevo's *La Coscienza di Zeno*, the barely suppressed hostility between the narrator and his father is expressed by the son's desire to kill his father. The relationship between father and son moves along the Hegelian dialectic of master and slave, which is to be repeated with important variations throughout the novel. Since Moscarda's father is already dead within the novel's time span, he carries out the murder by liquidating the bank that bore his father's name. But to destroy the image of his father's memory is to kill himself: Moscarda's red hair is that of his father's; the banker is another hated mirror double. In chapters of Book III like "Le Radici" ("Roots") and "Il Seme" ("The Seed"), the narrator admits to the mysterious ties of blood and heredity that prevent him from being an individual in his own right and bind him to the past:

> It was a moment, but it was eternity. I felt within it all the dread that is born from blind necessities, from things that cannot be changed: the prison of time; being born now, and not before or after; the name and body that is given; the chain of causes; the seed cast by that man: my father without his willing it; my coming into the world, from that seed; involuntary fruit of that man; bound to that seed; pushed forward by those roots. (P. 1257)

The circumstances of birth have made Vitangelo a prisoner of chronological time. The narrator sees still more profoundly into the relationship between parents and children when he notes how as offspring mature they begin to observe their parents and end by encroaching on their social identities and preventing them from being autonomous creatures. Moscarda always felt rejected by his father, for after his mother's early death—and there is no Oedipal triangle in this novel—the boy was sent away to a distant boarding school. Like Svevo's Zeno, Vitangelo proved inept in his studies, taking the courses his father suggested and never advancing in them. The son's failures, as also in Svevo's novel, reassured the father of his innate superiority as master figure. Instead of genuine affection, Moscarda remembered his father's bestowing on him smiles that were mixed with tenderness and derision. Along with the physical characteristics and mannerisms inherited from his father, the narrator also received the reputation of a usurer. To be at least partially free from the bondage of his past, Moscarda feels that he must strip himself of his patrimony: the bank, the rental properties, the house his father started to build but left unfinished out of contempt for his inept heir. Unlike Zeno Cosini, he is not motivated by guilt or remorse toward his father's memory, for he never suffered a traumatic experience similar to Zeno's being slapped by his dying parent. Moscarda desires to obliterate his inheritance and affirm a fully separate identity, recognizing that in so doing he will die to the social world and human time in which his self-assertive father was a victor.

Since the narrator has learned that every person is the marionette of another, he wishes to sever his puppet strings and walk away from the puppet show of everyday life. To accomplish his goal he must carry out experiments in cruelty and irresponsibility until society permits his withdrawal. Above all, his experiments must be made in public. He refuses to revolt in private, as did the protagonist of the novella "La Carriola" ("The Wheelbarrow," ca. 1916) against constricting social forms. The character in the novella is a prominent attorney, professor, and public official who one day experiences the absurdity of life upon returning home from a business trip; his nameplate on the front door with all his many titles suddenly works like a mirror to make him see how his life has been trapped in a rigid conventional structure. His various *personae* as husband, father, and public figure all at once appear hostile strangers to him. In order to rebel against the stifling pose of dignity that he must maintain in public and before his family, he locks himself in his study every day for a few moments and plays insane by lifting up his dog's hind paws and making the poor animal move like a wheelbarrow.[6] Moscarda's revolt has to be far more radical than the professor's, and it claims many more victims than a weary dog. His experiments will be articulated in the master/slave relationship, in which he will use his wealth to exercise cruelty. First he arranges for the eviction from a hovel on his property of the impoverished inventor and ex-sculptor Marco di Dio. Then, just before an enraged crowd is about to rush at Moscarda, a notary announces that the "usurer" has donated to the inventor a home and a large sum for a laboratory. As Marco di Dio enters his new home, he catches sight of his merciless benefactor and calls him a madman (*Pazzo!*) three times, only to have the crowd take up that appellation for another three times. Thus, on the final page of the novel's fourth book, the first major explosion occurs as the public discards the label *usurer* for that of *madman*. Along with ruining the bank and betraying its administrators, Moscarda violently shatters his marital image as the harmless, pleasant Gengé by seizing his wife by the wrists during an argument and hurling her into a chair. His violence is necessitated by his feeling that he cannot assume a new name and body and take up a new life while his wife and business associates remain content with their old image of him as a marionette that they can manipulate. Moscarda does not enjoy Mattia Pascal's good fortune of having another's corpse identified as his own; he must therefore resort to drastic measures to execute his experiment in destruction.

Like Pascal, Moscarda discovers that the price of freedom from others is a terrifying sense of isolation. After the initial experience of uncovering the stranger in the mirror, he had at first longed for solitude, the nature of which he expicitly states in the third and fourth chapters of Book I. Ordinary solitude, he explains, consists of living in other persons, giving one's thoughts over to memories and reflections of friends, acquaintances, and relatives; it is as if a window opens in the memory to permit others to enter— everyone with whom one has come into contact during his lifetime. The special solitude that Moscarda wishes to know can be attained only if a person succeeds in being alone "without himself," banishing the familiar memories that usually preoccupy one's thoughts in order to enjoy the company of the "stranger" that others are able to see in an individual. But to know the stranger inseparable from oneself involves seeing oneself living, and the attempt to see oneself living is in vain since it requires one to strike a static pose before a mirror or a camera, thereby freezing life, which never remains still. As Pirandello comments in "La Carriola," the effort to know oneself means death. From the moment that Vitangelo Moscarda was first forced to acknowlege the existence of the stranger whom others knew, he began to die as a member of a society that imposes masks on everyone. For his violent acts of rebellion he has to suffer the full agony of exclusion: ". . . To touch myself, to rub my hands would be equivalent to my saying 'I'; but to whom was I saying it? And for whom? I was alone. In all the world, alone. For myself, alone . . . I felt the eternity and cold of this infinite solitude. To whom to say 'I'? What value was there to say 'I' if for others that pronoun had a sense and worth that could never be mine; and for me, standing outside of others, to assume sense and value at once meant the horror of this void and solitude?" (p. 1311). Throughout this passage the key word is the preposition *per* ("for") used to point out the individual's relative existence for himself and for others.[7] The effort to know, and later to annihilate, the stranger in himself plunges Moscarda into an abyss of loneliness.

Only one person in Richieri is able to understand the

desperate aloneness that has taken possession of Vitangelo:
Anna Rosa, a solitary virgin of twenty-five who is a friend
of his wife's. An orphan who has turned down several marriage proposals, Anna Rosa cannot tolerate anything that
lasts. Life's constant mobility fascinates her as she changes
from one attitude to another. Her one abiding joy is her
body, which she never tires of studying in a mirror or having
photographed. Anna Rosa's vanity arises out of a coquettish
desire to play life as an actress, in the conviction that the
scenes she performs and the poses that she forms will be
of but brief duration, and by choice her inward existence is
one of long silences and extravagant visions. Dwelling in
the shadow of a gloomy convent that stands next to her
home, Anna Rosa alone can recognize the significance of
Moscarda's revolt against artificial conventions, because she
herself has succeeded in staying apart to a limited degree
from everyday society. Yet, the consoling company that she
brings Moscarda carries with it the threat of a furious outburst if their relationship should move toward intimacy or
permanence. From her Moscarda gains an astonishing insight into the character of his wife, who confided to Anna
Rosa the suspicion that her darling Gengé cherished a secret
passion for the girl. Vitangelo had always thought of his
wife as a mere doll, never attributing to her a total human
life of thoughts and sentiments until Anna Rosa's startling
words reveal Dida to him as a person and not his plaything.
By becoming Anna's friend, Moscarda acts as if to prove
the validity of his wife's suspicions, but in truth he had
never examined his feelings toward the young woman when
she was an occasional visitor at his home, so that Dida's
apprehensions about her Gengé might have been a superior
intuition of emotions that her husband concealed to himself.
Anna Rosa's fascination with Moscarda's radical ideas is not
unmixed with a deep sense of horror at the chaos he has
introduced into the lives of those dependent upon him. Although attracted to him for his almost mystical abnegation

of his wealth and social power, she resists the sensual conversion that their friendship promises. And at the moment when she at last appears to succumb to the hypnotic force of his words and stretches out her arms to embrace him, she characteristically recoils from the danger of an enduring commitment and shoots Moscarda. She not only protects the treasure of her body from violation but saves herself from the spiritual revolution that would come from accepting and following Moscarda's beliefs. The shooting preserves Anna Rosa's separateness from another, for love threatens to remove the barriers between persons by obliterating the boundaries of the self in an intimacy of communion. Vitangelo's failure to transcend his isolation through the love of Anna Rosa represents his definitive break from all others.

Throughout the novel the narrator traces an inner movement from passive participation in a false and deceitful world to a final ascetic retreat of noninvolvement. The turning point from a general dissatisfaction with mendacious society to an overwhelming desire for active withdrawal comes when Dida laughs at her husband because he no longer cares to be labeled a usurer. At that instant of derision Moscarda discovers God within himself as that feeling of self-respect which every individual should defend from the mockery and pettiness of others. Early in his reflections he had confessed to a vague dream of leaving the constructed life of the city with its deafening machines for the peace of the open countryside where he could lose all consciousness of existence:

Ah, no longer to be conscious of being, like a stone, like a plant! No longer remembering even one's own name. Stretched out on the grass, with hands interlaced at the nape of the neck, looking up in the blue sky at the white clouds that sail along dazzling with the sunlight; listening to the wind that up there in the chestnut grove imitates the crash of the sea. Clouds and wind. (Bk. II, p. 1244)

The key colors for Moscarda's pantheistic experiences are the white of clouds and purity; the azure blue of the sky and his father's eyes; the green of grass, foliage, and his woolen coverlet during the period of convalescence from the gunshot wound. Distinct images of persons and objects blur in a colorful haze of sense associations. Moscarda's yearning to be transformed into a thing like a stone recalls Freud's theory that the aim of organic life is a return to an inanimate state.[8] By the novel's end he has come as close as any living creature can to achieving his goal:

> No name. No memory today of yesterday's name; no memory tomorrow of today's name. If the name is the thing; if the name is in us the concept of everything located outside ourselves; and if without a name there is no concept, and the thing remains in us blind, indistinct and undefined; very well, let each man take this name which I bore among men and inscribe it like a funeral epitaph on the brow of that image in which I appeared to them, and then leave it in peace and do not speak of it any more. . . . Life does not know anything of names. This tree, tremulous breath of new leaves. I am this tree. Tree, cloud; tomorrow book or wind: the book that I read, the wind that I drink in. Wholly without, wandering. (Bk. VIII, p. 1342)

Differing from Dante's position in the *Vita Nova*, the narrator takes up his new life, "wholly without," affirming that names are not the substance of things but mere accidents that he has put behind him as part of a dead past: the ugly "Moscarda," which sounds like *mosca* ("housefly"), the "caro Vitangelo" with which his business partner used to address him, and, of course, that simpleton marionette "Gengé," who was so dear to Dida until a madman destroyed him. All those names were shadows that possessed more reality than the man himself. In contrast to Mattia Pascal, the liberated narrator has no need to fashion another name for himself to serve as a second mask in everyday relationships. He can also discard mirrors since his image no longer preoccupies him. The narrator has become "nobody" (*nessuno*), not as before when everyone else robbed him of his identity, but because he has now abandoned all forms of conventional identification.

While the realization of approaching death teaches the man with a flower in his mouth to appreciate the loveliness of outer Nature, and the semblance of death enables Mattia Pascal to acquire Adriano Meis's delicate sensitivity, the ultimately nameless central character of *Uno, Nessuno e Centomila* undergoes an all-encompassing death of the ego —the same self-annihilation that mystics have sought for centuries through ascetic discipline and that many still seek today to induce through drugs. The narrator attains a state of evaporation that Serafino Gubbio once scornfully described to Cavalena as a lyrical expansion above the crude limitations of life. It is a condition of dying and being reborn from second to second, a release from the torture of thought, a constantly renewing ecstasy of self-loss in the vastness of the universe, the sweet shipwreck of the soul in the ocean of infinity that tempted the nineteenth-century poet Leopardi. There occurs an interpenetration of all things with one another, to annihilate the isolation and discontinuity that are customary to human existence in conventional society. The nothingness that the protagonist of Pirandello's final novel experiences is a positive "abyss of divine enjoyment," similar to the liberation that Thomas De Quincey derived from opium but without the frightening nightmares that clouded the English writer's artificial paradise. What the Pirandellian character enters is a realm of instantaneous vision, with no mutual exclusion of individual places in space that become harmoniously interrelated. The barriers between dream and reality vanish into the super-reality of that moment of absolute poetic expression to which the surrealists aspired, as when the jubilant first inmate of the hospice performs a daily ritual of adoration to Nature: "I go out every morning at dawn because I now wish to preserve my spirit—fresh with the dawn—by immersing it in all that is barely emerging from the night's chill . . ." (p. 1342).[9] The funereal darkness of the self in the nighttime of society gives way to the dawn of a morning life. At last in a Pirandellian work a fugitive from life triumphs by escaping the temporal death of social form. Moscarda has transcended the "normal" adjusted state that comes from abdicating ecstasy. The protagonist has abandoned that false self and those false realities of life as "Gengé."

A truly humoristic interpretation of this novel, however, permits the reader to perceive the imperfection of Moscarda's final tranquillity of spirit. To what extent has he genuinely freed himself from compromise? Is he perhaps adapting another false self-system, perpetuating the masked form that he objectifies as the stranger who dwells in the hospice? Although the divinity that he worships is an interior sentiment, he has allied himself with the bishops who represent the "other God from without" who expects persons to erect buildings in His honor. Moscarda once asserted that he felt no need to house his sentiments in edifices. His hospice is certainly no shrine to pantheism, which has its temple in Nature's splendor. That charitable building differs little from the soup-kitchen shelter where Serafino Gubbio spent his first night in Rome. Even if the narrator considers himself nameless, others continue to call him Moscarda. Vitangelo might be judged as having avoided confinement in a mental asylum by making himself the tool of the Church, which appropriates his wealth and displays him for its own selfish ends as a convert from his father's evil practice of usury. His institutional garb of a visored cap, sky-blue blouse, and wooden sandals may be seen as another version of the mask—here that of madman. Unlike Fausto Bandini, Moscarda seems to persist in his madness and never returns to the wisdom of accepting society's avarice. But it must be observed that for Pirandello the way of "salvation" is frequently that of madness. Just as in the play *Enrico IV* the title character saves himself by retreating behind the mask of madness, so the narrator of this novel prefers escape in the insanity of social and material nothingness to the vanity of a constructed world. Pirandello's final narrative protagonist avoids Being through the non-being of becoming an inmate of the hospice. He overcomes the ontological insecurity of existing as Vitangelo Moscarda the usurer by petrifying himself in a new spatio-temporal reality of his own constructing.

Toward the "New Novel"

In its apparent formlessness *Uno, Nessuno e Centomila* anticipates by more than twenty-five years the "new novel" as advocated by authors like Alain Robbe-Grillet, Nathalie Sarraute, and Anaïs Nin. Robbe-Grillet asserts that each novelist has to invent his own form, that the stylistic movement of each new book might lead to the explosion of all rules of composition. Out of the destruction of the traditional novel will come a fresh departure for daring new explorations.[10] Pirandello completes in his last long narrative work a process of novelistic decomposition that began with *Il Fu Mattia Pascal*. The technique is again that of first person narration, like a diary without date headings. Moscarda attempts to tell the story of his rapid disenchantment, his illness, and his eventual liberation. Unlike Pascal, the fictitional narrator here does not wish to waste time on details of environment and eccentric local characters. All Veristic concern with concrete depiction of outer reality has disappeared. There are no long, detailed descriptions of saints' processions and quaint customs as in *l'Esclusa*, nor does the author try to attribute the inability of the characters to realize their talents to the lethargy of modern Sicily. Only those few details of interior and exterior distance that form part of the narrator's inner mood of anger, curiosity, or irony are recorded in his notes: the rotting garbage in narroy sidestreets, the fierce Richieri wind, the squalor and despairing melancholy of his bank, the feudal-dungeon atmosphere of the Great Abbey with its courtyard gardens, where half-crazed nuns await their death. The novel's stylistic movement is an inward one through the narrator's steadily disintegrating personality.

Because Moscarda's consciousness is forever moving away from historical time to eternity, Pirandello was free from the artistic challenge of reconciling humoristic analysis with historical synthesis that resulted in the stylistic disequilibrium of *I Vecchi e i Giovani*. Plot events serve as occasions for lengthy reflective digressions by the narrator, who at times seems to forget the particular situation at hand as he grows absorbed in his meditations. This method of novelistic structure has been compared to Sterne's in *Tristram Shandy*, with its deliberate manner of wandering from the main subject for an excursion on some side issue.[11] Sterne thought of the novel as a highly flexible art form where the author's fantasy could play freely to capture both the tragic and the whimsical fragments of life. In his final novel Pirandello similarly wrote a book of constant improvisations meant to carry the reader to surprising discoveries and startling insights. The narrator interrupts the narrative time and time again to make a parenthetical digression that may run for several chapters. What first impresses the reader as a lack of coherence is not the result of mere caprice but the outcome of humoristic investigation. The decomposition of the supposedly unified human personality —the subject of the novel—is expressed through the method of literary disarticulation.

As Nathalie Sarraute observes in *The Age of Suspicion*, the twentieth-century reading public has grown wary of the old-fashioned omniscient author who claims to be perfectly aware of what is happening in the minds of his characters. Wheras in a novel like *I Vecchi e I Giovani*, which has third-person narration, Pirandello took the responsibility of representing the thoughts of a vast number of characters across the various strata of Italian society, in *Uno, Nessuno e Centomila* his use of the first-person technique is an admission of the authorial impossibility of speaking for more than one person. Moscarda alludes to that difficulty as he prepares to embark on a lengthy parenthesis about Marco di Dio and his wife, Diamante: "But with what right can I speak of them? With what right can I grant countenance and voice to others outside myself? What do I know about them? How can I talk about them? I see them from outside, and naturally as they are for me, that is to say in a form in which they certainly would not recognize themselves . . ." (p. 1261). In his attempt to describe Marco's emotions on a sultry afternoon of several years before, when the inventor molested a child who was serving as a model for a statue, the narrator concedes that all he can present is his own version of another man's reality. All through the novel, as Moscarda writes down what someone else like Dida or Anna Rosa "thought," he is admittedly relating only what he believes another was thinking. In truth, all Vitangelo knows—and that to a very limited degree—is the phenomena of his own consciousness. As the narrator, Moscarda rejects the role of the omniscient author who manipulates his characters like marionettes.

It is the aim of the writers of the "new novel" like Sarraute to break away from the preoccupation of the traditional novel with giving a reasonable "likeness" of pedestrian reality. In place of a "formalistic" concern with presenting superficially convincing characters in a clearly structured plot full of action and imbued with a familiar atmosphere, Sarraute argues for a new realism that would reach the realm of the unknown and the hidden that lurks behind the façade that earlier novelists never penetrated. Rather than emphasizing plot and characterization, the new realistic novel aims at exploring the conflicts and gropings (or "tropisms," as Sarraute calls them) of an inner world. Instead of outmoded papier-mâché characters, there is an indefinable, anonymous *I* who engages in a continuous dialogue with other dreamlike figures that are frequently reflections of the narrator. The inner tropisms are revealed through the dialogue, which greatly resembles that of the theater—except, of course, for the absence of assigned parts and stage directions. What Sarraute wishes to create is a "subconversational" world of inner monologues.[12]

Pirandello in *Uno, Nessuno e Centomila* comes close to realizing the novel of subconversation. Although he occasionally resorts to the conventional "he said"-"she answered" devices that Sarraute eliminates through shifts in punctuation, the novel is largely a continuous monologue by Moscarda, an interior "monologue" of inner selves struggling against each other according to the conflicting identities that everyone else imposes on the narrator. Vitangelo lives in a state of dialogue as he tries to make contact with the stranger in himself. The text is made up of a series of statements by the narrator, questions to the reader, and imaginary answers. Usually the form of address that predominates throughout the novel is the second-person-plural *voi*, which the narrator employs to involve readers directly in his interior arguments, as in this passage from Book II:

> Be sincere: the idea never passed through your heads that you might desire to see yourselves living. You attend to living for yourselves, and you do well thereby, without giving yourselves a thought of what in the meantime you may be to others; not indeed because the judgment of others does not matter to you, for in fact it matters a great deal; but because you live in the blessed illusion that others, from without, must depict you to themselves as you depict yourselves. (P. 1233)

The readers' attention is immediately caught here by the opening imperative form. Moscarda thrusts upon the readers the blame for his own inability to see himself as others saw him; it is his own sincerity that he calls into question. This use of *voi* brings narrator and readers into a close relationship, compelling the latter to enter into Moscarda's battle to find and later destroy his alien identities. The readers participate in the processes of thought, memory, and dream, rather than merely observing them.[13] In this novel Pirandello approximates the subconversational technique by not contenting himself with telling stories about Moscarda but instead involving the reader in the central character's movement toward self-awareness.

The presence of an antagonistic is essential in order to render Moscarda's "subterranean" drama.[14] Generally the readers serve this function by acting as a partner in Vitangelo's inner conflicts; they constitute the "others" who are forever reducing him to a puppet. At one moment in the novel the general community constitutes the antagonist, when as a chorus it pronounces Moscarda a madman for the donation to Marco di Dio. At another time the antagonistic spirit is the narrator's father, who speaks in his own voice (Book III, Chap. 3) and addresses Moscarda with the familiar pronoun, *tu*, as he looks at his adult son from the perspective of the past and finds him to be as simple-minded as ever. The actual number of prolonged dialogue encounters between Vitangelo and true "flesh-and-blood" characters is extremely limited; those scenes are catalytic moments that set the narrator's thoughts and feelings in violent motion. With Dida he has two verbal skirmishes: on the novel's first page, when she demolishes his mental equilibrium by commenting on his crooked nose, and in the last chapter of Book II, where the wife showers her love on him as "Gengé." The other dialogues include talks with unnamed friends on the street (Bk. I, chap. 2) about physical defects, which individuals tend not to notice about themselves; arguments with his business administrators, Firbo and Quantorzo (Bk. IV, chap. 5; Bk. V, chap. 8); a "talk" with his dog Bibí (Bk. V, chap. 3), written almost entirely in the present tense except for one verb in the conditional and another in the present perfect; a heated discussion with Moscarda's father-in-law (Bk. VI, chap. 4); a visit with the bishop and a talk with a canon who addresses Moscarda with *tu* as he assumes charge of the contrite sinner's future (Bk. VII, chap 7); and last, a conversation with Anna Rosa (Bk. VIII, chap. 8) that culminates in the shooting. In addition there is a scene at a notary's office (Bk. IV, chap. 3) in which Moscarda speaks to the public official with the polite singular pronoun, *Lei,* and where the presence of yellowed documents recalls to the narrator that refuge from life's uncertainty which the fixed records of history offer—causing him to echo the sentiments of Enrico IV on the pleasures of history. The general effect of most of those verbal encounters is to demonstrate the barriers to communication as the supposedly sane conversational partners come to view Vitangelo as mad. In the rather brief interview with the bishop, that madness is rendered through what André Gide called *"composition en abyme,"* [15] the emblematic device of a scene-within-a-scene that mirrors the principal situation. Throughout his talk with the prelate, Moscarda observes through the window a man on a nearby terrace who is trying to fly, in the ferocious wind, with a red blanket. When the bishop dismisses the person on the terrace as just a harmless madman, Moscarda answers, "Like me." The impossibility of using words to make another understand the reason for his actions is easily illustrated by the exchange between Vitangelo and his father-in-law:

> "What! And you think all this is nothing? But my God, it's true then, isn't it?"
> "What's true?"
> "That you have gone mad! And what do you want to do with my daughter? How do you intend to live? With what?"
> "That's it all right: that does seem important to me. I'll have to study that." (P. 1314)

To Moscarda his father-in-law is nothing but a creature with the body of a tailor's mannequin and a head from a display model in a barbershop window, someone who cannot comprehend the thorough moral revolution that he is attempting; he fails to appreciate how infuriating his words are to a person who is thinking first of his daughter's financial welfare. That angry interchange shows how the author moves along the borderline between everyday conversation and the subconversation of Moscarda's withdrawal from banal economic concerns.[16]

In all of his conversations—with readers, with other characters, with himself—Vitangelo Moscarda is groping toward a showdown with the stranger, the novel's ultimate antagonist. He must face that threat to his existence in a dialogue (Bk. I, chap. 7) in front of the mirror. At first he succeeds in seeing only his usual image, which appears to take delight in that hide-and-seek game before the looking glass and teasingly smiles at Moscarda, who shouts back in irritation:

> "Be serious, you imbecile! . . . There isn't anything to laugh about!"
> The change of expression on my image was so instantaneous because of the spontaneity of my anger and such an astonished apathy immediately followed the change, that I was able to see there before me in the mirror my body separated from its domineering spirit.
> Ah, finally! There it is!
> Who was it?
> It was nothing. No one. A poor mortified body waiting for someone to take command of it. (Pp. 1229–30)

Here the novel's main paradox arises: Moscarda's realization of the innumerable selves within him and the coinciding fact of his intrinsic nothingness. This confrontation with the Other leads to the recognition of personal vacuity. The resulting impression is one of spiritual atrophy, the outcome of those unrelenting pressures working to undo Vitangelo's consciousness. Here the barely knowable tremors of the exploding psyche are rendered through the staccato notations of the prose. This mirror scene is one of those isolated moments of inner experience to which the advocates of the "new novel" are aspiring. Moscarda's effort here is to overcome a paradoxical situation similar to the one that frustrates the narrator of *Le Horla:* one between presence and absence, between the thinking *I* and the thought *I*, which Lacan has reduced to a dualistic formula: "I think where I am not, therefore I am where I think not." [17] Existential nothingness results from the breakdown of the *I-process* as the protagonist becomes involved in a whirlwind of unconscious irrationality. Lacan asserts that the imaginary is not imaginative in the eyes of a madman but that there is a world of images and double mirrors. Self-reflection arises only in relation to the observation of others. Attempting to objectify the *I* in the ego, the subject ceases to be an individual as it turns into a relationship of images. Unlike the character in Maupassant's tale, Moscarda does not find an empty mirror; instead, he finds the mirror of his own emptiness. He is *nessuno* until the Other takes possession of him.

All the symbols of alienation and the motifs of Pirandellian art are present in this novel: the mirrors, malformed noses, noisy machines, fixed forms of documents, the play between false realities and enduring illusions, the futility of every human construction. The continual repetition of those standard symbols and themes has led some critics to deny any originality in the work.[18] What such critics fail to appreciate is the wholly innovative inner structure of the novel as a collage in which the artist has assembled the component elements of the work in a dynamic relationship that illustrates graphically the central idea that humans are not finite, static, crystalline unities. Several brief chapters in each of the eight books constitute the pieces of the collage. Often chapters are only a few paragraphs in length. The various chapter titles frequently work in antithesis to each other, such as "My wife and My Nose" as opposed to the pointed interrogation of "And Your Nose?" or "A Fine Way of Being Alone!" in contrast to "How I Wanted to be Alone." As a collage, *Uno, Nessuno e Centomila* is a collection of pseudo-autobiographical fragments that become balanced in a whole that traces the development of an individual's alienation and distintegration. In his own manner, working with themes and symbols that are repeated throughout his writings. Pirandello anticipates the stylistic experimentation of Anaïs Nin in the novel *Collages* of 1964, where the apparently independent chapters gain coherence from the heroine's unifying quest to find meaning in animate and inanimate objects alike. Nin's definition of the novelist of the future would be appropriate for Pirandello: "The novelist becomes one who sees characters from within, catches the elusive flow of images which are the key to the character's inner reality and which are more revealing than his actions . . . far more interesting than the mask created by family, environment, mores, national ambiance, class and education, all of them imposed artificially over the natural self. . . ." [19] Pirandello always unmasks the hidden man and exposes the disorder of his interior world. Through the seemingly incongruous collage patterns of his last novel, the Sicilian author recaptures the pure relativity of the self. [20]

During a press interview in July 1922 Luigi Pirandello stated that *Uno, Nessuno e Centomila* should have appeared as an introduction to his theater. But, because of the novel's delayed publication, the writer admitted that the work would have to stand as a summary of his dramatic productions. For indeed, that final novel, with its first-person technique and anguished dialogues, represents an internal stage on which the self's dissolution into warring antagonists is reenacted. Just as Pirandello decomposed human personality and narrative structure in his seventh novel, so his dramas of *Naked Masks* were to undermine the illusionistic principles of conventional theater.

Conclusion: Shadows in Search of a Meaning

All of Pirandello's characters are involved in a desperate quest to impart meaning to their existence, to discover some guide out of the darkness and confusion of a world that is disintegrating about them, to find an author to rescue them from the emptiness of their trivial roles in a vitiated society. As a humorist the Sicilian writer offered his pathetic characters little consolation, for no sooner did he fashion a fictitious reality than he immediately began to question its validity. The author's analytical mind rejected all facile solutions for social and moral redemption, whether through scientific progress or a reawakening of religious faith. He examined contemporary social institutions—marriage, the family, the Church, the parliamentary state—and demonstrated that they all lacked the solidity that alone would have made possible the firm spiritual foundation that his characters needed. From the time Pirandello published his first collection of novelle, *Amori senza Amore,* in 1894, he pointed out that the myths of love and mutual respect were masks to conceal the selfish desire to manipulate others. In his first novel, *L'Esclusa,* the home is not Verga's sanctuary but a prison founded on jealous suspicions. Throughout Pirandello's tales and novels a constantly recurring motif is that of the dream of withdrawing from the contention and hypocrisy of society in order to find peace, perhaps in the fulfillment of the instinct of motherhood, in the delusions of insanity, or through an artificial system of evasion in the exotic charm of foreign lands or the remoteness of the stars. Yet, the only sure way out for all those characters is the total annihilation of Death—the ultimate, truly substantial reality, despite the insincere rituals of final vigils and pompous funerals that make it appear a carnival farce.

Although the author regretted that his mediocre age provided him with mere worrisome puppets instead of positive heroes, he considered it his responsibility to represent the oppressive situations that forced men to enclose themselves within the protective form of a puppet's nonbeing. The crisis that Pirandello explored was that of a middle class who lived without any concrete values, attempting to hide the absence of a moral order and the inconsistency of sentimental bonds behind a façade of respectability and material prosperity. Indeed, the Pirandellian personage is without character, if character is defined as a body of qualities possessing a supposedly permanent depth in morality, religion, philosophical outlook, and political allegiance. Pirandello showed how false the structure of society was when just a casual remark or the whistle of a distant train could destroy the delicate equilibrium of an individual character's existence. The unconscious bourgeois puppet who accepted his life of mechanical, inconsequential ceremonies and narrow prejudices was brought by the writer to the mirror confrontation where he would have to view his grotesque deformation. Having been made to distrust his own reality, the character could afterward return to society as a conscious puppet of conformity trying to tame the fury of his despair, or else he could seek the rebellion of a Mattia Pascal or a Vitangelo Moscarda. In his novels the author endeavored above all to depict the cases of characters cast outside an uncomprehending community that relied on the documentary evidence of apparently solid facts to determine the verdict of exclusion. Once the marionette security of their lives has been shattered by others, the outcasts are able to perceive from the vantage of their isolation the blatant disorder and hollowness of all social relationships and discourse. Of Pirandello's novels only *Il Turno* does not present characters who have been compelled to recognize the inauthenticity of their roles, since its characters hypnotically and unquestioningly travel the round of social ambitions. When the figures in novels or tales freely elect to break from the purely accidental forms of civilization, they experience the impossibility of preserving even the appearance of a coherent consciousness without having to construct new forms and language to fill the void created by their attempt at escape. The *espace vitale* always requires an *espace linguistique* for the ever renewing myths of the psyche. No individual character in the world of Pirandello's narrative writings—not even a puppet-master like Flaminio Salvo— actually feels free of the pressures of others. At the risk of spiritual suicide a few figures like Pascal, Gubbio, and Moscarda struggle within the desert of human relationships and the impersonality of the industrial age to overcome the broken sense of communication with others and reaffirm the genuineness of their individual identities. Among the novel's protagonists only Marta Ayala achieves reintegration within the structure of society. Pascal writes away in the dilapidated municipal library while Moscarda finances his own asylum. Retreat into psychical automatism and the blind serenity of privileged recollection usually provide evasion from the responsibility of existing.

Because of their inability to satisfy their yearning for the

absolute, most Pirandellian characters have to take part in a
continual masquerade of self-importance that the ridicule
of others can easily shatter. The formal language of deceiv-
ing oneself and others fails to shield the characters from the
humoristic corrective of a derision that in Pirandello is compassion itself. As in the novella "C'è qualcune che ride," the
harmless laughter of a father and his children suffices to
arouse the hostility of a somber crowd of masked guests
trying to conceal their disquietude under a grave demeanor.
What the majority of Pirandello's characters fear is the threat
of dispersion into the nothingness that oppresses their lives.
For without the shield of a mask or a puppet identity, those
characters are as insubstantial as fleeting shadows, mere
phantoms like those caught by Serafino Gubbio's voracious
camera. Throughout his entire literary career Pirandello felt
a deep sense of obligation toward his shadowy characters,
in the recognition of his duty as a serious writer to realize
in art those grievous situations (*casi*) in which the characters
presented themselves to him. The first full investigation of
the author's relationship with his characters is to be found
in the novella "La Tragedia d'un Personaggio" "The Tragedy
of a Character") of 1911. Pirandello relates in that tale the
imaginary audiences that he grants in his study every Sunday from eight in the morning to one in the afternoon to
the potential characters who desire a "part" of their own in
his writings. Often those characters, as they sit explaining
their situations to the author, observe that he seems to be
laughing; and with the easily wounded sensitivity of most
Pirandellian characters they mistake his laughter for cruelty
instead of understanding it as the compassionate indulgence
of a humorist. One Sunday a certain Dr. Fileno, a character
from another writer's second-rate novel, pushes his way into
the study demanding that Pirandello save him from ob-
scurity by setting him as a figure in a story worthy of his
singular intelligence. As a completely realized character, Dr.

Fileno declares he will be superior to any living man—including even the author who is to rescue him from a commonplace plot:

> No one can know better than you that we are living beings, more alive than those who breathe and wear clothes; perhaps less real but more true! One is born to life in many ways, my dear sir; and you indeed know that nature uses the instrument of human imagination in order to carry on its work of creation. And whoever is born through that creative activity which has its seat in the spirit of man is predestined by nature to a life that is greatly superior to that of anyone who is born from the mortal womb of woman. Whoever is born a character, whoever has the good fortune to be born a living character can dismiss Death. He is not to die! Man will die. The writer, the natural instrument of creation, will die; the created character will not die! And in order to live eternally he does not need extraordinary gifts or to accomplish miracles. Tell me, who was Sancho Panza? Tell me who was Don Abbondio? And yet they live eternally because—living seeds—they had the good fortune to find a fertile womb, an imagination that was able to rear and nourish them for eternity. (*Novelle per un anno*, 1:717)

Fileno's words were to be repeated ten years later by the Father in *Sei Personaggi* to prove that literary characters in a viable work of art possess an infinite advantage over flesh-and-blood actors and writers, for while real-life persons may appear to have a concrete vital form, their reality is one that changes from moment to moment. Fictional characters are elevated to an eternal form that redeems from the chaos and relativity of a world in flux. The world of literature knows a fixity that cannot be altered: on the same page, in the same act and scene, fictional figures perform the identical gestures, pronounce the identical words, and shed identical tears as compared to living persons who are never certain of what life will require of them or how they will react to unforeseen situations. Pirandello has to admit the limits of his ontological domination of his characters. Although as the author he holds the power of life and death over those creatures of pretence, he concedes that as soon as they acquire life in a novel or tale, they gain total independence of their creator. Like all other men, the writer will perish, while his creations live on through the centuries. Man lacks the ultimate self-sufficiency of the closed literary character. The greatest good fortune in our uncertain and decadent age is to be born a character. Art, then, is the instrument of redemption that Pirandello chose to liberate the middle-class marionette from the absurdity of his condition.

It would be the most dreadful tragedy for a character to remain unrealized in the twilight realm of an unfinished sketch that a writer for various reasons could never conclude. Writers, like other men, are vulnerable to numerous pressures that might rob them of the energy and the tranquility of mind to see their projects to completion. Therefore the potential characters frequently find themselves in the distressing position of pleading and vehemently insisting that authors subdue the emotions of a moment in order to concentrate on the labor of creation. Pirandello confesses in the first of the "Colloqui coi Personaggi" of 1915 that the impending Italian intervention in the First World War caused him to announce suspension of all interviews with potential characters. Intent solely on reading all the newspaper accounts of the imminent war, the author even granted his characters permission to seek out other writers whose patriotism did not interfere with their literary pursuits. One character, however, refused to go away, maintaining that wars were transitory events that would pass without leaving a trace. With the typical Pirandellian scorn for the "facts" that naturalists and positivists hold sacred, the obstinate character asserted that the only thing that mattered was to give to human passions a life *outside of time* and its vicissitudes by overcoming the ephemeral facts of the present to attend to the one important task of writing. It was for deliverance from history that the as-yet-unrealized character begged of the author. Torn between his anxiety as a patriot and his commitment to literature, Pirandello had to find a way out of his inner conflict. As the darkness of late afternoon invaded his study, the author slowly understood that only with his characters—the shadows born of his grief—could he communicate his sorrow. Through those characters the Sicilian writer was able to give expression to the pain of living in a world of futile actions.

In this age of arbitrary constructions all humans appear as shadows that are destined to fade into oblivion. But the literary character is a privileged shadow that transcends the compromising situations of everyday existence. The drama of Pirandello's art is that of Multiple-Selves-in-Performances, for the characters are always actors. With the insane lucidity of that most humoristic of all literary characters, Don Quixote, the human figures in Pirandello's works act out their suffering to save themselves from submerging in the terror of living. Marta Ayala, Marcantonio Ravì, Adriana Paleari, Don Cosmo Laurentano, Giustino Roncella, Varia Nestoroff, Anna Rosa, and the host of novellistic characters —all of them are actors in the shadow play of life that Luigi Pirandello's narrative writings reflect as in a mirror of our unending anguish.

Notes

INTRODUCTION

1. Joseph S. Kennard, *Masks and Marionettes* (New York, 1935), pp. 99–113, supplies a history of puppetry.

2. James T. Soby, *The Early Chirico* (New York, 1941), passim, discusses the mannequin figure in De Chirico's paintings. Some of the most illustrative canvases are *The Duo, The Jewish Angel, The Disquieting Muse,* and *Hector and Andromache*—all executed between 1915 and 1916.

3. Published in *Im Zeichen der Hoffnung,* ed. Erwin De Haar (Munich, 1961), pp. 257–63.

4. See E. G. Craig, *On the Art of the Theatre* (London, 1911), p. 81. The essay first appeared in the initial issue of Craig's magazine *The Mask,* March 1908. A good introductory article on Craig can be found in Norman Marshall, *Enciclopedia dello Spettacolo,* 3:1678–82.

5. (Paris, 1909), pp. 37–192. This edition also includes the founding manifesto of Futurism, which was first printed in *Le Figaro* on February 20,1909. The play is dedicated to Wilbur Wright for elevating men's hearts higher than woman's captivating lips. For an evaluation of Marinetti see D. Radcliff-Umstead, "Italian Futurism: The Rhythm of Modern Life," *Mondo Libero* 14, no. 4 (April 1969): 42–43.

301

6. See Rosa Clough, *Futurism, The Story of a Modern Art Movement* (New York, 1961), pp. 145–50, which examines the theories of Marinetti, Depero, and Prampolini. Recently Futurist theater has elicited a great deal of interest in the United States, as evidenced by an issue of *The Theatre Review* 15, no. 1 (Fall 1970) that included examples of several synthetic plays and manifestoes by Marinetti, Settimelli, and Corra, as well as an interpretive essay by Michael Kirby, "Futurist Performance," pp. 126–46. Also cf Kirby's text *Futurist Performance* (New York, 1971), pp. 91–119 and passim.

7. Background on the Grotesque Theater and Rosso di San Secondo can be found in these works: Adriano Tilgher, *Studi sul Teatro Contemporaneo* (Rome, 1928), pp. 165–67; Silvio D'Amico, *Il Teatro dei Fantocci (Florence,* 1920), pp. 77–82; Lander MacClintock, *The Age of Pirandello* (Bloomington, Ind., 1951), pp. 152–55; and Bruno Brunelli, *Enciclopedia dello Spettacolo,* 5:1806–7. The path from the Futurists to Pirandello by way of the Grotesque Theater is charted by Giovanni Calendoli, "Dai Futuristi a Pirandello attraverso il 'grottesco,'" *Sipario,* no. 260 (1967), pp. 14–16.

8. The grotesque manner of Valle-Inclán and his use of puppet figures are studied by Anthony N. Zahareas, "The Absurd, the Grotesque and the 'Esperpentos,'" *Ramon del Valle-Inclán, An Appraisal of His Life and Works* (New York, 1968), pp. 78–98 and passim. For the continuing use of larger-than-life puppets in the American underground theater, consult Peter Schumann, "The Bread and Puppet Theatre (An Interview)," *TDR* 12, no. 2 (Winter 1968): 62–73; also cf. *The Drama Review* 14, no. 3 (Spring 1970): 33–96, for a survey of the Bread and Puppet movement.

9. Letter cited by Gaspare Giudice, *Luigi Pirandello* (Turin, 1963), p. 94.

10. Kennard, *Mask and Marionettes,* p. 106, provides information on the origin of Italian names for puppets. Olga Ragusa, "Pirandello and Verga," *Le Parole e Le Idee* 10 (1968): 17–18, n. 5, notes the writer's use of the Sicilian dialect verb *impuparsi* in the novella "Lontano" with the meaning "to dress up like a puppet" and considers it to be the origin of Pirandello's concept of the man-puppet. While it remains true that Pirandello had available to him two cultures—Sicilian and European—his vision of the puppet-man results not only from the traditions of his native island but even more from the romantic revaluation of man begun by Kleist and Schiller. See Eberhard Leube, "Der Zauber des Spiegels," *Romantisches Jahrbuch* 17 (1966): 163–66; and D. Radcliff-Umstead, "Pirandello and the Puppet World," *Italica* 44 (1967): 13–27.

11. The original text of the essay can be found in the volume

Saggi, Poesie, Scritti Varii, ed. Manlio Lo Vecchio-Musti (Milan, 1960), pp. 842–52. Giuseppe Giacalone, *Luigi Pirandello* (Brescia, 1966), pp. 33–34, comments on the author's disappointment with contemporary literature.

12. Italian text in *Saggi, Poesie, Scritti Varii,* p. 874.

13. Frank Kermode, *The Sense of an Ending, Studies in the Theory of Fiction* (New York, 1967), pp. 107–8, studies Yeats's support of Italian Fascism and the correlation between modernist literature and totalitarian politics.

14. Sergio Pacifici, *The Modern Italian Novel from Manzoni to Svevo* (Carbondale, Ill., 1967), pp. 98–128, studies Verga's treatment of the primitive world of Sicilian peasants. Vincenzo P. Traversa, *Luigi Capuana, Critic and Novelist* (The Hague, 1968), pp. 23–28, discusses Capuana's theories. E. A. Walker, "Structural Technique in Luigi Capuana's Novels," *Italica* 42, no. 3 (September 1965): 265–75, points out that Capuana anticipated the techniques of flashbacks and geometric construction of the present-day "new novel."

15. Fausto Montanari, "La Tragedia dei *Sei Personaggi,*" *Studium* 55, no. 4 (1959): 320–31, comments on the similar situation between the drama of 1921 and the early tale.

16. I am using the text in the Lo Vecchio-Musti edition, pp. 16–160, which is taken from the 1920 augmented revision of the original 1908 treatise.

17. Pirandello returned to this definition of philosophical irony in an article that appeared in the newspaper *L'Idea Nazionale* of February 27, 1920, in which he called the productions of the contemporary Grotesque school transcendental farces and parodies of tragic situations. René Wellek and Austin Warren, *The Theory of Literature* (New York, 1956), pp. 212–13, speak of the "romantic-ironic" mode of narration of German authors like Tieck and Jean Paul Richter that demolishes the illusion of life by emphasizing the role of the narrator who interrupts a narrative to point out its artificial nature.

18. It is no wonder that *Umorismo* baffled the Neapolitan philosopher Croce, who admired above all logical exposition. During the same year that *Umorismo* appeared in print, Pirandello attacked Croce's aesthetic theories in an essay called *Arte e Scienza,* thus beginning a polemic between the two writers that ended only with their deaths. See Antonio Illiano, "Momenti e problemi di critica pirandelliana: *L'Umorismo,* Pirandello e Croce, Pirandello e Tilgher," *PMLA* 83 (March 1968): 135–50. Croce judged Pirandello's fiction as "neither philosophy nor art."

19. Walter Starkie, *Luigi Pirandello* (Los Angeles, 1967), pp. 272–73, refers to Pirandello's analysis of the Cantoni story; in Starkie's opinion Pirandello should be classified with the bitter modern humorists. Pirandello

studied Cantoni at length in the essay *Un Critico Fantastico* of 1905.

20. For an English translation of the Cervantes passage, see Olga Ragusa, "Pirandello's Don Quixote," *Cesare Barbieri Courier* 9, no. 1 (Spring 1697): 13–15. Victoriano García Martí, "Pirandelismo anticipado," *Don Quixote y su mejor camino* (Madrid, 1947), pp. 101–6, compares the art of Cervantes to Pirandello. Cervantes's vision does anticipate Pirandello's; in the second book of the Spanish masterpiece Don Quixote and Sancho know that they are already famous literary characters whose adventures in the first book have made them known to "real" persons like the Duke and Duchess of Villahermosa. Americo Castro, "Cervantes y Pirandello," *Hacia Cervantes* (Madrid, 1960), pp. 377–85, contrasts the rejected figures in *Sei Personaggi* with Quixote and Sancho. Ragusa's translation tends frequently to be grotesquely awkward. A. Illiano and Daniel Testa have prepared a complete English translation of *Umorismo*, which will be published by the University of North Carolina Press.

21. Illiano, p. 138, mentions Croce's extreme displeasure with and inability to appreciate Pirandello's style. Nicola Chiaromonte, "Pirandello e l'umorismo," *Tempo Presente* (May 12, 1967), pp. 11–17, comments on how the need to respond to Croce's criticism compelled Pirandello to develop fully the theory of humorism. In the best of the essays on humorism Dante Della Terza, "Veins of Humor," *Harvard English Studies* (1972): 17–33, asserts that the *"sentimento del contrario"* effects an emotional explosion that undermines the privileged heritage of sentiments.

22. In *Studi sul Teatro Contemporaneo* (first published in 1923) Tilgher neatly "packaged" Pirandello's main ideas in a series of thirty-one axioms with formulas like Life versus Form, and Reality versus Illusion, which have become the clichés of Pirandello criticism and which worked a detrimental effect on the spontaneity of Pirandello's own works that originally avoided a clear and logical systemization. For a few years the illogical (or anti-logical) Pirandello accepted Tilgher's schematic presentation.

23. Throughout this text I shall use lower case letters for *others* and the *other* to indicate the pressure that other persons can exert upon an individual as he or she structures a personal image. I shall use a capital to indicate the voice of the unconscious as the discourse of the *Other*. Anthony Wilden, the American literary exponent of Lacan, notes in "Death, Desire and Repetition in Svevo's 'Zeno'," *Modern Language Notes* 84 (January 1969): 98–119, how modern man is divided from himself according to Heidegger's authentic or inauthentic *Gewissen*, Freud's *id* and *ego*, Lacan's *je* and *moi*.

24. Oscar Budel, *Pirandello* (London, 1966), pp. 66 ff., traces Pirandello's debt to German humoristic theorists like Theodor Lipps.

to a surrounding apartment house appeared in the literary sketch "Alberi Cittadini" ("City Trees"), published in *Marzocco* on March 4, 1900.

8. Franco Loriggio, "Life and Death: Pirandello's Man with a Flower in his Mouth," *Italian Quarterly*, 47–48 (1969): 151–60, discusses the essentially poetic method of Pirandello's language in this novella. Zina Tillona, "La Morte nelle novelle di Pirandello," *Forum Italicum* 1, no. 4 (1967): 279–88, examines the predominance of death throughout the novelle.

9. Hemingway's comment in *Death in the Afternoon* (New York, 1932), pp. 122, on the role of death for the serious writer would also hold true for Pirandello: ". . . all stories, if continued far enough, end in death, and he is no true story-teller who would keep that from you."

10. Cited by Wilden, "Death, Desire and Repetition," p. 116.

11. Janner, p. 91, speaks of Didi's suicide as the act of an automaton. The novella "Pubertà" of 1926 explores the unconscious mind of an adolescent girl who longs for an older man, a prince charming, to come and marry her. After compromising her fully innocent English tutor, the girl hysterically hurls herself from a second-floor ledge. The novella is a portrait of a pubescent girl's fatal inability to adjust to the mysterious changes in her body and the arousing of sensual desires. Both Didì and the girl in "Pubertà" reject the prolongation of a life that cannot measure up to their immature fantasies. Pirandello viewed the adolescent, especially girls, in their struggle toward adult identity as resembling a garden that is partly cultivated but also to a large extent left in a wild state.

12. Tillona, p. 283, speaks of the Pirandellian woman as remaining faithful to her natural instincts. She compares Eleonora's suicide to that of Zia Michelina, the title character of a novella of 1914 who, because of the incest taboo, kills herself rather than consummate a marriage with an adoptive son.

13. G. Giudice, "Pirandello e Verga," *Galleria* 15, nos. 1–2 (1965): 19–32, unfavorably compares Pirandello's grotesque portrayal of the *caruso* to Verga's sympathetic depiction of the boy Rosso in the novella "Rosso Malpelo," who, though brutalized by labor in the sulfur mines and persecuted unjustly as an evil person because of his red hair, never sinks to Ciàula's subhuman level. Giudice judges as sadistic and repulsive those traits which the humorist Pirandello regards as part of life's deformation. Claude Perrus, "Les Nouvelles de Pirandello," *Situation*, no. 14 (Paris, 1968), p. 70, notes that while Rosso's life is passed without surprises, the Pirandellian tale is structed up to the moment of startled discovery. Terracini, p. 352, points out that the world of Pirandello's

NOTES

CHAPTER 1

1. E. K. Bennett, "The Novelle as a Literary Genre," *A [...]
the German Novelle* (Cambridge, Eng., 1949), pp. 1–19, dis[...]
novella as an art form that reflects a fatalistic view of life[...]
traces, pp. 24–27, the origin of the modern German "Novelle" to[...]
of the *Decameron*. For the emergence of the modern short na[...]
Italy see the dissertation (Columbia, 1973) by S. Austerlitz, "T[...]
Short Story Between 1830 to 1850," passim.

2. Percy Lubbock, *The Craft of Fiction* (New York, 1957[...]
makes the distinction between *drama* and *picture*. For the [...]
commentary that follows see Freud, *Jokes and Their Relatio[...]
Unconscious*, trans. James Strachey (New York, 1963), passim. [...]

3. For the term *narrated monologue* see Dorrit Cohn, [...]
Monologue: Definition of a Fictional Style," *Comparative Liter[...]
no. 2 (1966): 97–112. "Narrated mololoque" is the same thi[...]
technique of rendering a character's thoughts in his own langu[...]
philologists also call *Erlebte Rede, style indirect libre, reported[...]
represented speech, or substitutionary speech*. Cohn observes[...]
that "whenever the thoughts of the character are rendered [...]
discourse (referring to the self in the first person and to the[...]
moment in the present tense) we have interior monologue."[...]
Janner, *Luigi Pirandello* (Florence, 1967), pp. 245–48, analyzes[...]
person interior monologue technique as used in the novella "[...]
del Malato" of 1915. Benvenuto Terracini, *"Le Novelle per [...]
di Luigi Pirandello," Analisi stilistica* (Milan, 1966), contends[...]
that narrated monologue (which he calls *discorso indiretto liber[...]
key to Pirandello's narrative style. Part of my interpretation of "[...]
matto" follows a model established by Gian-Paolo Biasin, "Lo [...]
di Moscarda," *Paragone* 23 (June 1972): 44–68. Barthes's r[...]
Foucault's *Histoire de la Folie* can be found in *Essais critiqu[...]
1964), pp. 173 ff.

4. D. Radcliff-Umstead, "Foscolo and the Early Italian Ro[...]
Italica 42, no. 3 (September 1965): 231–46, contrasts the two[...]
dictory romantic tendencies. Austerlitz, p. 18, quotes Tomma[...]

5. Janner, p. 85, makes such an examination of the volume *Il [...]

6. Giudice, pp. 33–34, mentions an incident in Pirandell[...]
childhood when he made a visit to a morgue and, besides v[...]
corpse, witnessed a man and woman engaged in the act of l[...]
in a darkened corner of the room. The repulsive association [...]
and sexual intimacy stayed with Pirandello all his life.

7. The account of the tree that died when new stories wer[...]

writings is full of those moments of astonishment (*stupore*) similar to Ciàula's. It almost seems as if Pirandello's novella were written in response to Verga's where the protagonist hated moonlit nights because they made the landscape appear more desolate than ever.

14. Prostitution is the way out of economic straits for the heroines of "Volare" ("Flight," 1907) and "Spunta un Giorno" ("A Day Dawns," ca. 1927). Enzo Siciliano, "Per Alcune Novelle di Pirandello," *Nuovi Argomenti* 11 (1968): 74–75, compares Pirandello's contrast in "La Balia" between the ingenuous attitude of the Southern girl and the hypocritical calculation of the Roman employers to the contrast in cultural values between Americans and Europeans in the novels and stories of Henry James.

15. See the novella "Zafferanetta" of 1911, where a husband deserts his pregnant wife to take his half-breed baby daughter back to the Congo because she was languishing in Italy.

16. Frederick May, *Pirandello's Short Stories* (London, 1965), p. xxiii, calls Petix one of Pirandello's beggars who, like Candelora or Henry IV, are refused admittance into the lives of others.

17. Janner, pp. 159–79, analyzes the novella "Pena di Vivere Così" and judges it as Pirandello's masterpiece of subtle psychological revelation. Terracini, pp. 285–92, starts his exacting linguistic examination of Pirandello's style of significant silences and conflicts in identity with a study of "Pena di Vivere Così."

18. Anna Balakian, *The Literary Origins of Surrealism* (New York, 1947), p. 6, cites a passage from Eluard's *Les Dessous d'une vie ou la Pyramide humaine* on the loss of personality in a mirror.

19. See Janner, p. 276, for his evaluation of the style. Terracini, pp. 369–76, considers the tale a prime example of the language of evasion to which Pirandello's style always aspired.

20. For an Oedipal interpretation, consult May, pp. xxv–xxvi. Terracini, p. 340, discusses the language of eyes and silence in the tale; he also notes the importance of colors for the dreamlike harmony of Anna's visit.

21. Budel, pp. 28–29, sees the Fascist government as the object of Pirandello's wit.

22. The German author Heinrich Böll in his short story "Sad Face" tells of a man who was imprisoned for several years by the government because he had a happy expression on his face at a time when official policy required seriousness; shortlly after his release he was arrested again for going around with a sad face when the government wanted reflections of contentment.

CHAPTER 2

1. For a discussion of the style and themes of Foscolo's novel see D. Radcliff-Umstead, *Ugo Foscolo* (New York, 1970), pp. 44–76.

2. Robert A. Hall, Jr., "Fogazzaro's Maironi Tetralogy," *Italica* 42, no. 2 (June 1965): 248–59, examines Fogazzaro's appeal to the middle class and the symbolic function of his fictional characters.

3. Giorgio Pullini, *Le Poetiche dell'Ottocento* (Padua, 1959), pp.337–42, cites the preface to *Il Trionfo della Morte*.

4. For the definitive study on mediated desire see René Girard, *Mensonge romantique et vérité romanesque* (Paris, 1961), passim.

5. Luigi Russo, "Il noviziato letterario di Luigi Pirandello," *Ritratti e disegni storici*, 4th ser. (Bari, 1953), p. 381, finds Pirandello a writer without mercy and expresses his perference for Verga's more gentle depiction of death. Domenico Vittorini, "The Reaction to Naturalism: Luigi Pirandello," *The Modern Italian Novel* (Philadelphia, 1930), p. 142, stresses the pity beneath the irony.

6. Sarah D'Alberti, *Pirandello Romanziere* (Palermo, 1967), p. 32, in particular cites D'Annunzio's tale "l 'Eroe" ("The Hero").

7. Ibid., pp. 42–43, examines the Capuana tale.

8. Proxemics, the communicative use of human space, is studied by Edward Hall, *Hidden Dimension* (Garden City, N.Y., 1966), passim. Man's loving attachment to a spatial area is of course the subject of Bachelard's *The Poetics of Space*.

9. Giacalone, pp. 119–20, and D'Alberti, pp. 33–34, discuss the importance of landscape in the novel.

10. E. Allen McCormick, "Luigi Pirandello: Major Writer, Minor Novelist," *From Verismo to Experimentalism* (Bloomington, Ind., 1969), pp. 76–77, analyzes the Jué episode as a *bozzetto* that can stand independent of the novel. He holds that those "comic-grotesque" figures constitute a structural weakness.

11. D'Alberti, p. 37, compares Anna to the schoolmistress and calls her the most human of the minor figures in the novel.

12. Starkie, p. 66, calls him a Don Juan. D'Alberti, p. 41, declares that he is lacking in true and sincere humanity. McCormick, p. 63, sees the lawyer as a cold and lifeless mouthpiece character. Alvignani delivers in Palermo a public lecture with the same title as Pirandello's early essay *Art e Coscienza d'Oggi;* for the connection between Pirandello's theoretical writings and this novel see Gosta Anderson, *Arte e Teoria: Studi sulla Poetica del Giovane Pirandello* (Stockholm, 1966), pp. 76–98.

13 Glauco Cambon, "Pirandello as Novelist," *Cesare Balbo Courier* 9, no. 1 (Spring 1967), compares Marta to feminine rebels like Nora in *A*

Doll's House and Dreiser's *Sister Carrie*; he states that she chose her solitude, but isolation was society's punishment for Marta. The verdict of others was cast upon the heroine. She never deliberately "turned the tables" on society; rather, the irony of her readmittance after becoming an adulteress resulted from the absurdity of the social honor code and the community's nonthinking adherence to it.

14. Starkie, *Luigi Pirandello*, p. 71, compares *Il Turno* to *Mastro Don Gesualdo* and *Il Marchese di Roccaverdina*, as well as declaring that in the second novel: ". . . the author tries to observe more closely the surroundings of his characters without attempting to delve too deeply into their subconscious minds."

15. McCormick, p. 79, compares *Il Turno* to *La Ronde* as a treadmill or continuing circle for the characters. In her translation, (New York, 1964) of the novel Frances Keene wished to stress the carousel movement with the title *The Merry-go-round of Love*.

16. Filippo Puglisi, *Pirandello e la Sua Lingua* (Rocca San Casciano, 1968), p. 145, discusses the construction of dialogue and narrated monologue in this novel.

17. Antonio Di Pietro, "Luigi Pirandello," *Letteratura Italiana: I Contemporanei* (Milan, 1963), p. 55, points out how Ravi endeavored to impose a logical line of development upon a chaotic situation.

18. D'Alberti, p. 53, states that Stellina's personality is an absence of personality.

CHAPTER 3

1. Renato Poggioli, "Pirandello in Retrospect," *The Spirit of the Letter* (Cambridge, Mass., 1965), p. 154, mistakenly attributes the Russian play to Pirandello's influence. Glorija Rabac. "*Il fu Mattia Pascal e Il Defunto* di Branislav Nusîc," *Atti del Congresso internazionale di Studi pirandelliani* (Venice, 1967), pp. 598–609, compares Pirandello's novel with the play *The Dead Man* (1937) by the Serbian Branislav Nusîc.

2. Joseph Warren Beach, *The Twentieth Century Novel: Studies in Technique* (New York, 1932), p. 408, compares Pirandello's technique of restricted vision to Joseph Conrad's impressionistic method. Terracini, p. 351, cites the novella "Mal di Luna" ("Moon Sickness") as another example of limited perception used to create suspense and terror, where a peasant bride hides behind a locked door while her husband is outside on the ground barking like a wild dog during an epileptic seizure; too horrified to look outside, the woman perceives the terrifying scene only through the sense of hearing.

3. Loriggio, "Life and Death," p. 160, n. 8, contrasts this adherence to matter with Freud's hypothesis in *Beyond the pleasure Principle* that the end of organic life is a return to inanimate form.

4. For this judgment see Benedetto Croce, "Luigi Pirandello," *Letteratura della nuova Italia* (Bari, 1950), 6:357.

5. Janner, p. 53, discusses the ease of international travel before the First World War.

6. Luis Leal, "Función de los personajes espannñoles en *Il Fu Mattia Pascal*," *Forum Italicum* 1, no. 4 (December 1967): 325–35, examines the role of Spanish characters in the novel with their half-Italian and half-Spanish jargon, their cosmopolitanism, and their exaggerated manners.

7. McCormick, pp. 77–74, compares Pirandello's use of the shadow to Chamisso's depiction of his character's loss of being on account of his infernal bargain. McCormick also interprets the shadow as another version of the social mask.

8. Giacomo Debenedetti, *"Il Fu Mattia Pascal," Paragone* 19 (1968): 69–93, considers Pascal's inability to transcend himself through the beyond as a sign of Pirandello's failure to create a positive characater. For Debenedetti, the novel's weakness rests in the protagonist's essential negativity. But Pirandello himself in that early novella "La Scelta" admitted to the impossibility of fashioning positive characters. Jacques Lacan, "The Insistence of the Letter in the Unconscious," *Yale French Studies* 36–37 (1966): 143, also speaks of a beyond zone, "If I have said elsewhere that the unconscious is the discourse of the Other. . . ., I meant by that to indicate the beyond in which the recognition of desire is bound up with the desire of recognition." Man usually identifies with or against another person; Meis momentarily was about to escape the vicious circle of identification.

9. Debenedetti, pp. 70–76, judges the Montecarlo episode as an example of journalistic travelogue literature.

10. Franco Fido, "Una Novella Siciliana," *Belfagor* 17 (1962): 335–38, notes the ironical divergence of Pirandello from Verga's form of Verism through Guarnotta's liberation in captivity. Also cf. Enzo Siciliano, "Per Alcune Novelle," p. 76, with his statement that Guarnotta's kidnapping represents a metaphorical death.

CHAPTER 4

1. Claude Lévi-Strauss, "History and Dialectic," *The Savage Mind* (Chicago, 1966), p. 254, speakers of the need of the contemporary Frenchman for the myth of the French Revolution to inspire practical

action. He then proceeds to dissect the history of the Fronde and disclose it historical vanity. For Lévi-Strauss the chronological structure of events is irrelevant. For Pirandello events in time reveal a humoristic absurdity.

2. For the complete letter see *Saggi, Poesie, Scritti Varii*, p. 1245.

3. Biographical details in Giudice, *Luigi Pirandello*, pp. 6–11. Also consult Giudice, "Pirandello in Sicilia: I Paesi dell'Infanzia," *Belfagor* 15, no. 2 (1960): 338–50, where he relates the author's Sicilian childhood to his later literary productions. Leonardo Sciascia, *Pirandello e la Sicilia* (Rome, 1961), passim, talks at length of Pirandello's Sicilian heritage.

4. D'Alberti, p. 123, studies the four novelle and their thematic connection with *I Vecchi e i Giovani*.

5. For multiple selective omniscience see Norman Friedmann, "Point of View: The Development of a Critical Concept," *PMLA* 70 (1955): 1160–84.

6. McCormick, p. 68, summarily dismisses the work in this manner: "this long and meandering account of the Sicilians, from Garibaldi's campaigns to the present, is hardly a novel at all. . . ." Gloria Gaetano, "Realismo e Umorismo nella Narrativa Pirandelliana," *Filologia e Letteratura* 10 (1964): 304–20, comments on the defective technique. Leone Tatulli, *'I Vecchi e i Giovani nella Narrativa di Luigi Pirandello* (Trani, 1955), pp. 20–21 speaks of a superior synthesis that overcomes stylistic weaknesses. Giacalone, p. 174, also discovers unity of conception and execution. Georg Lukács, *The Historical Novel* (Boston, 1963), p. 54, opposes an author's world view with the "correct" (Marxist-Hegelian) reflection of reality in a novel.

7. D'Alberti, pp. 140–41, comments on the despotism of the Uzeda family in *I Vicerè*. Luigi Russo, "Analisis del *Gattopardo*," *Ritratti*, 4th ser., pp. 433–57, stresses that Lampedusa's novel is predominantly political. Richard Kuhns, "Modernity and Death," *Essays on the Affinity Between Philosophy and Literature* (New York, 1970), pp. 177–214, analyzes *Il Gattopardo* as a literary attempt to integrate death with life, history and the state.

8. Poggioli, "Pirandello in Retrospect," pp. 148–53, contrasts Verga's presentation of the intimate relationship between man and nature to Pirandello's analysis of wealth as an instrument of strife. Russo, *Ritratti*, 4th ser., p. 235, and *Giovanni Verga* (Bari, 1955), pp. 280–330, examines Gesualdo's faith in acquiring possessions as a desperate act to gain immortality. Thomas Bergin, *Giovanni Verga* (New Haven, Conn., 1931), pp. 72–84, describes the pathetic helplessnes of many of Verga's characters even after they have won power. Giudice, "Pirandello e Verga," pp. 19–32, accuses Pirandello of being anti-literary in style and cerebral in attitude.

312   THE MIRROR OF OUR ANGUISH

9. Franz Rauhut, *Der Junge Pirandello* (Munich, 1964), p. 381, speaks of Salvo's economic power. Cesare Guasco, *Regione e Mito nell'Arte di Luigi Pirandello* (Rome, 1954), p. 48, demonstrates how the industrialist is one of life's victims. Janner, pp. 138–40, examines Salvo's motives. Marziano Guglielminetti, *Struttura e Sintassi del Romanzo Italiano del Primo Novecento* (Mondovi, 1964), pp. 90 ff., analyzes the soliloquies of the financier as moments of inner monologues that reveal the pointlessness of his everyday acts. Tatulli, pp. 49–53, relates Salvo to the characters of the *Maschere Nude*.

10. Janner, pp. 140–41, comments on the relationship between husband and wife. Tatulli, pp. 71–72, regards the portrait of the lawyer as an enlarged *macchietta*.

11. Puglisi, *l'Arte di Luigi Pirandello* (Florence, 1958), p. 151, relates the prince to Enrico IV, although he does not notice the puppetlike similarity of the courts. Ferdinando Pasini, *Luigi Pirandello (Come mi pare)* (Trieste, 1927), pp. 267–79, compares Ippolito's withdrawal to that of the Popes after 1870 to the Vatican Palace; the Swiss Guards are the papal marionettes. Gaetano Trombatore, "Pirandello e i Fasci Siciliani," *Riflessi Letterari del Risorgimento in Sicilia* (Palermo, 1962), pp. 45–46, mentions the political strength of Ippolito's position. The prince has the same program as Marquis Giglio D'Auletta in *Il Fu Mattia Pascal* to restore the Bourbons by defeating the central government through an alliance with the clerical party. Carlo Salinari, *Miti e coscienza del decadentismo italiano* (Milan, 1962), pp. 254 ff., gives a Marxist interpretation of the novel's political significance and the social roles of the different characters.

12. Tatulli, pp. 108–12, compares the prince to Manzoni's Don Ferrante, but Ippolito is a genuine scholar and no pedant. A. Pallotta, "*Il Gattopardo:* A Theme-Structure Analysis," Italica 43, no. 1 (March 1966): 57–65, mentions astronomy as Don Fabrizio's morphine.

13. Aldo Vallone, *Pirandello*, trans. Delfín Garasa (Buenos Aires, 1962),p. 48, shows how Pirandello uses realistic details to make a moral portrait of Donna Caterina. The way Donna Caterina reacts at the sight of the miniature is similar to Enrico IV's disgust before the portrait of himself as a youth.

14. Trombatore, pp. 49–51, discusses her disillusionment with the new Italy. Di Pietro, "Luigi Pirandello," p. 61, speaks of Caterina's closed soul. Tatulli, p. 25, criticizes Pirandello for his lack of artistic detachment since Caterina's speeches are exceedingly polemical.

15. For a lengthy and detailed study of Don Cosmo see Antonietta Gaglio, "*I Vecchi e i Giovani*, Girgenti, Don Cosmo," *Nuovi Quaderni del Meridione* 1 (1963): 442–77. Di Pietro, *Pirandello* (Monza, 1951),

p. 81, studies the programmatic role of this character. Janner, p. 129, studies Cosmo's philosophy of retreat. Giacalone, pp. 157–58, comments on the bitterness that follows youthful idealism.

16. For the text of *Pier Gudrò* see *Saggi, Poesie, Scritti Varii,* pp. 689–701.

17. The soldiers' question brings to mind the conclusion of Prince Fabrizio in *Il Gattopardo,* Feltrinelli edition (Milan, 1960), p. 137, that the falsified returns of the plebescite for Sicilian annexation to Italy in 1860 had killed a new-born babe: faith in democratic institutions. Trombatore, pp. 51–53, discusses Mauro as a political symbol. Rauhut, p. 380, sees Mauro as a miniature Garibaldi. Tatulli, pp. 137–38, describes the old soldier's nobility before a corrupt society.

18. Giuseppe Lanza, "Modernità di Pirandello," *Tempo Presente* 9, no. 12 (1964): 20–30, relates *Umorismo* to *I Vecchi e i Giovani* as parallel developments of Pirandello's thought.

19. Giudice, *Luigi Pirandello,* pp. 96–97, discusses the autobiographical source for Auriti.

20. Auriti's case anticipates that of the Father in *Sei Personaggi* who becomes equally hooked because of one self-incriminating act. Trombatore, pp. 46–47, analyzes Auriti's political significance.

21. D'Alberti, p. 121, draws attention to Pirandello's distrust of socialist demagoguery.

22. McCormick, p. 75, with his usual insensitivity, asks, "What . . . is the import of Dianella Salva's visit to the *camerone,* that decaying reminder to old Mauro of his hero, General Laurentano?" Dianella is the one person that the warrior peasant admits to his shrine because he knows that she will respect his adoration of the general and never violate the *camerone's* sacred atmosphere.

23. Salinari, pp. 264–66, investigates Lando's involvement with the socialist party. Tatulli, pp. 100–101, finds fault with the characterization of Lando, who should embody all the despair of his youthful generation but who in Tatulli's opinion turns out to be a rather coldly constructed figure.

24. Sciascia, p. 67, details the autobiographical elements that Pirandello placed in the portrait of Antonio Del Re.

25. Salvatore Battaglia, *Lezioni su D'Annunzio e Pirandello* (Naples, 1963), pp. 11–13, demonstrates how Pirandello reflects the breakdown of all social ties in Italy during the era of Giolitti. Giuseppe Petronio, *Pirandello Novelliere e la Crisi del Realismo* (Lucca, 1950), passim, points out that in an age of social lies sensitive souls like Pirandello withdrew inwardly to escape hypocrisy. Carlo Lagomaggiore, "*I Vecchi e i Giovani,* romanzo sociale di L. Pirandello," *Realismo lirico* (July 31, 1962), pp. 79–82, con-

siders the novel as being constructed in scenes in anticipation of Pirandello's later dramas. Pieter de Meijer, "Una fonte de *I Vecchi e i
Giovani*," *La Rassegna d. Lett. Ital.*, 67 (1963): 481–92, contends that a
source for the socialist sections of the novel is Napoleone Colajanni's
Gli Avvenimenti di Sicilia e le loro cause of 1896.

CHAPTER 5

1. Giudice, pp. 150–51, gives the background of the offense to Grazia
Deledda.
2. Janner, pp. 203 ff., refers to the work as a *romanzo mancato*.
Giacalone, p. 177, declares that the novel has nothing new or interesting
to offer.
3. Giudice, p. 150, n. 2, suggests that the novel was perhaps written
several years before 1911, and he cites some of Pirandello's notes from
1901 and 1903 as evidence. Those two related novelle, "Gioventù" and
"Il Sonno del Vecchio," would surely suggest an earlier date. Terracini,
pp. 328–29, n. 58, points out the stylistic relationship between "Gioventù"
and the Piedmontese passage in the novel; he notes how Silvia cannot find
herself in the area's unreal atmosphere. The use of dialect, according
to Terracini, p. 347, is a sign of characters' seeking shelter in their native
traditions, but in the novel dialect suggests the exotic quality of the region
where Silvia is exiled, and renders difficult communication. Guglielminetti,
p. 100, comments on the use of narrated monologue by Silvia in her
reflections in the lonely valley.
4. Cambon, p. 18, refers to "the self-denying figure of the
husband. . . ."
5. See Roger Brown and Albert Gilman, "The Pronouns of Power and
Solidarity," *Readings in the Sociology of Language*, ed. J. A. Fishman
(The Hague, 1968), p. 254. Janner, pp. 208–19, analyzes the Frezzi-Gueli
enclave as Pirandello's first elaboration of the multiplicity of other truths.
Pirandello confessed to his official biographer, F. V. Nardelli, the derivation from his own marriage for the Frezzi-Gueli episode.
6. Cambon, p. 18, speaks of a "funeral gaudiness, Sicilian baroque
style . . ." for the death watch.
7. Giudice, pp. 510–14, discusses Pirandello's early experiences with
the motion-picture industry and his view of the camera as another
instrument of separation.
8. Gubbio's situation resembles that of Kierkegaard's protagonist in
Repetition, trans. Walter Lowrie (Princeton, N. J., 1946), p. 114: "My life
has been brought to an *impasse*. I loathe existence. . . . One sticks one's

finger into the soil to tell by the smell in what land one is: I stick my finger into existence—it smells of nothing. Where am I? Who am I? How came I here? What is this thing called the world? . . . How did I obtain an interest in this big enterprise they call reality? . . . And if I am to be compelled to take part in it, where is the director? I should like to make a remark to him. Is there no director? Whiter shall I turn with my complaint?"

9. Beach, p. 408, compares Pirandello's method in *Si Gira* to the subjective style of Henry James, but perhaps a parallel with Joyce would be more appropriate.

10. Arcangelo Leone de Castris, *Storia di Pirandello* (Bari, 1962), p. 136, n. 22, notes the similarity in attitude between Pirandello and Svevo. Wilden, "Death, Desire and Repetition," p.118, notes of Svevo's novel that it "does not end on this personal plane, it ends with a world-war and a society facing destruction. . . . it is *society* which is discovering its own historicity and finitude in the convulsions of the war to end all wars."

11. Vittorini, pp. 147–48, calls the villa's inhabitants "outcasts," but they are not individuals rejected by society so much as persons who wished to live apart in a private world of their own. For Pirandello's memory device for recapturing the past, see Gilbert Bosetti, "Le Thème du Retour au Passé Mythique dans l'Oeuvre de Pirandello," *Revue des Etudes Italiennes* 14 (1968): 42–50.

12. Kermode, *The Sense of an Ending*, p. 47, distinguishes between *chronos* as "passing time" or "waiting time" and *kairos* as a significant moment of crisis. Ordinarily Gubbio is merely passing time, but then, as he records his journals, he grows aware of certain points in time that are charged with meaning because they relate to life's end.

13. D'Alberti, p. 148, notes the parallel with *Trovarsi*. Jan Miel, "Jacques Lacan and the Structure of the Unconscious," *Yale French Studies*, 36–37: 109, describes the mirror-stage in the early development of a child.

14. Guidice, p. 253, mentions the autobiographical source.

CHAPTER 6

1. McCormick, p. 70, calls the novel "a clever psyschological study in growing insanity."

2. Starkie, p. 111, contrasts St. Francis's love of humanity with Moscarda's conversion because of spite for the world.

3. Brewster E. Fitz, "The Use of Mirrors and Mirror Analogues in

Maupassant's *Le Horla" French Review* 45, no. 5 (April 1972): 954–63, studies the contradictory interpretations of the French tale and offers a structural interpretation using the Saussurian terms *signifiant* and *signifié* respectively for the text and the events to which it refers. My student Judith L. Ecker had drawn to my attention the works of Brendan A. Maher, *Principles of Psychopathology: An Experimental Approach* (New York, 1966) and R. D. Laing, *The Divided Self* (New York, 1965), for their respective discussions of overinclusion of pronouns and false self-systems.

4. Cf. Kermode, *The Sense of an Ending,* p. 145, on the problem of justifying fictive ends: "The novel will end; a full close may be avoided, but there will be a close: a fake fullstop, an 'exhaustion of aspects'. . . ."

5. Dominique Budor, "Les Romans de Pirandello," *Situation,* no. 14 (1968), p. 56, speaks of the motif of the exterior mask as expounded in *Umorismo.*

6. Giudice, p. 191, states that the nameplate can serve as a mirror. Budel, p. 49, points out that the rebel is significantly nameless, for he possesses no identity of his own. Leube, "Der Zauber des Spiegels," p. 151, cites "La Carriola" as an example of Pirandello's treatment of the *Doppelgaenger* figure. Leube notes that, for Moscarda as for Donata Genzi, the eyes of others work as distortion mirrors.

7. Budel, p. 75, interprets the function of the preposition *per.*

8. Loriggio, "Life and Death," p. 160, n. 8, cites Freud. Pirandello extracted the passage quoted here from an earlier tale "Canta l'epistola."

9. De Castris, p. 204, relates the novel to Breton's manifestoes.

10. See A. Robbe-Grillet, *For a New Novel: Essays on Fiction,* trans. Richard Howard (New York, 1965), p. 12.

11. Starkie, pp. 111–112, speaks of Sterne's ability to reproduce the flow of natural speech through his rambling method. Georges Poulet at the structuralist symposium held at Johns Hopkins University in October of 1966 commented that *Tristram Shandy* is distinguished by a painful lag between slowness of speech and rapidity of thought, so that Sterne's technique worked to represent the failure of language to communicate thought; see *The Languages of Criticism and the Sciences of Man* (Baltimore, Md., 1970), p. 177.

12. Cf. especially "What Birds See," *The Age of Suspicion,* trans. Maria Jolas (New York, 1963), pp. 121–47. Sarraute in particular admires the dialogue novels of Ivy Compton-Burnett.

13. Michel Butor's novel *Modification* (1957) carries this method to its fullest conclusion by being written entirely in the *vous* form.

14. D'Alberti, p. 168, comments on the presence of antagonists in the

novel to serve as debating partners for the narrator. Sarraute, pp. 94–95, interprets the role of "partners" in the new novel.

15. See Justin O'Brien, "Gide's Fictional Technique," *Yale French Studies*, 7 (1951): 88.

16. I take this occasion to express my gratitude to a former student, Donald A. Longo, for several fine remarks on Pirandello's dialogue in this novel. To Mr. Longo I owe the idea of this work as a collage of vari-colored pieces.

17. "The Insistence of the letter," p. 136. Cf. Fitz, pp. 160–61, for his application of the same Lacanian paradox to the structure of reflection in the Maupassant tale.

18. De Castris, pp. 198–203, contents that in thematic material this novel presents nothing new. McCormick, p. 69, working from a very limited and traditional idea of the novel as an art form, states that this work "pleases no one as a novel."

19. *The Novel of the Future* (New York, 1968), p. 59.

20. Sergio Pacifici, *The Modern Italian Novel, From Capuana to Tozzi* (Carbondale, Ill., 1973), p. 133, relates the novel's style to Sartre, Ionesco, Beckett, and Albee.

Selected Bibliography

TEXTS OF PIRANDELLIAN WORKS

Novelle per un anno. Edited by Corrado Alvaro. 2 vols. Milan, 1959.

Tutti i romanzi. Milan, 1945.

Saggi, Poesie, Scritti Varii. Edited by Manlio Lo Vecchio-Musti. Milan, 1960·

Maschere Nude. 2 vols. Milan, 1958.

GENERAL STUDIES

Anderson, Gosta. *Arte e Teoria: Studi sulla Poetica del Giovane Pirandello.* Stockholm, 1966.

Angioletti, Giovan Battista. *Luigi Pirandello narratore e drammaturgo.* Turin, 1958·

Battaglia, Salvatore. *Lezioni su D'Annunzio e Pirandello.* Naples, 1963.

Beach, Joseph Warren. *The Twentieth Century Novel: Studies in Technique.* New York, 1932.

Bergin, Thomas. *Giovanni Verga.* New Haven, Conn., 1931·

Bosetti, Gilbert. "Le Thème du Retour au Passé Mythique dans L'Oeuvre de Pirandello," *Revue des Études Italiennes* 14 (1968): 42–50.

Budel, Oscar. *Pirandello.* London, 1966.

Budor, Dominique. "Les Romans de Pirandello," *Situation,* no. 14 (1968), pp. 56–61.

Calendoli, Giovanni, "Dai Futuristi a Pirandello attraverso il 'grottesco,'" *Sipario,* no. 260 (1967), pp. 14–16.

Cambon, Glauco. "Pirandello as Novelist," *Cesare Balbo Courier* 9, no. 1 (Spring 1967): 16–19.

Cantoro, Umberto, *Luigi Pirandello e il problema della personalità* Bologna, 1954.

Castro, Americo. "Cervantes y Pirandello·" *Hacia Cervantes.* Madrid, 1960.

Chiaromonte, Nicola. "Pirandello e l'umorismo." *Tempo Presente* (May 12, 1967), pp. 11–17.

Clough, Rosa. *Futurism, The Story of a Modern Art Movement.* New York, 1961.

Cohn, Dorrit. "Narrated Monologue: Definition of a Fictional Style." *Comparative Literature* 18, no. 2 (1966): 97–112.

Craig, Edward Gordon. *On the Art of the Theatre.* London, 1911.

Croce, Benedetto. "Luigi Pirandello." *Letteratura della Nuova Italia.* Bari, 1950.

D'Alberti, Sarah. *Pirandello Romanziere.* Palermo, 1967.

D'Amico, Silvio. *Il Teatro dei Fantocci.* Florence, 1920.

De Castris, A. Leone. *Storia di Pirandello.* Bari, 1966.

———. "Il Problema di Pirandello dalla filosofia alla storia." *La Rassegna d. Lett. Ital.* 66 (1962): 63–80.

———. "Ragione ideologica e proiezione drammatica del

'personaggio senza autore.'" *Convivium* 30, no. 2 (1962): 175–85.

Di Pietro, Antonio. *Pirandello*. Monza, 1951.

―――. "Luigi Pirandello," *Letteratura Italiana: I Contemporanei*. Milan, 1963.

Fido, Franco. "Una Novella Siciliana." *Belfagor* 17 (1962): 335–38.

Friedmann, Norman. "Point of View: The Development of a Critical Concept," *PMLA* 70 (1955): 1160–84.

Gaetano, Gloria. "Realismo e Umorismo nella Narrativa Pirandelliana." *Filologia e Letteratura* 10 (1964): 304–20.

Gaglio, Antonietta. "*I Vecchi e i Giovani*, Girgenti, Don Cosmo." *Nuovi Quaderni del Meridione* 1 (1963): 442–77.

Giacalone, Giuseppe. *Luigi Pirandello*. Brescia, 1966.

Giudice, Gaspare. *Luigi Pirandello*. Turin, 1963.

―――. "Pirandello in Sicilia: I Paesi dell'Infanzia." *Belfagor* 15 (1960): 338–50.

―――. "Pirandello e Verga," *Galleria* 15, nos. 1–2 (1965): 19–32.

Guasco, Cesare. *Ragione e Mito nell'Arte di Luigi Pirandello*. Rome, 1954.

Guglielminetti, Marziano. *Struttura e Sintassi del Romanzo Italiano del Primo Novecento*. Mondovi, 1964.

Illiano, Antonio, "Momenti e problemi di critica pirandelliana: *L'Umorismo*, Pirandello e Croce, Pirandello e Tilgher." *PMLA* 83 (March 1968): 135–50.

Janner, Arminio. *Luigi Pirandello*. Florence, 1967.

Lagomaggiore, Carlo. "*I Vecchi e i Giovani*, romanzo sociale di L. Pirandello." *Realismo lirico* (July 31, 1962), pp. 79–82.

Lanza, Giuseppe. "Modernità di Pirandello." *Tempo Presente* 9, no. 12 (1964): 20–30.

Leal, Luis. "Función de los personajes españoles en *Il Fu Mattia Pascal*," *Forum Italicum* 1, no. 4 (December 1967): 325–35.

Leube, Eberhard. "Der Zauber des Spiegels." *Romantisches Jahrbuch* 17 (1966): 155–69.

Loriggio, Franco. "Life and Death: Pirandello's Man with a Flower in his Mouth." *Italian Quarterly* 47–48 (1969): 151–60.

Lugnani, Lucio. "Genesi ed evoluzione del personaggio pirandelliano." *Belfagor* 21 (1966): 269–96.

MacClintock, Lander. *The Age of Pirandello.* Bloomington, Ind., 1951.

McCormick, E. Allen. "Luigi Pirandello: Major Writer, Minor Novelist." *From Verismo to Experimentalism,* edited by Sergio Pacifici. Bloomington, Ind., 1969.

Martí, Victoriano García. "Pirandelismo anticipado." *Don Quixote y su mejor camino.* Madrid, 1947.

May, Frederick. Introduction to *Pirandello's Short Stories.* London, 1965.

Meijer, Pieter de, "Una Fonte de *I Vecchi e i Giovani.*" *La Rassegna d. Lett. Ital.,* 67 (1963): 481–92.

Montanari, Fausto. "La Tragedia dei *Sei Personaggi.*" *Studium* 55, no. 4 (1959): 320–31.

Pacifici, Sergio. *The Modern Italian Novel from Manzoni to Svevo.* Carbondale, Ill., 1967.

———. *The Modern Italian Novel, From Capuana to Tozzi.* Carbondale, Ill., 1973.

Pasini, Ferdinando. *Luigi Pirandello (Come mi pare).* Trieste, 1927.

Perrus, Claude. "Les Nouvelles de Pirandello." *Situation* no. 14 (1968), pp. 63–94.

Petronio, Giuseppe. *Pirandello Novelliere e la Crisi del Realismo.* Lucca, 1950.

Poggioli, Renato. "Pirandello in Retrospect." *The Spirit of the Letter.* Cambridge, Mass., 1965.

Puglisi, Filippo. *L'Arte di Luigi Pirandello.* Florence, 1968.

———. *Pirandello e la sua Lingua.* Rocca San Casciano, 1968.

Pullini, Giorgio. *Le Poetiche dell'Ottocento.* Padua, 1959.

Radcliff-Umstead, Douglas "Italian Futurism: The Rhythm of Modern Life." *Mondo Libero* 14, no. 4 (April 1969): 42–43.

―――. "Pirandello and the Puppet World." *Italica* 44, no. 1 (March 1967): 13–27.

―――. "Pirandello, An Author in Search of God." *Mondo Libero* 13, no. 2 (February 1968): 28–31.

―――. "Pirandello and the Ideal Society." *La Parola del Popolo* (October-November 1968), p. 28.

Ragusa, Olga. "Pirandello and Verga." *Le Parole e le idee* 10 (1968): 1–22.

Rauhut, Franz. *Der Junge Pirandello.* Munich, 1964.

Russo, Luigi. "Il noviziato letterario di Luigi Pirandello." *Ritratti e disegni storici,* 4th ser. Bari, 1953.

―――. *Giovanni Verga.* Bari, 1955.

Salinari, Carlo. *Miti e coscienza del decadentismo italiano.* Milan, 1962.

Saurel, Renée. "Beffe nella vita di Luigi Pirandello ou Pirandello sans Pirandellisme." *Les Temps Modernes* 11 (1953): 723–41.

Sciascia, Leonardo. *Pirandello e la Sicilia.* Rome, 1961.

Siciliano, Enzo. "Per Alcune Novelle di Pirandello." *Nuovi Argomenti* 11 (1968): 71–78.

Starkie, Walter. *Luigi Pirandello.* Los Angeles, Calif., 1967.

Tatulli, Leone. *'I Vecchi e i Giovani' nella Narrativa di Luigi Pirandello.* Trani, 1955.

Terracini, Benvenuto. "Le 'Novelle per un anno' di Luigi Pirandello." *Analisi stilistica.* Milan, 1966.

Tilgher, Adriano. *Studi sul Teatro Contemporaneo.* Rome,, 1928.

Tillona, Zina. "La Morte nelle novelle di Pirandello." *FI* 1, no. 4 (1967): 279–88.

Trombatore, Gaetano. "Pirandello e i Fasci Siciliani." *Riflessi Letterari del Risorgimento in Sicilia.* Palermo, 1962.

Vallone, Aldo. *Pirandello.* Translated by Delfín Garasa. Buenos Aires, 1962.

Vittorini, Domenico. "The Reaction to Naturalism: Luigi Pirandello." *The Modern Italian Novel*. Philadephia, 1930.

Zahareas, Anthony N. "The Absurd, the Grotesque and the 'Esperpentos.'" *Ramón del Valle-Inclán, An Appraisal of His Life and Works*, New York, 1968.

Index